Marketing Channel Management

MARKETING CHANNEL MANAGEMENT

People, Products, Programs, and Markets

Russell W. McCalley

Foreword by Ray Goldberg

Westport, Connecticut
London

Library of Congress Cataloging-in-Publication Data

McCalley, Russell W.
    Marketing channel management : people, products, programs, and
markets / Russell W. McCalley ; foreword by Ray Goldberg.
        p.   cm.
    Includes bibliographical references and index.
    ISBN 0–275–95439–0 (alk. paper)
    1. Marketing channels.   2. Marketing—Management.   I. Title.
HF5415.129.M383   1996
658.8'4—dc20   95–26517

British Library Cataloguing in Publication Data is available.

Library of Congress Catalog Card Number: 95–26517
ISBN: 0–275–95439–0

First published in 1996

Praeger Publishers, 88 Post Road West, Westport, CT 06881
An imprint of Greenwood Publishing Group, Inc.

Printed in the United States of America

The paper used in this book complies with the
Permanent Paper Standard issued by the National
Information Standards Organization (Z39.48–1984).

10 9 8 7 6 5 4 3 2 1

To my wife Grace, whose computer skills, encouragement, perseverance, and inspiration made this book possible.

Man is the only animal that laughs and weeps; for he is the only animal that is struck with the difference between what things are, and what they ought to be.

—*William Hazlitt*

It is through the management of change that companies either succeed or fail. If management does not direct and control the changes in their business environment, they will forever be at the mercy of those who do.

—*Russell W. McCalley*

Contents

Tables

Foreword

This volume is a detailed account of the functions to be performed in moving products and services through the value-added chain from the product source to the ultimate consumer. The changing trends in demographics, as well as globalization, technological advances, and new governmental and social priorities, significantly affect the business economy. Marketing managers must consider how these changes affect the quality control of products, the product packaging, the logistics, and the need for control of their marketing programs throughout the marketing channel.

As important as these changes are, one cannot understand their impact on developing and managing the marketing channel unless one is aware of how that system currently works and how it will evolve in the future. The marketing channel concept is a shorthand way of focusing the reader's attention on what needs to be done when considering products and markets as comprising an integral and inseparable marketing system. This volume offers a detailed understanding of this system's operations. The marketing process is effectively presented, with factual examples and illustrations for specific management actions in the marketing channel.

It is rare to have one individual who is employed at a senior management level in both consumer and industrial leading companies and, at the same time, is able to translate that experience in a practical and meaningful way to others, but such is the case with the author of this volume, Russell W. McCalley. There is no doubt that what is described and analyzed, in an effective and detailed way, will be useful to students, up-and-coming managers, and established business professionals alike. This volume will also be extremely helpful to the researcher who wants to understand how the functions and structure of the marketing channel system may change in the future.

—*Ray Goldberg*
Harvard University

Preface

In over thirty years of high-level corporate management, and with a decade of teaching at the university level, I have observed that too many managers believe progress is made through the management of people. Regardless of its skill and perseverance, management cannot expect more from employees than what they are prepared to give based on their experiences and knowledge. It is through learning that the potential for progress is born. Through the repeated application of what we learn, experience is gained. Many successful experiences result in the acquisition of knowledge. In time, with sufficient insight, we may develop the ability to predict the outcome of actions accurately without actually experiencing them. This is called wisdom. We start by learning from others what is already known and applying it to whatever we are attempting to accomplish.

In reality, progress is achieved, not by managing people, but by managing their energies and intellects into productive actions. It is my hope that this book will facilitate the process of learning, provide a better understanding of how to perform complex marketing jobs, and foster the inspiration of great ideas.

Acknowledgments

The greatest contribution any person can offer to another is encouragement. I received sufficient encouragement from Dr. George Seperich, As-
sociate Professor, School of Agribusiness and Environmental Resources,
Arizona State University, to follow this task to its conclusion. He also
provided insights that were most valuable in developing the organization of the material for presentation to students. Dr. Seperich is a great
teacher. I have learned much from him.

Dr. Michael W. Woolverton, Continental Grain Professor of Agribusiness, American Graduate School of International Management, provided
a much-needed and most helpful critique of the materials in this text.
He also is the one who encouraged me to become a teacher. With his
guidance I was able to make the shift from the boardroom to the class-
room.

Introduction

Those who manage the marketing channel know that it runs swiftly with frequent changes and is influenced by channel members at many levels. This study identifies how the channel is structured and how it can be managed to allow manufacturers to complete their marketing objectives successfully. The focus is on the marketing activities in the channel. The author recognizes that the primary function of physical distribution is one of facilitating marketing objectives. From the consumer to the manufacturer of a product, all the channel members have specific actions to perform if the channel is to work without conflict. The influences of consumers, retailers, wholesalers, and those who manufacture (or market) products are presented as they affect the channel structure and the channel management activities. Those functions that are manageable are the elements of the *marketing mix*: products, prices, marketing programs, physical distribution, and people.

The Marketing Channel Manager is the title given to whoever performs the jobs related to channel management. Chapter 6, Effective Responsibility without Authority, provides these managers with a method for performing their job that will substantially improve the probability of success.

Every management function needed to manage the marketing channel is discussed in sufficient detail to encourage the learning of the basic marketing skills in managing the marketing channel. In place of general case studies, many specifically targeted marketing scenarios provide examples and illustrations to improve understanding of complicated actions and functions. In addition, the language of the text is that of the marketplace rather than that of academia.

PART I

Physical Elements of the Marketing Channel Structure

ONE

Marketing Channel Overview

The structure and functions of a marketing channel are not complicated. There are only two essential parts: the *physical distribution structure* and the company's *marketing programs*.

STRUCTURE AND FUNCTIONS OF THE MARKETING CHANNEL

1. The channel structure employed for physical distribution moves products from the manufacturer or marketer to the consumer or user. The manufacturer or marketer is the product source.
2. Marketing programs created to achieve the company's business objectives affect all the channel members. The physical distribution structure must support the marketing programs and all channel participants.

Complications arise when a company tries to select a simple, effective, and easy-to-manage physical distribution structure while, at the same time, preparing the most appropriate marketing programs for a competitive market. Organizing an effective physical distribution structure, as well as selecting channel members who will work to accomplish the company's marketing objectives, is the challenge. The channel members' capabilities must be realistically evaluated, with consideration given to the effects of competition on their ability to perform. The marketing objective, for most manufacturers of physical products and marketable services, is to profitably reach as many potential users or consumers of their products as is realistically possible.

To accomplish the task of moving products from one or more points of origin to hundreds of destinations that reach thousands or even millions of consumers requires a formal structure for both marketing and physical distribution. The unified structure, which must accomplish the objectives of these functions, is the *marketing channel*. The marketing channel includes every aspect of business, from product concept to the guarantee of its value or usefulness to the buyer. It is the obligation of the marketer or manufacturer to create or employ a marketing channel capable of ensuring that all these functions are accomplished.

Marketing Channel Definition

> *A business structure, reaching from the point of product origin to the consumer, through which a manufacturer or marketer motivates, communicates, sells, ships, stores, delivers, and services the customer's expectations and the product's needs.*

ACTIONS IN THE MARKETING CHANNEL

The tasks to be accomplished in the marketing channel are these:

1. *Communicating* to all members of the channel.
2. *Selling* through intermediaries in the channel.
3. *Shipping and storing* to provide product availability.
4. *Servicing* both products and customers.

All these actions are a part of the channel marketing programs, with the exception of shipping and storing that are a part of the physical distribution function.

Communicating

All forms of communication are included in marketing communications: advertising, literature, product promotions, mail, telephone, training, and any contact related to marketing information. Even billings and follow-up on complaints can be a part of communication among the channel members. Of critical importance in serving the marketing channel, communicating must be timely and accurate. It is also recognized that each channel member has an obligation to maintain communications within the channel. Channel communications are a two-way system, with information also flowing from the user back to the manufacturer.

Selling

Selling is the act of transferring title to a product from one channel member to another. The marketing programs created by the manufacturer will determine some conditions under which products are sold by all channel intermediaries. Wholesalers, brokers, agents, and retailers may all be involved in the task of selling, however, in the corporate structure selling may be a function independent from marketing. Whether the sales force acts as an independent group or as a part of marketing, the conditions under which the transfer of title (sales) takes place are articulated through the marketing programs the sales force must follow.

Shipping and Storing

The selection of channel members may be contingent upon their capabilities to receive, store, and ship products. Shipping usually includes the capability to perform the order entry function and also frequently provides or generates documents to initiate the billing action. The function of physical distribution may also be performed by facilitating agencies such as public warehouses and common freight carriers, which will create one or more steps in the channel of distribution. Frequently, manufacturers use common carriers (truck, air, sea, or rail companies) to ship products to regional public warehouses. From these points, wholesalers or other channel intermediaries may pick up products with their own trucks or be serviced again by common carriers. Shipping and storing of products takes place at every level of the channel, with the exception of the user. In some specific situations, product handling, transporting, and storage may be performed by users of industrial products. This occurs when companies purchase and store frequently consumed supplies or other materials used in manufacturing or packaging products.

Customer Service

The need for customer services can vary greatly from product to product and from company to company. In general, customer services include those tasks needed to inform channel members about company programs and to train them how to promote product features and benefits. In addition, the service function fulfills legal and regulatory requirements and provides facilitating services, such as credit extension. Direct product service and technical advice may also fall under the umbrella of customer services. Companies such as International Business Machines (IBM) and major automobile manufacturers have made customer service and equipment maintenance a part of the product line they actively sell to their customers.

Review

Communicating, selling, shipping and storing, and providing customer services are carried out by the members of the marketing channel. Some of these actions are facilitated by companies that are not direct members of the channel but that do play a part in providing special services that make the action effective or efficient. These facilitating agencies include banks, truckers, advertising agencies, market research groups, equipment maintenance specialists, and the like. (The specifics of each facilitating action are discussed later and will deal with those channel members who perform or use these services.) Others who use the facilitating agencies are channel members such as manufacturers' representatives, agents, brokers, wholesalers, retailers, and sometimes even the user.

MARKETING CHANNEL INTERMEDIARIES

Most marketing channels are created with one or more intermediaries between the manufacturer and the consumer or user. The intermediaries will perform specific functions the manufacturers cannot, or prefer not, to do themselves. By employing other companies to perform a part of the marketing or physical distribution task, manufacturers give up some control over the products and markets involved and pay a part of their profit for the services rendered.

Probably no element in the marketing of products or the development of markets is as devoid of insight and understanding as is marketing through wholesalers, distributors, jobbers, agents, brokers, dealers, retailers, or whatever one calls the direct intermediary member of the marketing channel. The business relationships developed by the utilization of a marketing channel are those where independent businesses act as the funnels or filters through which manufacturers market their products. We use the term *funnel* or *filter* because a market intermediary or channel member may act as the manufacturer's direct representative, using all the materials and following the policies and programs established by the manufacturer. Conversely, some intermediaries may filter and selectively combine the policies and programs of one manufacturer with those of another, or those of its own independent company. As a result, manufacturers may be significantly frustrated by their limited marketing influence and capability to direct and manage their company's impact on the market. The manufacturer must realize that all members of the marketing channel, at every level, are the company's customers. The policies and programs of the manufacturer must therefore support all members of the marketing channel—whether they are direct members or indirect members.

To further complicate the marketing of products through intermediaries, manufacturers must deal with the fact that to be consistent with their own objectives, the intermediaries need to balance and blend the many different products, programs, and ambitions of their suppliers. Frustrated by this requirement, some intermediaries will need to acquire new capabilities to perform the necessary marketing or physical distribution tasks. For this reason, manufacturers must carefully evaluate the capabilities of the intermediaries they select. Intermediary selection and qualification is an important part of marketing channel development; indeed, it is critical to the maintenance of effective channel management. Compatibility is difficult to find in a competitive business environment.

CHANNEL STRUCTURE

The channel structure is defined by the names of the activities that take place in the channel. Although the marketing channel can have many different structures, the activities that will take place are consistent: manufacturing or marketing, wholesaling, retailing, and consuming, as well as physical distribution, which is involved in all these activities. There may be several members who make up the channel structure or as few as two. Manufacturers who sell to the users or consumers of their products have a direct or one-step channel structure with only themselves and the consumers as members. Other channel structures may contain six or more steps between the manufacturer and the consumer. Table 1.1 shows a one-step, two-member channel structure and a three-step, four-member channel.

The length of the marketing channel is influenced by many factors, which will be discussed in detail in chapter 3 (see especially Table 3.2). As an overview, remember that the marketing channel for industrial products tends to be shorter than the marketing channel for consumer product industries. This is true because vastly fewer consumers use industrial products compared to most other products. Also influencing the length of the industrial product's channel is the fact that the users are more easily reached and will usually buy more costly products in much greater volume per purchase than mass market consumers. In addition, the need for greater control over the product's movement throughout the channel, because of governmental regulations, influences the channel to be shorter. A high cost ratio between freight and handling charges and product worth requires greater control over the product and fewer

Table 1.1
Steps in the Channel Structure

Manufacturer
        to   One step, two members
        Consumer

Manufacturer
    to
    Wholesaler
        to   Three steps, four members
      Retailer
        to
          Consumer

intermediaries involved in product shipping, storage, and delivery. This subject is presented in detail in chapter 3.

WHOLESALERS, RETAILERS, CONSUMERS, OR USERS

As shown in Table 1.1, many marketing channels will be structured with wholesalers and retailers between the manufacturer and the consumers of its products. Every channel member has specific obligations to the others. These obligations must be met if the channel is to function properly. The channel manager must be aware of each channel member's obligations and make sure that what is expected of them is performed.

Wholesalers

Wholesalers may have as their suppliers only a few manufacturers or marketers or several hundred. Wholesalers must satisfy not only the needs of each supplier but also those of the retailers they expect to service. Retailers are the wholesaler's customers. When wholesalers are a part of the marketing channel, they usually represent the first step in the channel structure. Manufacturers who do not sell to wholesalers assume both the manufacturing function and the wholesaling function in the marketing channel. Likewise, wholesalers who sell directly to the user are also functioning as a retailer. One of the most important functions for most wholesalers is to provide physical distribution for the manufacturers they represent. When selecting wholesalers to become channel members, manufacturers first consider the wholesalers' ability to sell their products. Following the ability to sell, the wholesalers' shipping, handling, storage, and order-processing capabilities become of prime importance.

Retailers

Retailers usually need to have several wholesalers to make up their sources of supply. The retailer's first concern is to satisfy customer needs. To offer users or consumers a satisfactory product selection, retailers may stock products from a few manufacturers or from several hundred. There may also be requirements, established by the manufacturer or the wholesaler, to which retailers must conform. If retailers plan to stock and sell specific products of their choice, they will readily comply with the channel action requirements of their suppliers.

Consumers

Consumers or users make up the final members of the marketing channel. We note a distinction between the two because it is frequently the case that the final buyer of industrial products and services will not consume those products as one consumes toothpaste or corn flakes, for example. If the product in question is equipment, such as a tractor or a forklift, it is used over a period of time, worn out, and replaced. Everyone who owns an automobile buys motor oil, but that motor oil is not consumed in the usual application of the word. When consumption means product disappearance, then the designation *consumer* may be universally applied. Most industrial products such as fertilizers, chemicals, steel, paper, medical supplies, and trucks and tractors are consumed as they are used, over a period of time in the course of the user's business. The purchasers of these products do not normally think of buying them for consumption, but rather for use. Since all products that are used are not necessarily consumed, but all products that are consumed are used, this text will generally refer to consumers as product users.

MANUFACTURERS AND MARKETERS

As previously stated, the manufacturer or marketer of a product is considered to be the product source. A company may offer only one product, but usually most manufacturers offer a line of products. The primary obligation of marketers and manufacturers to their channel members is always to be competitive to other product sources. The competitive obligation will include new and in-line products, prices, marketing programs, and services. Effective communication that comes from the product source is essential to facilitate all channel actions. This is especially true for the implementation of marketing programs.

Industrial Products Manufacturers

Industrial products manufacturers include any company that manufactures or markets a product or service not intended to be used exclusively for mass consumer marketing. The manufacturer or marketer of the product is considered to be the product source whether it actually produces the product or has it produced by contract. Industrial product manufacturers and the companies who market their products need to develop specific relationships with each of their channel members, learning their needs and facilitating their capabilities.

Products for industrial uses are normally researched and produced for the specific needs of the markets they serve. Markets are *not* created for products; rather, products are researched and developed for the markets. This relationship is not as common in industries that produce for the nonindustrial market. In many of the industrial product industries, the users of the manufactured products are themselves producers or manufacturers. These users buy products from the marketing channel not for personal consumption but for the operation of their business. This relationship to the products used affects the development and management of the marketing channel structure differently than with end users who are not producers themselves, but are true consumers. The primary difference is centered in the *measurable* value of the industrial product whose use is motivated by need rather than by want. These products are purchased for their utility. The satisfaction of the need is measured by product value and intrinsic worth.

Industries involved with the manufacture and marketing of industrial products are also those that tend to be highly regulated by state and federal governmental agencies. The channel members and participants serving these industries must frequently perform services mandated by governmental regulations. The channel members' capability of satisfying these regulations significantly influences the manufacturers' ability to manage their marketing channels for compliance and effectiveness. Many consumer products also come under state and federal regulations. The significant difference for the channel member is that consumer product regulatory compliance is often completed at the point of processing or packaging, whereas for industrial products, compliance follows each step in the marketing channel.

Consumer Product Manufacturers

The marketing channel for consumer products recognizes the consumer as the most controlling factor in channel structure and product development. The marketing company must be able to reach a large number of consumers capable of purchasing their products. This requires the development of a marketing channel that can accomplish this significant physical distribution task.

Channel members in the mass consumer markets must also be able to provide many special services related to handling and storage of perishable products. Communications through advertising and product promotion are also important and costly in consumer product marketing. The selection of channel intermediaries in the consumer products industries will be highly dependent upon their ability to satisfy these and other special product-handling and marketing requirements.

FREIGHT, STORAGE, AND HANDLING FACTORS

Another consideration that significantly affects industrial products is the generally high cost of freight and the frequent need for special handling of these products. The ability to handle, store, and ship products such as drugs for animal use, lubricants, chemicals, explosives, lumber, gasses under pressure, and equipment plays a highly significant role in the selection of marketing channel members and the type of physical distribution system that is developed and managed. In many cases special use permits or licenses are required for the storage, handling, shipment, and application of these products. In the case of explosives, pesticides, drugs, and other regulated compounds, permits or a prescription for use may be required before they can be purchased.

Perhaps one of the most significant factors affecting the management of industrial products is that many are used infrequently or seasonally, and consequently purchasing may occur only once or twice each season or year. Compounding this channel management problem is the impact of unpredictable weather that will affect *when* products will be used, *which* products will be used, or *if* a product is to be used at all. Both the construction industry and agricultural industries are very weather sensitive. The availability of the right product at the right location and in the needed quantity presents inventory and storage management problems unique to these enterprises. For infrequently used products, physical distribution and suitable marketing programs for purchasing are crucial to channel management considerations.

THE MARKETING MIX

All the marketing functions, managed through the marketing channel, are found in the marketing mix. The marketing mix is the common designation for these elements:

1. products
2. prices
3. programs (or promotions)
4. physical distribution
5. people

Managing the marketing channel is the job of those in marketing positions. This text will cover the impact of each of the marketing mix elements on channel development and management tasks. Those who manage the marketing channel know that the effectiveness of its operation is dependent upon each member doing its part, whether as a direct or indirect participant.

The marketing channel concept embraces the proposition that there are two distinct activities that take place. One is the establishment of a physical distribution system. The other is the management of marketing objectives related to products, prices, programs, and *people*. This added element, people, represents the organizational choices that are possible in the marketing channel and the need to couple people to specific marketing responsibilities required in marketing planning.

The physical distribution system and channel structure is established as a fairly fixed system through which products flow in the marketing channel. Marketing actions and programs are the means by which the channel manager may stimulate, educate, regulate, and communicate with channel members. Both physical distribution and marketing actions may contribute to provide services for channel members and the products in the channel. Marketing actions control the productivity of the channel, whereas the physical distribution structure facilitates product flow between the channel members.

Marketing Management Actions

One of the most important marketing management actions is planning. Marketing management must plan to make the current channel environment competitive and profitable. In addition, managers must also plan for the future needs of the marketing channel. Planning for product and marketing needs will ensure that the company will continue to be an important product source to its channel members.

Marketing management is involved with all the activities in the marketing channel. Channel managers must fulfill the obligation of providing a consistent product source, offer competitive marketing programs, manage pricing, and motivate the people in the channel to perform their tasks. These marketing mix tasks are accomplished by effective communication, motivational marketing programs, and delivery of services

Table 1.2
Marketing Mix Activities

Marketing Management		Physical Distribution	
Communicating	Servicing	Shipping	Handling
• Product features	• Customers	• Provide carriers	• Equipment
• Pricing policies	• Products	• Delivery	• Wrapping
• Marketing programs	• Intermediaries	• Negotiate rates	• Packaging
• Motivation		• Handle claims	• Regulatory
		• Documentation	• OSHA regs
Selling	Motivating	Storing	Order Process
• To wholesalers	• Consumers	• Proper facility	• Order entry
• To retailers	• Wholesalers	• Inventory control	• Order trace
• To consumers	• Retailers	• Regulatory	• Document
• Intermediaries	• Facilitators	• Facilitators	• Feed back

needed by all channel members. Table 1.2 shows the marketing mix functions and actions.

Physical Distribution

Many systems of physical distribution—the storage, handling, order processing, and shipping of products in the channel—are available to those who plan the marketing channel. The actual physical distribution system employed will to a great extent be determined by the capabilities of the manufacturers and the intermediaries they select to be members of their marketing channel. Physical distribution is costly yet important, since the functions of distribution can significantly affect the product service aspects of marketing programs. Because physical distribution has a direct relationship to product and customer services, it is considered a part of the marketing mix. The efficient management of the physical distribution function is therefore very important to the smooth and effective application of marketing programs and channel management.

Since the major actions of physical distribution operate independently from most other marketing activities, channel managers must create a physical distribution plan independent of marketing mix elements except for product or customer services. This is not intended to imply that physical distribution is an end unto itself. In fact, physical distribution exists only to act as a facilitator for the marketing actions in the channel. Marketing actions work in concert with physical distribution to ensure that marketing activities take place as planned. A complete method for physical distribution analysis and marketing planning is presented in this text.

THE MARKETING CHANNEL MANAGER

Throughout this book, reference is made to the marketing channel manager. In most marketing organizations, there is no specific position titled Marketing Channel Manager. This designation is used as a catchall title for anyone involved with the management responsibilities of the marketing channel. The managers who will usually be involved in the marketing area range from the vice-president, who is responsible for marketing, to marketing directors, marketing managers, product managers, advertising and sales managers, market research managers, and all others involved in sales and marketing management. Those channel managers responsible for the physical distribution functions may include managers of materials handling and logistics, distribution services, distribution centers of public warehouses, and for some companies, those managers responsible for specific manufacturing activities. From time to time reference is made here to specific managers such as product managers or market managers. This designation is intended to indicate the position with the primary responsibility for a specific marketing activity.

MOTIVATION OF CHANNEL MEMBERS

Motivating channel members takes many different forms in order to satisfy the different needs at each level in the channel. Since wholesalers can buy products from many sources, profitability is the prime motivation for product selection. Assuming the profit motivation has been satisfied, the wholesaler becomes concerned with the marketing programs the manufacturer offers to help sell the products to retailers. Wholesalers will look at the credit options and the terms of payment when evaluating the profit potential of doing business with a specific supplier. Retailers are usually first concerned with the maintenance of product supply and availability. When consumers cannot find the products they want at one retailer, they will frequently seek out another that has what they are looking for. Retailers do not like losing customers. The second interest of a typical retailer is with the profitability of the products they carry. The only way for a retailer to remain in business is to be profitable. The primary motivational considerations for wholesalers, retailers, and product users are listed in Table 1.3 in their general order of importance.

Table 1.3
Motivational Considerations for Channel Members

For Wholesalers	For Retailers	For Product Users
Profit	Product availability	Product utility
Credit & terms	Profit	Value received
Marketing programs	Credit & terms	Credit & terms
Competitiveness	Marketing programs	Retailer service
Policies	Competitiveness	Product info.
Training	Training	Guarantees
Legal & regulatory	Legal & regulatory	Legal & regulatory

Note: Technical Service is considered to be a part of the marketing programs planned for wholesalers, retailers and product users.

MANAGING PRODUCTS AND MARKETS IN THE CHANNEL

The typical marketing organization provides four basic functions:

1. marketing planning
2. product and market management
3. advertising and promotion
4. market and marketing research

The members of the marketing channel will play a role in discerning how the manufacturer's marketing organization can or should manage these functions. It is therefore essential that the selection of channel members and the development of channel programs be consistent with the objectives of the marketing organization that will manage the channel. It is equally important to be assured that the channel intermediaries have the capabilities to implement and sustain the actions of the marketing programs.

Product management and market management functions are given special attention in this text concerning their influence in the development and management of the marketing channel. The impact different product line strategies and market actions have on channel members is of specific interest to those who manage the marketing channel. New product introductions and the development of new markets affect channel members differently at each level in the channel structure. The effects of the product life cycle on channel management and the decisions to be considered by the channel managers are discussed in a later chapter. How these decisions affect the company's marketing channel members is of critical importance to the maintenance of a competitive channel.

Market and marketing needs are also discussed in relationship to the role played by each of the channel members in identifying and helping to satisfy these needs. In a real sense, the capabilities of channel members and the depth of their commitment to their suppliers affect the alternatives available to manufacturers in managing the marketing mix at all channel levels.

SUMMARY

For most manufacturers and/or marketers, the choice of a marketing channel for their products and services is already established. The need to develop or design new marketing channels is uncommon and is almost always an expensive alternative to using channels that already exist. The modification of an existing channel structure to suit the unique needs of a marketer or manufacturer is not a difficult task. The marketing channel structure may consist of many members or it may function as a direct manufacturer-to-user channel. The channel manager must realize that an effective and satisfying relationship between manufacturers and marketing intermediaries (channel members) is a difficult one to establish and maintain. This is true because so many people at different levels in the marketing channel have their own priorities of needs to satisfy. Manufacturers who provide the proper incentives to encourage channel members to keep their products, programs, and communications near the top of their list of priorities will establish the most effective and productive marketing channel.

The most challenging aspect of channel management is the maintenance of control over all parts of the distribution flow and marketing activities. Controlling the most major elements of the marketing channel is sometimes a difficult and involved task. Marketers must consider the legal problems in channel control. Marketers must also develop channel programs that will stimulate the actions planned without creating conflict among participating or even competitive channel members. Legal, regulatory, and other governmental considerations are covered as a separate topic in this text.

Each of the marketing channel members, whether manufacturers, marketers, wholesalers, retailers, or users, has obligations to perform if the marketing channel is to work efficiently to the satisfaction of all. In chapter 2 we discuss the roles of channel members as well as the roles of nonmember channel participants (facilitating agencies). The nonmember participants are those who may ship, warehouse, insure, package, service, finance, or in any other way aid direct members of the marketing channel. Also discussed is a special group of channel members designated as brokers and agents. Brokers and agents, like wholesalers and retailers, are direct members of the channel and are not facilitating agencies.

This overview of the marketing channel and how it is managed should leave the reader with the perception that there are two parallel channels working together in tandem. One is the physical distribution channel, and the other is the marketing channel. The marketing channel embraces everything that happens to the product, the market, and all the intermediaries who play a part in successfully and profitably moving a product from its source to the consumer or user. Management of the marketing channel involves all the functions of the marketing mix, which we know as marketing, sales, and distribution. These subjects are covered in detail in this text from the point of view of the manufacturing and/or marketing company that is the product source.

QUESTIONS FOR DISCUSSION

1. Define *marketing channel*.
2. What are the four actions in the marketing channel?
3. What is meant by channel intermediaries? Name them.
4. When manufacturers sell directly to the retailer, who performs the wholesale function?
5. Channel intermediaries must serve many suppliers. How does this affect a manufacturer's point of view as to who his customers are?
6. For a wholesaler, what are the top three motivational considerations that can be offered by a manufacturer or marketer?
7. Are industrial products researched to fit into existing markets, or are markets developed for the products that are discovered through research?
8. Many industrial products are used as necessary tools in the maintenance and operation of the buyer's business. For this reason, buyers make a critical analysis concerning the product's_____.
9. What is meant by physical distribution? What function does it perform in the channel?
10. List the five elements of the marketing mix. All start with the letter *P*.

TWO

Marketing Channel Participants and Their Functions

The potential exists for many different participants to operate in the marketing channel. It is also likely that in each channel, the participants will perform a variety of functions even if those functions have similar names. Therefore, the names used here and the functions assigned to each are not fixed or unchangeable; rather, they reflect the most usual and logical players and their functions. The point of view is that of the product source. Most of the marketing channel structure and management concepts presented here can easily apply to either industrial or consumer markets. A distinction is made between the two markets primarily to emphasize the difference between the marketing channel functions. Industrial products may be different for channel members who use the products they purchase in the production of their own materials.

MARKETING CHANNEL PARTICIPANTS

Any company or agency involved with the marketing or physical distribution activities of a product is a participant in the marketing channel. Further, channel participants may be defined as direct participants or indirect participants. Direct participants are channel members, and they, too, are divided into two types. Table 2.1 shows the types of marketing channel participants.

The designations of channel members and facilitators listed in Table

Table 2.1
Marketing Channel Participants

Direct Channel Participants (Members)	Indirect Channel Participants
Merchants	*Facilitators*
Manufacturers, Producers, Marketers	Wholesalers, Distributors
Retailers, Dealers, Branches	Advertising Agencies
Users, Consumers	Sales Promotion Agencies
	Merchandising Specialists
Agents	Public Relations Firms
Brokers	Transportation Companies
Manufacturer's Representatives	Public Warehousing and
Commission Agents	Storage Companies
	Insurance Companies
	Service Companies
	Market Research Agencies

2.1 may not include all possible functions, but they are representative of commonly used terms. The direct channel members, who are also divided into two distinct groups, are segregated by the functions they perform. One significant fact concerning all direct merchant channel members is that they must own the products they sell.

> *Merchant channel members always take an ownership position with the products they sell, whereas agents, brokers, and manufacturer's representatives do not normally take title to products even though they participate in the selling function.*

Merchant Channel Members

Those channel participants we identify as merchant members, sometimes referred to as merchant middlemen, have specific tasks they must perform to be called merchants. The most singular qualification is that they take title to the products they sell. In addition to buying products from manufacturers, merchant channel members perform many important activities in the channel. It is their ability to perform these functions that makes merchant middlemen of value to the manufacturers they represent. In general, the merchant members perform more services than any other channel members. It is because merchant members are capable

Table 2.2
Services Provided by Merchant and Agent Channel Members

Merchant Members	Agent Members
Provide needed products as suppliers.	Act as the selling agent.
Offer depth and assortment of products.	May offer training.
Extend credit	Give customer assistance.
Perform bulk breaking.	Extend billing services.
Provide customer services.	Offer order processing.
Fulfill channel selling needs.	Provide storage and delivery.
Offer training.	Supply product information.
Maintain storage and delivery capabilities.	

of doing many more things for the manufacturer that they are paid more for their services. Agent members may be paid a commission ranging from 5% to 15%. Merchant members are usually paid 10% to 25% or more depending upon the services they perform.

By consulting Table 2.2, one can see that some services performed by merchant members of the marketing channel may also be performed by member agents. The size of the trade discount, or the gross profit margin that is offered, depends upon how many of the services needed are provided by the merchant members or agents. The decision to use merchant members or agents to provide services depends upon the ability of the manufacturers to perform these services for themselves. Almost all the market support services listed in Table 2.2 are required for the marketing channel to function. If manufacturers cannot offer the services, or prefer not to, they will have to pay a channel member or facilitating agency to provide them.

Most wholesalers, whether merchant or agent, will provide a selling function for their suppliers. If wholesalers sell the product, they will usually bill or invoice the product. The bill may be sent as payable to their own account, if they have title to the product, or to the manufacturer's account, if they have not taken title to the product but are acting as a commission agent for the manufacturer. The values of these marketing services as they apply to the chemical industry are listed in Table 2.3. These are representative values, not absolute, as they vary significantly among different types of businesses.

The costs listed in Table 2.3 are those that would occur whether the manufacturer is providing these services or the services are performed by one or more of the channel members. The percentages shown are then

Table 2.3
The Value of Marketing Services

1.	Market-level inventory costs	7%
2.	Storage or warehousing costs	2%
3.	Transportation and delivery costs	3%
4.	Order-handling costs	3%
5.	Credit costs	2%
6.	Selling costs	_8%_
Total		25%

Source: Chemical industry survey. R. W. McCalley & Assoc., Inc. (revised 1993).

relative to the value or cost they represent to the manufacturer. Another way of expressing these values is to say that the percentages represent the "add-on" costs manufacturers would experience were they to provide these services themselves.

A channel member in the chemical industry who provides all the listed services for a manufacturer supplier may expect to be paid up to the full value of these services, or 25%. In many situations the wholesaler may perform these functions or services for much less money than it would cost the manufacturer. Wholesalers perform the same marketing services for many suppliers at about the same cost these suppliers would encounter for themselves.

KEY SERVICES OF MERCHANT WHOLESALERS

Product Supply Source

The merchant wholesaler will usually buy products from several manufacturers. The types of products purchased are most often bought in families of products that will be stocked for resale by many of the wholesaler's retail customers. Because wholesalers offer many products, they have many selling opportunities each time their sales representative calls on a retailer. A hardware store may carry everything from cat food to precision tools. Thus wholesalers seeking the hardware retailer's business may offer one or several product lines to the retailer. Retailers expect wholesalers to act as their buyers, offering them the opportunity to fulfill their product requirements with competitively priced products. The ability to supply products fulfills the wholesaler's role as the product source for much of the merchandise the retailer requires. To maintain this commitment to retailers, wholesalers must have a supply relationship with many manufacturers.

Product Assortment and Depth

Retailers and wholesalers also know that consumers look for a selection of brands from different manufacturers. This marketing channel requirement forces the retailer to represent several manufacturers with similar products under different brands. Wholesalers must offer retailers the convenience of product assortment available from one source. The assortment must also represent the most needed products in sufficient *depth* to accommodate the user or consumer. Product depth relates to the sizes, colors, styles, or other specifications for a specific product or brand. As an example, retailers may offer an assortment of four different makes or brands of paint. The depth of inventory for each may vary in the many container sizes, types of paint, and color choices of preferred brands to only a few choice options for lesser brands. Retailers may choose to carry both complementary and competitive lines of products from several wholesalers. Most retailers will also offer products representing both premium pricing and economy pricing to satisfy the diverse buying preferences of their customers.

Bulk Breaking

The merchant wholesaler is required to perform the task of bulk breaking for retail channel members. As an example, bulk breaking is facilitated by wholesalers who buy a truckload of motor oil for their inventory and then sell it to retailers a few cases per order. The retailer, in turn, may sell a few quarts of oil to the user. Wholesalers buy in bulk quantities from many suppliers. They then offer their retailers an assortment of products from many manufacturers. Some wholesalers will even break cases of certain products to fill their retailers' orders.

Credit and Terms

Wholesalers are frequently asked by retailers to extend credit or provide special terms of payment. This is a competitive necessity in most industries; nevertheless, it provides a service to the retailer that is a cost to the wholesaler. The size of a wholesaler's accounts receivable can be significant and will affect the wholesaler's option for buying the assortment and the depth of products needed by retailers. Manufacturers, who supply many wholesalers, look for those who are financially strong. The wholesaler's ability to carry credit and offer extended terms of payment to retailers may in turn affect manufacturers, who may be required to have credit policies that complement the needs of their wholesalers.

Storage and Delivery

One of the most important services wholesalers must provide to their retailers is prompt and complete delivery of all products ordered. The commercial term that applies to shipping the complete order on time is *order service-level percentage*. If a company ships all products ordered in the time allowed for order completion, their order service-level percentage is 100%. If five of one hundred items ordered is not shipped but placed on a "back order" to be shipped at a later date, the original service-level percentage is 95%. If only two of the five back-ordered products are subsequently shipped, then the order completion percentage would go to the 97% service level. If all five of the remaining products were shipped, even at a later time, the service level would still be considered to be 100%.

Retailers have limited storage space for products, and usually they must stock on open shelves much of what they buy. Users who come into retail stores can find what they want with little involvement by the store clerk. The fact that most retailers have a limited depth of inventory strains their ability to satisfy all their customer's needs from stock on hand. For this reason, the retailer looks for the wholesaler to maintain a high service level for products ordered. As previously noted, users like one-stop shopping and will frequent the retailer who can satisfy this expectation.

Customer Services

Most wholesalers will provide a variety of customer services. These may be services provided or supported by the manufacturer, or they may be unique to the wholesaler. Customer services to retailers cover a wide range but fall into two categories: those services directed to the customer and those services directed to the product. Product services may include training in product use, product maintenance, and provision of technical information. Services directed to the retailer would include training in selling skills, store management, display techniques, product promotion, and financial and inventory management. It is also not uncommon for wholesalers of industrial products to offer direct product services to consumers (or users) who are the retailer's customers.

Table 2.4
The Wholesaler's Obligations to Manufacturers and Retailers

To Manufacturers	To Retailers
Selling capabilities	Product availability & delivery
Storage & shipping	Product selection
Financial strength	Credit & terms
Support marketing programs	Marketing programs
Competitive pricing	Competitive pricing
Management capabilities	Customer services
Operating programs	Training & business advice
Technical capabilities	Accurate communication
Bulk breaking	Technical services
Legal & regulatory compliance	Legal & regulatory compliance

Merchant Wholesaler Services to the Manufacturers and Retailers

The merchant wholesaler and the retailer are true middlemen. As the intermediary company between the supply source and the retailer, the wholesaler must satisfy specific marketing channel requirements in two directions: down to the retailer and up to the manufacturer. The obligations placed on wholesalers by manufacturers and retailers are shown on Table 2.4. Wholesalers and retailers may perform some or all of the services listed. Services not provided by either of these channel members will have to be fulfilled by the manufacturer or a facilitating agency.

AGENTS, BROKERS, BRANCHES, AND EXCLUSIVE DEALERSHIPS

The true merchant intermediaries are the wholesalers and the retailers. The other market intermediaries, called agents, may be brokers, manufacturer's representatives, or branch operations. Since these marketing channel representatives are also middlemen, they must be considered before the obligations of the manufacturers and users are discussed. Agents, whether brokers, manufacturer's representatives, or factory branches, perform the wholesaling and/or retailing functions for manufacturers who may not have other intermediaries in the marketing channel.

Commodity Brokers

Commodity brokers are limited in their product scope to the special interests they represent. Brokers who deal with raw produce or unprocessed agricultural commodities such as apples and small grains may deal with the *spot market*—today's business—or sell contracts for future delivery. This is a special type of marketing channel over which the producer has little management control and in which only limited marketing expertise is applied to the product. The limited commodity market channel will not be covered in this study because commodity trading and marketing of raw unprocessed products differ from the marketing of manufactured products such as corn flakes, applesauce, or alcohol. The channels developed to support the needs of commodity marketing are also unique. For the most part, agricultural commodities are grown under strict governmental regulations and sold under loan guarantee programs that change frequently. Those involved in commodity marketing channels must consult the latest information available.

Independent Brokers

Brokers who represent manufacturers of products rather than producers or growers of products may have a variety of relationships depending upon the needs of the manufacturers they represent. Brokers may have exclusive representation for all the company's products sold anywhere in the world, or they may represent the manufacturer only for a specific product category or for a single product in a restricted geographic area. In general, brokers are hired by marketers or manufacturers when the markets into which the products are to be sold are seasonal or not large enough for manufacturers to afford their own sales force. Seasonal products may be those that are infrequently purchased. It is common for brokers to operate in market segments where high-volume purchases are made directly by retailers or users and no other channel intermediary is involved. In these cases, the broker assumes the wholesaling and/or retailing function in the marketing channel. Such brokers or agents do not take title to the products they sell; thus they are not merchant wholesalers.

When brokers are acting in behalf of a retail chain, rather than the producer or manufacturer, they will contact several product sources to determine if they can fill an order of a specific product. In this way, the broker represents both the manufacturer and the retailer. Even in these situations, the broker is paid by the manufacturer. The following statement explains how brokers are identified.

> *Brokers represent manufacturers on a transaction-by-transaction basis.*
> *Each sale or transaction is a separate business deal. Brokers may handle*

many deals each year for a manufacturer, but every transaction is completed independently of all others.

It should be noted that food brokers, as well as others who represent the consumer products manufacturers, may act almost as manufacturer's representatives. These brokers may provide storage, delivery, and service retailers with the manufacturer's promotional programs. This is an *ongoing,* probably contractual, relationship with the supplier, and not a transactional one, as is more the case with industrial products brokers. Even in food brokerage relationships, the broker will not take title to the product but may bill the retailers to whom they sell in the name of the manufacturers they represent. Brokers who do take title to the products they sell become merchant wholesalers.

Manufacturer's Representatives or Agents

Manufacturer's representatives or agents differ from brokers in several important ways. Manufacturer's agents, or "reps," will usually represent only one manufacturer of a product category, whereas brokers will often represent several manufacturers. Agents may also perform more of the marketing functions for a marketer or manufacturer than will a broker. Agents may handle order processing and billing for the manufacturer's account. They may also arrange shipping, storage, and credit conditions and facilitate product guarantees for the manufacturer. Agents will sometimes sell their manufacturer's products through merchant wholesalers as well as directly to retailers or users. Seldom will agents or reps represent the retailer to their manufacturer, as is the case with brokers.

Manufacturer's agents are paid in the same way as a broker, that is, on a commission basis. The primary difference between the two is that the "factory reps" will also perform market-building functions related to product introductions, customer prospecting, account servicing, account building, and limited market information gathering. The manufacturer's agents will represent the manufacturer as though they were direct employees or a branch office of the company. Reps are restricted to specific territories for their manufacturers and must follow the company pricing and promotional programs.

Brokers will frequently set prices and negotiate the conditions of sale independently of the manufacturers they represent. The manufacturer is not committed to accept the broker's deals, whereas the manufacturer's agent is subject to his or her supplier's policies, programs, and direction. The manufacturer's rep offers only those conditions of sale (deals and prices) that are authorized by the marketers or manufacturers they represent. Occasionally, some manufacturer's representatives will buy products and take title to them as a merchant wholesaler. This is not a usual situation, yet it does occur.

Branch Operations

Branch offices are owned and operated by the manufacturer. These locations will perform the function of the wholesaler and/or the retailer. Branches are established by manufacturers for many reasons. Sometimes, but not frequently, the reason is that the branch can be operated with less cost than traditional merchant intermediaries. There are more compelling reasons that lead manufacturers to establish branch operations even when they are more expensive to operate than to use established channel intermediaries.

Manufacturers' Reasons for Establishing Branch Offices

1. *To establish exclusive representation.*
   No other manufacturer's products are sold at the same location (e.g., franchises).
2. *To perform highly technical tasks.*
   To service and repair specialized equipment. IBM makes this function into a product.
3. *To ensure legal or regulatory compliance.*
   The use or application of toxic or regulated chemicals may require licenses or permits and trained personnel to handle or apply these products (e.g., pest control operations).
4. *To provide specialized storage or product handling facilities.*
   Refrigerated storage, explosive materials, gases under pressure, toxic compounds, and even drugs may come under this special handling requirement.

There may be other reasons for establishing branch operations—such as not being able to find available alternatives. The listed reasons for operating branch operations can be summed up in one word: *control.* When it is necessary for manufacturers to exercise optimum control over their marketing channel, the answer may be a branch office or operation that provides either or both the wholesale and retail functions. Branches are expensive to operate, and for this reason the manufacturer who creates them must have a serious need.

Exclusive Dealerships

Exclusive dealerships, similar to franchises, are also a form of branch operations. In these arrangements, the manufacturer will help to estab-

Table 2.5
Characteristics of Brokers, Agents, and Branches

Brokers	Agents	Branches
Work for a commission	Commissioned	Salaried staff
Transactional deals	Long commitments	Company owned
Sell few products	Sell many products	Sell all products
No defined territory	Defined territory	Assigned area
Offer few services	Many services	Company services
Acts independently	Follow direction	Controlled
Never owns the product	Seldom owns product	Company product
May represent retailer	Seldom rep. retailer	Channel member

lish a local business as its exclusive branch operation. Major automotive and farm equipment manufacturers use this channel very frequently. Other exclusive dealerships may be represented by brokerage houses, insurance agencies, hardware retailers, oil companies, and beverage companies. Company branch operations and exclusive dealers will usually sell their products directly to the user. An exception to this is the beverage industry, where local or regional bottlers and distributors will sell to retailers. When the exclusive branch sells directly to the user, complete control over the product is maintained throughout the marketing channel. Consult Table 2.5 for a list of the characteristics of brokers, agents, and branches.

Franchise operations are also exclusive dealerships or retailers. Special purchasing conditions, selling and marketing commitments, and service requirements are specified in contracts between the supplier and the franchisee. Some of these conditions are discussed in chapter 12.

MANUFACTURERS AND PRODUCT USERS

The extremes of the marketing channel are represented by (1) the manufacturer as the product source, and (2) the user as the final product destination. Some marketing channels are comprised only of the manufacturer and the product user. Whether or not there are intermediaries in the marketing channel, the manufacturer and the user are obligated to perform certain tasks in developing and maintaining the channel. Often the fulfillment of these obligations to the marketing channel members is accomplished through intermediaries. The obligations of manufacturers are these:

1. Establish a profitable and reliable product source.
2. Give reasonable product guarantees.
3. Create and maintain a favorable identity for their brand of products to the users and to the whole marketing channel.
4. Maintain effective communications to users and all channel members through advertising, promotions, informational bulletins, and whatever means is necessary.
5. Fulfill regulatory and legal needs at all levels in the marketing channel.
6. Provide training, technical product information, and all necessary customer services.
7. Maintain a favorable competitive position in the marketing channel concerning all elements of the marketing mix.

User's Obligations to the Marketing Channel

Users in the marketing channel have few obligations, and only three can be considered important. Businesses that are closely regulated must instruct product users concerning their obligations regarding product usage, container disposal, and any other governmental regulations that apply. Agribusiness, power generation, mining, industrial manufacturing, and waste disposal are a few such industries watched by the Environmental Protection Agency (EPA), the Occupational Safety and Health Administration (OSHA), the Office of Economic Opportunity (OEO), the Food and Drug Administration (FDA), and many other governmental regulatory agencies.

The obligations of product users or consumers are these:

1. Use all products according to the manufacturer's recommendations.
2. Inform a responsible channel member promptly of any problems.
3. Pay for the products purchased according to the terms agreed.

All other responsibilities in the marketing channel are those of the manufacturer, wholesaler, retailer, broker, or agent. All channel intermediaries should be dedicated to achieving the user's satisfaction with the products.

Facilitating Channel Participants

Those in the marketing channel who are not directly involved with products may be considered facilitating agencies. (A representative list of such agencies as indirect channel participants is noted in Table 2.1.) Facilitating agencies may be utilized at any level in the channel structure, from the manufacturer to the user of the products involved. Those who use these services will pay for them. If the service is provided by the manufacturer, it adds value to the product because it removes the expense of the service provided to channel members. The cost of the facilitating service will result in a higher product cost to the user and lower profit for the channel member paying for the service.

The need for facilitating services depends on whether the channel members are capable of providing these services. A manufacturing company may not have the ability to create advertising copy and graphic layouts to give a print media representative for publication. In such a case, the manufacturing company would find it necessary to hire an advertising agency to perform this service. A marketing-oriented company may have an "in-house" advertising agency of its own to save the cost of a facilitating advertising agency.

Many companies do not manufacture any of the products they sell. They obtain their products by contract with selected manufacturers that produce for companies who are marketers of their own brands. These marketing companies may have their own advertising, graphic arts, product promotion, or market research capabilities, but no manufacturing facilities. They will not need to employ outside agencies to develop or place ads for them, but they do have the cost of paying a contract manufacturer for their products.

As an example of company strength and the utilization of facilitating services, consider Merck and Company, a large pharmaceutical company dedicated to basic research, developmental research, manufacturing, and several types of marketing. Merck is a strong, highly integrated company that uses many facilitating agencies to find and employ the highest quality of services available. Merck knows its own strengths and how it can best invest its money for the future of the company and at the same time manage its several marketing channels. Maintaining an in-house advertising agency is not one of the activities that attracts corporate investment by Merck.

The Value of Facilitating Services

The value of facilitating services to wholesalers or retailers is based on what is needed and what it would cost the channel member to provide these services for themselves. In most situations, a facilitating agency may charge less than what it would cost a channel member to provide a particular service for itself. This is possible because the facilitating agency can spread the costs over a base of many clients. Examples of cost spreading include making legal, accounting, advertising, and shipping services available to channel members from facilitating agencies.

In most cases, the facilitating agency will provide its expertise to a channel member *as needed*, rather than as an ongoing service. Market research, sales promotion, recruiting, market audits, and shipping represent the *use-as-needed* types of facilitating actions. The more fixed-services, or ongoing facilitating agencies used, may be represented by advertising, public relations, billing services, warehousing, and accounting services and by the provision for open lines of credit with banks or other financial institutions.

Most companies will also develop long-term relationships with insurance companies and legal firms. For the most part, facilitating agencies will provide services rather than products for those companies who use them. With today's high cost of specialized and infrequently utilized equipment, such as that used in construction jobs, farming, and natural resources exploration, an equipment-leasing agent may be found to provide a facilitating service that handles or carries a product needed for only a limited period of time.

In some instances, the wholesaler or retailer may also provide a facilitating service. It is common for wholesalers and retailers to extend credit for their accounts. In many cases, technical service and training is also available as a facilitating service. The important point to remember concerning facilitating services is this:

> *All members of the marketing channel may use some type of facilitating agency at one time or another in their relationship to the marketing channel. The deciding factors are whether assistance is needed and whether the channel members can perform the services themselves as effectively and at less cost than the facilitating agent.*

SUMMARY

All members of the marketing channel must perform their function properly and in harmony with the other channel members. Because marketing channels with many members are more difficult to manage, manufacturers try to keep the channel as short as possible. However, even if the channel used is directly from the manufacturer to the user, none of the necessary functions of the wholesaler and retailer are eliminated. In this case, manufacturers must assume the responsibility for the performance of the essential channel functions. As long as there is a competitive or economic justification for the existence of an intermediary member in the marketing channel, the intermediary will exist. Wholesalers as well as retailers, who both accept some of the marketing costs in the channel from the manufacturer, will perform a necessary service and will earn their profit according to the extent of the services they perform.

Channel managers employed by a marketing or manufacturing company must evaluate the need and worth of all services required in the channel, whether available through a direct channel member or an indirect channel member. They must then determine how these services will be performed, who will perform them, and what the cost will be to the company.

QUESTIONS FOR DISCUSSION

1. Define *merchant wholesaler* and *merchant retailer*. What are their functions in the channel?
2. Why are facilitating agencies needed in the marketing channel?
3. What is the clear distinction between agents and merchant channel members?
4. What are the notable differences between brokers, manufacturer's reps, branch operations, and exclusive wholesalers or retailers?
5. What are the primary reasons for establishing branch offices?
6. Automobile companies and manufacturers of large equipment, such as John Deer and Caterpillar, may assign exclusive dealerships. Give at least three reasons why a manufacturer would establish this type of representation.
7. List the key obligations of the manufacturer to the marketing channel.
8. Will all channel members use the same facilitating services? Give your reasons.
9. Who pays for facilitating services?
10. When a manufacturer sells its products directly to the user, are the services performed by the wholesaler and retailer eliminated? Explain.

THREE

Marketing Channel Structure and Physical Distribution

In planning the structure and physical distribution of the marketing channel, two basic questions must be answered by manufacturers or marketers. The first question deals with channel structure: "What is the best way to profitably sell my products to users?" The second question, "How can I most effectively and efficiently deliver the product into the user's hands?" covers the subject of physical distribution. To answer these questions requires the formation of a carefully planned organizational structure. This structure *is* the marketing channel. Individually, the actions indicated by these two questions point to different objectives, yet they must work together to accomplish the marketing goals. Remember that the physical distribution structure exists only because it is needed to help accomplish the marketing objectives. The channel structure, independent of physical distribution, is established to serve the marketing objectives of the manufacturer.

One must first make critical *marketing* decisions before a channel structure can be conceived that is suitable to accomplish the manufacturer's goals. These decisions will lead to the formation of a concept for the marketing channel structure. Reaching the established marketing goals, according to plan, is dependent upon a sound marketing and physical distribution channel structure. Experienced channel managers know that plans to accomplish both the marketing objectives and the physical distribution objectives are frequently modified by the availability of intermediaries capable of performing these essential functions.

SELLING PRODUCTS TO THE USER

If we assume that products similar to those the manufacturer wishes to sell are already being purchased by consumers, it is logical to believe that where these products are now being purchased is the established and preferred retail channel. It is almost always a successful strategy for manufacturers to include in their channel structure those channel members who are now supplying the users whom they want to buy their products. Users must buy their products either directly from the manufacturer or from a wholesaler, a retailer, or some other channel intermediary. There are no other options. Those intermediaries who sell to consumers are acting as retailers, no matter what other channel functions they perform. The most crucial consideration for manufacturers is to provide a way for the consumers of their products to buy them as easily as possible.

SHIPPING TO THE USER

The determination of an effective physical distribution channel is provided in part by the resolution of how the company will sell to retailers. When one knows which retailers are involved, finding the channel intermediary that sells to them is the next step. Although the marketing channel intermediaries that perform the selling function may also deliver products to the retailers, this is not always the case. Many wholesalers never deliver products to retailers but depend upon facilitating agencies such as public warehouses and common carrier truckers to do the physical distribution job.

Always keep in mind that the satisfaction of the marketing objectives is the primary goal. Making the best plan for marketing channel structure and physical distribution will require a significant amount of information. This chapter presents methods for gathering the information necessary to accomplish this difficult task.

MARKETING CHANNEL STRUCTURE

From chapters 1 and 2, we know the basic marketing channel structure consists of three components:

1. product source, the manufacturer, or the marketing company
2. the channel intermediaries (wholesalers, brokers, agents, retailers, or branches)

3. the users or consumers of the products—identified earlier as the direct channel members

The previous chapters also informed us that the marketing channel structure may consist of two or more members with one or more steps in the channel. The number of channel members is determined by the need for intermediaries to perform all the tasks required. Chapter 2 provided a list of potential marketing channel participants and their functions. The channel structure will be formed from this list. As a rule, the more participants used in the channel structure, the more cost is added to the marketing process. All channel members must be paid for the services they provide. It is therefore important for manufacturers or marketers to clearly identify *all* the channel services that are needed. Following this evaluation, manufacturers must determine the company's ability to provide these services. Where capabilities are lacking, the manufacturer must locate either direct or indirect channel participants to provide them. The first place to look is to the wholesalers in the channel.

The Wholesale Function in Channel Structure

Merchant wholesalers, or agents, represent the first possible intermediary step between the marketing or manufacturing company and the user in the marketing channel structure. Whether the marketing company manufactures its products or not, it is the first channel member. Wholesalers represent the first step in the channel. Channel structures using wholesalers or agents recognize them as the second member of the channel but as the first step in the channel structure below the marketer or product source. Wholesalers are direct members, whereas agents are indirect members.

Whenever the first step in the channel structure is represented by an intermediary who sells to a retailing company, that channel intermediary is a wholesaler. It makes no difference whether the wholesaler is a merchant member or a nonmerchant agent. If they sell to retailers, they fill the marketing function of wholesaling. In cases where the manufacturer sells directly to the retailer, the manufacturer also provides the wholesale function. In these cases, wholesaling is a step in the channel assumed by the manufacturer or marketing company.

There may be many wholesalers in the marketing channel. Usually a manufacturer will develop or select a channel with only one intermediary wholesaler, but not uncommonly a marketing channel may have two or more wholesaling intermediaries. As an example, companies who utilize agents will frequently employ those who sell only to merchant wholesalers. In these cases, the agent represents step 1 in the channel structure and is the second member of the channel. The agent's customer, who may be the merchant wholesaler, is the second step and the third member in the marketing channel. If the merchant wholesaler sells the product to yet another wholesale intermediary, such as jobber or distributor who buys in lesser quantities, the next intermediary becomes step 3 and member four of the marketing channel.

The wholesaling function may be performed by the manufacturer or an agent, distributor, jobber, contract buyer, small-lot wholesaler, or anyone who sells the product to another wholesaler or retailer—whether a merchant wholesaler, an agent, or a manufacturer's direct representative.

All wholesalers resell either to other wholesalers or to retailers. Wholesalers do not sell to the product user. If they do sell to users, they become known as retailers for that part of their business. Some wholesalers sell to retailers as well as users. Companies that sell directly to the user are more likely to sell through retail stores they own and operate themselves. It is difficult for wholesalers to develop both direct user business and retail business in the same market, since retailers do not want to buy from wholesalers who may also become their competitors.

Even more commonly, wholesalers sell to independent retailers along with their own branch retailers in the same market. Companies entangled in these marketing situations create conflict in the channel. Retailers who must compete with their supplier's retail branches reasonably feel they are at a competitive disadvantage. This practice prompts retailers to shift their support to the products of manufacturers who will not permit their wholesalers to cause direct retail competition. Manufacturers must keep this situation in mind when selecting channel intermediaries.

The Retailing Function in Channel Structure

Any member of the marketing channel who sells to the user is performing the retailing function. This function can be performed by the marketing company or by the manufacturer of products who acts as a retailer in the channel, as is the case with many mail order businesses. Company branches may also sell directly to the user and thus fulfill the retailing function. Companies involved with products that are bulky, heavy, perishable, or low profit are candidates for short, direct marketing channel structures. Some examples of such products are animal feeds, fertilizer products, cement block products, fruits, vegetables, and chicken products. Companies such as major tire manufacturers, automobile companies, and large-equipment producers may sell directly to product users. Leasing agencies and fleet buyers will not usually buy cars from the local dealership.

The traditional retailer is an independent retail store or a branch store of a retail chain. These retail stores buy their products from several wholesalers, who may be merchants or agents. Except for users, retailers present the largest group of all channel members; they are also the largest group of *direct* channel intermediaries.

There are two important aspects to retailing as far as marketing channel structure and management are concerned. The first is the support retailers give to manufacturers by stocking, displaying, and recommending their products to the users. The second important job of retailers is to fill their customers' needs for various products and services. Retailers who fail to take care of their customers' needs will have no customer base in the market and, consequently, will not be able to offer competent representation for their manufacturers or wholesalers.

Retailers who are part of a large chain of stores will buy, stock, and sell products according to the chain's management guidelines. The wholesale buying will usually be done at a central location, and the retail chain store will order from the company facility responsible for physical distribution and/or wholesaling to their area.

Independent retailers buy directly from their wholesale suppliers and depend upon them to deliver products as needed as well as providing all wholesale services. Making plans to ensure sufficient inventory of needed products is the retailer's responsibility. However, retailers depend on the advice of their wholesalers to help make these plans. Independent retailers will need more services than will branch operations of chain retailing companies. Unlike independent retailers, most branch retail operations have little flexibility in deciding which products to buy—this is determined by the purchasing department at the chain's headquarters.

In channel structure considerations, a chain retailer purchasing in large quantities may be a bigger potential customer to the manufacturer than some of its wholesalers. For this reason, some retailers may be designated as "house accounts" or contract buyers. This means they will buy directly from the manufacturer rather than through a wholesaler. The prices that retailers pay for the manufacturer's products may be the same as wholesale or they may be a contract price based on an annual volume of purchases. Whatever the pricing, the house account will buy below the normal retail purchase price. House accounts earn a discount because of the services they render to the retail branches and because of the volume of their purchases.

The retail step in the marketing channel structure is the last one before the user of the product takes possession and ownership. Once again, a manufacturer may sell directly to the user. When this is the case, the manufacturer assumes the function of the wholesaler as well as the retailer in the marketing channel. When wholesalers sell directly to the user, they also assume the retailer functions. Whether there is a one-step marketing channel or a six-step marketing channel, the wholesaling and retailing functions, with the services they represent, must be provided by the channel members.

Manufacturers of products that require the use of a long marketing channel involving many members must remember that retailers have the final impact on the potential users of their products. This makes it highly important for manufacturers to maintain good relationships with the retailers, either directly or indirectly, through the intermediaries in the channel.

The retail step in the marketing channel for industrial products manufacturers is often performed by a wholesaler or a manufacturer who sells directly to the user. The high cost of maintaining several levels in the channel is one of the reasons for this consolidation in the marketing structure. Another reason is to maintain control over regulated products. The volume of business from individual industrial and agribusiness producers is growing dramatically, while at the same time the number of accounts is shrinking. The volume of trade from the large corporate farming operations accounts is increasing while small farms and industrial businesses are disappearing. Many producers can buy products in larger quantities than a local retail store and will find wholesalers or manufacturers eager to sell to them directly and create an alternative branch channel. Consumer products sold by chain retailers and the rapidly growing number of factory outlet malls produce significant competitive pressures on independent retailers and wholesalers and provide the manufacturers ample justification for selling their products directly to these large retailers and bypassing traditional wholesalers.

Branches in the Channel

Recall that the marketing channel runs parallel to the physical distribution channel, and that each may have different functions. The physical distribution channel may involve separate branches feeding into or bypassing the main channel of distribution. The branch channels are the manufacturer's branch channel, the wholesaler branch channel, and the retailer branch channel. Manufacturers may also use a separate branch in their own channel of distribution to conveniently locate inventories of their products at strategic market locations. The need and function of branches in the physical distribution channel will depend upon the capabilities of the members of the channel and the marketing programs they provide.

The Manufacturer's Branch Channel. The manufacturer's branch channel is used when the wholesaler asks for direct shipment to retailers or users. Usually wholesalers will perform part of the physical distribution job. Most wholesalers receive products from the manufacturer, take title, and then store the products in their own warehousing facilities for shipment again to retailers. This activity provides wholesalers with the opportunity for bulk breaking, collecting assortments of products ordered by their retailers, and reshipping them to the retailer.

Table 3.1
Branch Channel Shipping and Billing

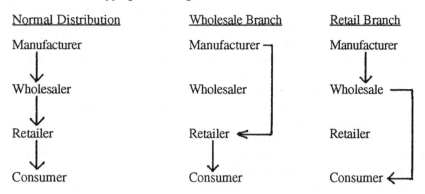

_____ Shipping path; Billing path follows the same path as normal

distribution in both branch channels.

As just mentioned, some manufacturers will keep products in conveniently located warehouses from which wholesalers will either pick up or have an order shipped from the warehouse to the wholesaler. In these situations, the wholesaler still performs its normal distribution functions once it receive the products ordered. There may also be branches in the normal channel prompted by marketing programs that enable wholesalers to have the manufacturer ship products directly to retailers or to users—a procedure known as _drop shipping_. These are usually large orders such as full truckloads, or rush orders for a critical spare part to repair a piece of disabled machinery, or special products manufactured for a specific user. When manufacturers ship products for a wholesaler directly to a retailer or the user, the manufacturer uses a branch channel to bypass the wholesaler. The cost of this service may be charged to the wholesaler if it exceeds what is normal for similar shipments. The wholesaler saves the "in-and-out" costs related to taking products into the warehouse and reshipping them. The wholesaler may also save the shipping costs if they are paid by the manufacturer. The decisions relating to cost sharing on direct shipments are a part of the marketing programs and are usually tied to competitive pressures. See Table 3.1 for a diagram of the structure established for branch channels.

Wholesaler's Branch Channel. The merchant wholesaler has several options for the development of a branch channel. One option is to ship directly to the retailer's customer as a service for the retailer. This service is not uncommon in industrial products that are bulky or require special handling equipment. For example, a manufacturer of special types of bricks sold through wholesalers may deliver directly to a contractor's building site for the wholesaler that sold the bricks to the contractor. As with the manufacturers, wholesalers will normally offer this service only for large and special orders. The primary purpose for using a branch channel is to save money, save time, and stay competitive. Product handling is costly and may cause wear and tear on certain products. In most situations where the branch channel is used, all or part of the cost of reshipping will be saved by the channel member's asking for this service.

A second option, used by some wholesalers, is the competitive retail branch. Some wholesalers not only will perform the wholesaling function in the channel but will operate retail stores as well. Frequently these wholesaler retail branches will be located at the wholesaler's warehouse. Most retailers do not like their suppliers to be in competition with them and will look for wholesalers that do not operate retail branches as their source of supply. It should be noted that when wholesalers do operate a retail store, they will usually mark products at the full retail price in order to prevent imposing a disadvantage on the retail accounts they sell. The advantage to the wholesaler is a larger profit.

Retailer's Branch Channel. Branch channels are common in industrial product marketing but are infrequently found in mass consumer product channels. Usually branch channels are linked to the large retail chains that establish their own wholesale channel serving the chain's retail stores exclusively. Since this branch channel is internal, not serving the general public or other retailers, it is not competitive with other wholesalers selling competitive retailers. However, the competitive relationship may occur with other shippers and warehousing companies, the facilitating agencies.

Consider the Wal Mart operation as an example. This retailer establishes regional warehouses where it stores products purchased directly from the manufacturer. Each regional warehouse serves approximately six Wal Mart retail stores. A delivery schedule is established for each store in the region, and using Wal Mart trucks, regular delivery is made from the regional warehouse to the retail stores. This system provides an integrated channel from the manufacturer to the user. Acting as wholesalers, the company owns the warehouses as well as the trucks that do the delivery. The company also owns the retail outlets. When the manufacturer, the product source, will not deliver the product to the regional warehouse without charge, Wal Mart will sometimes pick up its orders at the factory with its own trucks. These services and their costs are all a part of the price negotiation with the product source.

PRODUCT SOURCE

Manufacturers and/or marketers are the product source. As far as the direct channel members are concerned, there is no basic difference between the manufacturer and the marketer. The brand name owner is the product source. Many companies do not actually manufacture the products they market. When a marketing company hires other companies to manufacture and package the products marketed under its label, it engages in *toll* or *contract* manufacturing. These manufacturing companies are known as *private label* manufacturers. This type of marketing and manufacturing arrangement is common for companies who wish to sell a complete line, or family of products, but have the capabilities to manufacture only part of the products. For example, a manufacturer of tractors and other farm equipment may wish to offer a complete line of lubricants and oils for its equipment. It is unlikely that the tractor manufacturer would have the capability to produce petroleum products. However, this company can go to any number of petroleum product manufacturing companies that would be glad to formulate products according to given specifications and package them for marketing under the tractor company's brand name. The petroleum manufacturer's name may or may not appear on the label. Statements such as "manufactured for" or "distributed by" preceding the marketer's name may fulfill the labeling requirements.

Regulated products such as pesticides, drugs, and toxic compounds must display a regulatory code number on the label. By this procedure the regulatory agencies can trace a product to the manufacturing and marketing source.

Those who perform the product source function may also be the manufacturer's agents. They represent one manufacturer for a specific product category in a given market area. In the name of the manufacturer, agents carry out all the functions of the product source for their wholesale, retail, or user customers. As mentioned in chapter 2, these arrangements are usually entered into when the manufacturer is not a major factor in a market and does not wish to commit its own people to develop and maintain a market presence.

For the members of the marketing channel, the product source is considered to be the company whose name appears on the label. This is the *brand identity*. It is the marketing company, or brand owner, that establishes the prices, programs, and physical distribution for the products it markets. The channel intermediaries will participate in the channel performing the familiar functions of selling, communicating, shipping, and storing as well as providing customer service. These actions are controlled by the marketing policies and practices under which the marketed products are moved through the marketing channel. The channel structure must accommodate the policy mandates of the company.

THE USER'S IMPACT ON CHANNEL STRUCTURE

One may think that because they are at the end of the distribution line, users would have little impact on how the channel is structured. The fact is that the user has more effect on channel structure than any other channel member. How well manufacturers accommodate user wants and needs—and how well they manage marketing programs directed to the users of their products—will determine the degree of success for the channel structure.

Consumer marketing programs are established to cause actions in the marketing channel that will accomplish the manufacturer's objectives. Some of the most important channel marketing programs are sales promotion, advertising, product guarantees, product quality, credit or terms of sale, and the competitive influences the manufacturer or marketer attempts to develop.

From the channel structure point of view, the last step is easy to locate. In fact, the whole channel structure is developed to provide an avenue for the manufacturer to influence, serve, and satisfy the consumer. The total number of potential users, their geographic location, and the frequency with which they purchase a manufacturer's products are the primary demographics that dictate the selection of a channel structure that can best serve users. Factors such as product cost, profitability, and customer service needs will also affect the channel structure.

The channel structure is obviously developed to serve users, and it must start with their purchasing habits, not the manufacturer's desire to develop a specific channel structure. Marketers are usually obliged to engage the marketing channel frequented by the consumers they wish to sell to—unless they are offering a completely new product or service for which there is no marketing channel developed. The need to develop a completely new marketing channel is most unusual. The design and creation of a completely new channel structure is also very costly. Building a new channel is time consuming and presents uncertainty about the new intermediaries' capabilities to perform as expected in the channel. Marketers and manufacturers are usually best served by existing marketing channel structures that are currently functioning and serving the users they hope to reach.

However, there are some valid reasons for becoming involved with the development of a new channel. A new channel structure may be considered when the manufacturer (1) wants to exercise more control over how the product is marketed than an existing channel will allow and (2) can design a channel that will do the job for less cost than is

Table 3.2
User Impact on Channel Structure Length

	High	Moderate	Low
Number of potential users	Long	Shorter	Short
User Density in the market	Short	Longer	Long
Product cost (including freight)	Short	Longer	Long/short*
Profit margin or mark-up	Long	Shorter	Short
Frequency of purchase	Long	Shorter	Short
Service needs	Long	Shorter	Short
User's regulatory obligations	Short	Longer	Long

*Note: This dichotomy in channel length occurs because products with a low freight to product cost can be sold by direct mail. High freight cost and low profit, or product cost, can also lead to a short marketing channel, whereas low cost and low freight may result in a longer marketing channel.

possible with existing channels. In some situations existing channel members will not permit a new product or manufacturer to participate effectively. (These situations are discussed in chapter 4, Market Characteristics and Channel Management.)

Users have great impact on the marketing channel structure, as shown in Table 3.2. The larger the number of channel members, the longer the channel becomes. Remember, it takes two members to make a one-step channel. Each additional member adds another step in the marketing channel. The more steps, the longer the channel. In addition, when viewing Table 3.2, remember that whoever sells to the user must perform all the necessary channel member functions of the retailer.

Market Characteristics and Channel Structure

The importance of market volume, size, and density are discussed in detail in chapter 4. The following list of channel-length influences is followed by details regarding the other market characteristics.

1. The larger the number of potential users, the longer the channel structure.
2. High user density normally influences a shorter channel structure, but this factor alone will not be the determining element for channel length.
3. The higher the product cost, the shorter the channel structure. Low cost relates to a longer channel structure.
4. Low profit margins mean a short channel structure. High profit margins can support a longer structure.

5. Products that are purchased frequently require a long channel to assure their availability. High purchasing frequency usually indicates a low product cost. Special situations involving product freshness in high-density markets may indicate a shorter channel structure.

6. Frequent nontechnical service allows the channel to be longer. Less frequent, specialized, or very technical service requirements influence a shorter channel structure.

Market Size. A distinction is made in the descriptive nomenclature of market size: Size relates to the number of potential users, not to dollars of potential sales. The number of product units sold in a market is also used to express the market size when this is a more reliable and significant figure.

User Density Influence on Channel Structure. Markets are characterized by the density of potential users in specific retailing areas. In general, the more concentrated the user potential, the easier it is to reach users and the shorter the market structure required to service them. Conversely, the more scattered the potential users, the more probable a longer channel structure.

Product Cost Influences on Channel Structure. The cost of a product may directly influence channel structure. The unit cost of a forklift or automobile is high and may be considered investment spending. These types of products are used over and over again for many years, and financing their purchase may be a deciding factor that influences when to buy and what brand to buy. Major equipment products, such as forklifts and automobiles, are generally sold by exclusive retailers for specific brands or by company branch retailers. Because of the high purchase price, the direct incentives offered by the manufacturer to the user—the manufacturer's discounts—are of considerable importance. In some instances, special options are offered and must be specified by the manufacturer in advance of product delivery. These market characteristics require a short line of communication, no storage or warehousing for wholesale distribution, and the frequent involvement of the manufacturer with the retailer. Periodic customer and product services may also be required for maintenance. In addition, providing replacement parts to support the marketing channel structure may be necessary as a customer service consideration.

The market for automobile parts and services is aptly called the *after market*, since the products or services follow the original purchase. Consideration of the after market requirements should be a part of the initial channel planning. For the automotive industry, for example, the manufacturer is both the product source and the wholesaler. The only channel intermediary is a retailer that may be a company branch or an exclusive retail operation.

Products that cost only a few dollars, such as hand tools, consumable supplies, and maintenance items, may be purchased on impulse or with little thought concerning "best buy" shopping, credit, or product service. The channel for these items tends to be long because the cost is low and purchasing is more frequent. The convenience of the purchase location is more important than the comparative price of the product.

Profit Margin Influences on Channel Structure. The impact of profit on channel length, as shown in Table 3.2, may be expressed as the *gross profit margin* or as the *gross profit markup.* The gross profit margin is based on the *selling price* of the product and is derived by dividing the dollars of gross profit per unit of sale by the unit selling price. The markup percentage is based on product *cost* and is calculated by dividing the profit dollars by the cost of the product.

Example

1. Gross Profit
   - A product sells for $400
   - The product cost is $300
   - The gross profit is $100
2. Gross Margin
   - The gross profit is $100
   - The selling price is $400
   - $100 ÷ $400 = 25% gross profit margin
3. Gross Markup
   - The gross profit is $100
   - The product cost is $300
   - 100 ÷ $300 = 33 ⅓% gross profit markup

The gross profit margin for most products will vary from sale to sale, season to season, or year to year. Most manufacturers will set a minimum acceptable level of gross profit beyond which they will refuse to compete on a regular basis. Considering that the cost of managing and maintaining the marketing channel increases in proportion to the number of participants involved, it is reasonable to believe that a product with a low profit margin cannot support a long and elaborate channel structure. The impact of the profit margin on channel structure is quite consistent for low-profit products. Low profit margins lead to short channels.

Products such as tractors, automobiles, and forklifts have a short channel. The gross profit on cars and equipment may be high in the dollars involved per unit of purchase, but not in the margin of profit as a percentage of the selling price. A tractor that sells to the farmer for $80,000 may bring the manufacturer $20,000 to $25,000 in gross profit. This is not a high margin of profit. It is only a 25% to 31.25% profit margin on the selling price. Pharmaceutical products, on the other hand, may make their marketers a gross profit margin of only a few dollars per unit of sale, but those few dollars will represent 60% to 85% or more of the selling price. This is a high margin of profit per unit of sale. Markups exceeding 200% of cost are not at all unusual for pharmaceutical products. These companies can afford a longer channel structure than the equipment or truck manufacturer, who makes more dollars per sale but makes fewer sales. There is also less margin of profit. The effect of profits and prices in the marketing channel are discussed in detail in chapter 10. The frequency of purchase, our next topic, also significantly affects this situation.

The Influence of Purchase Frequency on Channel Structure. Products consumed or used up on a frequent basis require many retail supply sources. The primary impact of purchasing frequency on the channel structure is the need for product availability at the user level. Frequently purchased products are usually lower-cost products with high user density, that is, with many potential users in a specific area. The frequency of purchase and the product cost are usually linked in their influence on channel structure. Profits may also be lower because of competitive pressure related to high product demand. Supply items, such as bath soap and toothpaste, are usually low in cost and can be purchased through many different retailers who buy from several wholesalers. This ensures that a variety or selection of these products will be conveniently in stock at many places at all times.

Perishable items, such as food products that do not remain fresh and nutritious when stored for long periods of time, present special considerations for the channel structure. These products are usually purchased every week of the year. Yet the channel structure will be as short as the retailer can reasonably establish. The channel structure created for fresh lettuce, tomatoes, potatoes, and carrots may include a producer, a broker, and the retailer. Sometimes retailers will have their own produce buyers, who take the place of the broker in the channel structure. In these illustrations, the influences of market density and product perishability are greater than that of high purchasing frequency.

Service Influences on Channel Structure. Service factors, related to product users, have the least influence on channel structure. Product service requirements vary from technical advice to repair and maintenance. Usually a service will influence the channel structure only when the product service factor is of major importance or is related to physical distribution. Factors such as recommendations for correct product selection and methods for its use or application are provided by a retailer to facilitate the buying decision. The repair of equipment is a less frequent service, and when not specialized, it is considered to be the kind of service available through a facilitating agency rather than a direct channel member. Direct channel members become involved when they provide specialized or very technical services, such as those provided by IBM to their commercial computer customers. These kinds of services call for a shorter channel structure.

Influences of Facilitating Agencies on the Channel Structure. Facilitating agencies, with one exception, play no direct part in channel structure. These operations are independent agents servicing the market for their own gain. The one exception is for physical distribution. Facilitating agents play a direct part in channel structure when the product source employs a warehousing and shipping agency that can provide local availability of the company's products. In this situation, the manufacturer may be able to eliminate one or all of the wholesale intermediaries. This has a direct influence on the channel structure. Many public warehouses allow orders to be picked up at their locations by wholesalers or retailers. Such direct pick up has a dramatic influence, since it will significantly shorten the channel structure. Facilitating warehouses act either as company agents or service wholesalers, not as merchant wholesalers, when they provide these services. The critical factor for manufacturers is to consider who will sell their products if there are no wholesalers to call on retailers. This thought leads one to determine whether or not an organization of manufacturer's representatives can perform the sales function. Manufacturer's reps, or agents acting as direct channel members, fit well into this situation. In addition, brokers or commission agents acting as facilitating agencies may also provide the selling function. When physical distribution is accomplished by a facilitating agency, the manufacturer has several options in determining the most effective and efficient channel structure.

Manufacturers of industrial products often use public warehouses strategically located throughout their marketing areas as the first level of physical distribution. Products may be shipped to local merchants by trucks owned by the warehouse; or more usually, a warehouse will call a trucking company to pick up and deliver as instructed. Many *common carriers*, or facilitating shippers, are available to deliver products of all types. Examples are railroads, truckers, air freight, sea freight, mail, Parcel Post, United Parcel Service, and special handling and delivery services. These agencies provide a wide variety of services for their customers.

Frequently channel members are selected because of their ability to ship and store products at the wholesale or retail level in the manufacturer's markets. These members may provide most or all of the needed physical distribution services. When this is not possible, or when it is too expensive for the manufacturer to do so, facilitating agencies may provide the logical answer to provide all or part of the physical distribution services needed.

CHANNEL STRUCTURE REVIEW

Channel structure is influenced by many factors. Building a new channel structure or selecting an existing channel structure should start from the bottom, with the users, and work its way up to the manufacturer.

Knowledge of the users and their buying habits is critical to the design of a channel structure. The total number of potential users in the market and their location, that is, their market size and density, have a major influence on channel structure. All the functions of the product source, wholesaling, and retailing must be satisfied whether the channel is short or long, direct, or with many intermediaries. Thus a large variety of factors affect the channel structure.

> *The structure of a marketing channel is determined by the manufacturer's need to profitably sell to as many users of its products as possible and to employ the most effective and efficient way to deliver these products into the user's hands.*

PHYSICAL DISTRIBUTION

> *Physical distribution is the means by which a product is handled, packaged, shipped, stored, warehoused, transported or delivered from the source of origin to the channel members.*

Note that in the definition of physical distribution, there is no mention of who performs these services. It may be the manufacturer or the marketer, a distributing intermediary, a retailer, a facilitating agent, or all channel members collectively. The objective is to get the product in the hand of the user as efficiently and effectively as possible. One should never lose sight of the fact that it is the duty of the physical distribution structure to help marketing in reaching its objectives. Physical distribution may be accomplished by facilitating agencies alone or in concert with some or all of the channel members. However it is accomplished, meeting the physical distribution needs in the channel must be satisfied in order for the marketing structure to function successfully.

Manufacturer/Marketer Capabilities

Most manufacturers have the capability to store their products for specific periods of time. They may need to hold inventories for quality assurance tests and collect an assortment of types or sizes in order to fill the orders they receive. Manufacturers do not usually have storage or shipping facilities that are designed to collect small orders for direct shipment to a large number of customers. Manufacturers who sell by direct mail would be an exception, but such situations would be unusual for industrial products. Direct mail marketers are not usually manufacturers.

In general, marketers and manufacturers are able to bulk ship the products they make or market. That is, manufacturers may package by the case, but they ship by the truckload. They can also provide order processing and shipping to only a limited number of customers. This limitation requires intermediaries in the channel to help with both physical distribution and marketing.

Physical Distribution and Facilitating Agencies

All nonmember channel participants are facilitating agencies (see chapter 2). Those agencies involved with physical distribution play two specific facilitating roles: warehousing (storage) and transportation (delivery). In some cases, you will recall, special product handling is also needed. To help in determining what is needed and whether or not these services are available, the channel manager should ask the following four key questions as they apply to each level in the channel (manufacturers, wholesalers, agents, and retailers):

1. What basic services are required?
2. Are there special product factors to consider in shipping and handling?
3. What are the capabilities channel members must have to satisfy distribution needs?
4. What is the availability, cost, and suitability of the needed facilitating agencies?

Only after these physical distribution questions are considered and answered can the source of the needed service be located and identified in the physical distribution planning process. The manufacturer's desire for all, several, none, or even alternative physical distribution services not listed depends upon the manufacturer's ability to provide key physical distribution services in the marketing channel. Table 3.3 identifies common services required in physical distribution.

Physical Distribution Planning Process

There are three steps in the planning process of physical distribution:

1. Determine who can best sell to the potential *users* of your product (retailers).
2. Determine who are the preferred suppliers to the selected *retailers* (wholesalers).
3. Determine the types of marketing programs required to entice *wholesalers* to buy your products (manufacturer's programs).

Table 3.3
Common Services Required in Physical Distribution

Handling, Storing, and Customer Services	Shipping
• Receiving products	• Secure carriers
• Storing and Warehousing	• Place shipping orders
• Inventory control and reporting	• Trace orders
• Bulk breaking and assortment gathering	• Handle freight claims
• Order handling, assembly, and processing	• Provide documentation
• Packaging and protective wrap	
• Direct customer services	
• Administration	
• Returns and replacement	

Marketing Scenario Consumer Product (not a factual case study)

In order to more easily understand how the physical distribution planning process is established, the following scenario for B&B Manufacturing is presented.

Your company, B&B Manufacturing, is a leading manufacturer of backing and bulking fiber products for use in the manufacture of upholstered furniture. Some employees call the company the "Stuffing Store." This informal company name gave a new employee in the product development department the idea to experiment with a new product. She found that some of the scrap materials from normal production were ideal to make soft, lightweight, stuffed pillows. These scraps were too soft to be commercially viable in the pillow industry, but she had another idea. In the product development lab, she produced ten very soft, lightweight pillows in five different shapes and colors: yellow star, a green crescent, a black square, a blue triangle, and a red circle. Each pillow measured approximately six to eight inches. An additional five pillows of each shape were two-colored, using the single colors in combination. The ten different pillows were packaged in a mesh bag adorned with a picture of two children throwing pillows at each other. The name on the bag was "Pillow Fight." With each bag came simple rules of a game that entailed choosing two teams of pillow fighters. Each team would have a bag of the ten different pillows, and the two teams would throw pillows for a short period of time. At the conclusion of the pillow fight, the children would be told to collect one each of the ten different pillows and put them back into their bag. This exercise was supposed to teach recognition of the differences in pillow shapes, colors, and combinations of colors. At the same time, the children would have some harmless fun throwing very soft pillows at each other.

The company product development person took two Pillow Fight bags to her daughter's preschool, two others to the daycare centers near her home, and another two to a nationally franchised play school. She planned to check back in a week to see what had happened. Within four days all three of the test schools wanted more bags of the Pillow Fight game. The children loved the pleasure of doing in school what was not allowed at home—throwing pillows at each other—and wanted their own bag of pillows for the game. Teachers also felt the instructional value of the game was evident in that children quickly learn to distinguish the right shapes and colors to collect in the bags so another pillow fight could take place.

A new consumer product was born. B&B Manufacturing, an industrial products company, had no idea how to market the new consumer product but felt it should do the job itself to give itself an opportunity to branch into new markets. B&B hired a consumer products marketing manager and began planning for the new product introduction. The most challenging problem was the development of a physical distribution channel for the product.

Step One. Determine who can best sell your products to the potential users. Whoever sells to the user is performing the retail function in the channel.

After much discussion and a small amount of market research, B&B decided that Toys R Us would be the most desirable retail chain to approach. Toys R Us was located in all the major markets, and in addition, the toy retailer bought products from many toy manufacturers and manufacturer's representatives. A major attraction to B&B Manufacturing was that consumer acceptance of the Toys R Us mass retailing methods was very favorable. B&B was convinced that many of its potential customers were already buying similar products from Toys R Us retailers.

Step Two. Determine the preferred suppliers that sell to the selected retail channel members. Whoever sells to the retailer provides the wholesale function.

It was also learned that the buying function was centralized at a regional level and that there were only four regions in the United States. Initially B&B thought it would need to sell directly to individual Toys R Us retailers, but when the company learned about the retailer's centralized buying structure, B&B felt the job would be much easier. However, later it was learned that the four regional buying locations purchased only what the individual stores ordered. In addition, the stores could order only those products appearing on a list of approved products established at headquarters.

Buying in large quantities and shipping to individual stores in smaller lots, a process known as *bulk breaking* and *assortment gathering*, the regional buying centers were acting as wholesalers. But unfortunately for B&B, they were not performing the selling function that most wholesalers provide manufacturers. The approximately 600 Toys R Us and Kids R Us stores would have to be approached individually, after B&B received approval from Toys R Us headquarters and Pillow Fight was added to the Toys R Us approved products list.

B&B decided to find a good manufacturer's representative organization to discuss its selling capabilities. Several were interviewed, but it soon became apparent that B&B would have to enlist the services of over a dozen such organizations to reach less than half the Toys R Us stores. In addition, these rep organizations were not excited about pioneering a new product for an unknown manufacturer, offering a one-product line, and looking for distribution to only one toy retailer.

In the end, the decision was made to explore the possibility of supplying another toy manufacturer with Pillow Fight, to be sold under a recognized manufacturer's brand. An exclusive five-year contract was signed with a recognized toy manufacturer for a specific minimum number of products to be purchased annually. B&B settled back into its familiar mode as a manufacturer.

The product development group at B&B continued to successfully research other toy products for their growing consumer products business. The long-range plan was to sell directly to Toys R Us when B&B had developed a family of toy products the stores wanted to order.

> *Step Three. Determine what marketing programs are required to entice wholesalers to buy your products. The holder of the brand name on the product is recognized as the product source.*

In this marketing scenario, the wholesaler was the Toys R Us regional offices. Authorization to add a new product was controlled by headquarters. Headquarters control indicates that Toys R Us is concerned about product safety, prefers to buy from known manufacturers, and chooses to buy a selection of several products from the same source.

Analysis of Marketing Scenario. The utilization of existing physical distribution channels is competitively impossible for B&B to accomplish. It had one good product but needed several to be competitive. B&B was unknown in the toy market. It is easy to see that manufacturers will have difficulty developing a channel of distribution independent from the marketing commitments that must be made. You will recall that the channels for distribution and marketing must be developed together.

The physical distribution consideration, which is independent from the marketing programs, relates *only* to shipping. Having selected an established toy manufacturer to sell its new product, B&B will have included in the contract a minimum level of purchases, prices, delivery, and terms of payment. The manufacturer who bought the product, Pillow Fight, from B&B was recognized as the product source and B&B became a contract manufacturer.

It should be obvious to those who manage the marketing channel, whether it be an industrial channel or a consumer channel, that merchant wholesalers and retailers require much less in the way of physical distribution services than do agents and brokers. Intermediaries who buy and sell products usually have both storage facilities and shipping capabilities. Brokers and agents, on the other hand, act primarily as sales representatives rather than product handlers. Agents will find buyers and may include delivery schedules and specific freight carriers as conditions of the sales agreement. They will advise the manufacturers of these needs but will not usually provide them.

Freight and Product Handling Factors in Physical Distribution

Freight costs and product-handling factors affect most businesses. Probably the most directly affected are the manufacturers of products whose bulk or weight make handling and shipping a difficult task. In these situations, the cost of freight and product handling can represent a significant amount of money as compared to product costs. Companies that make or market large pieces of equipment, chemical products, metal products, cement, furniture, fertilizer, and lumber and paper products, as well as companies involved with perishable products, are good examples.

We differentiate the freight factor by referring to products as being *freight-intensive* or *freight-nonintensive*. Products classified freight-nonintensive are those where the shipping cost is added into the cost of the product. This is sometimes referred to as the *delivered price*. Freight-intensive products are those where the freight cost is added onto the price of the product. The freight and handling factors are critical in both physical distribution considerations and in creating competitive marketing programs. Here are two short examples.

Example One

A manufacturing company that produces screws, nuts, bolts, washers, and nails ships its products all over the country by common carrier. Building supply wholesalers order from the factory, in quantity, and are shipped freight prepaid at fixed freight-on-board (F.O.B.) prices. The cost of freight, though prepaid by the manufacturer, is added onto the order and is a cost to the wholesaler. Wholesalers located at significant distances from the manufacturing plant experience a higher product cost (freight add on) than those close to the plant.

The wholesaler will also have to charge outgoing freight when delivering products to retailers. Wholesalers will usually prepay this charge and add it to the retailer's bill. The retailer must factor the freight charges into his product cost before adding his profit markup. Here again, the farther the retailer is from the wholesaler, the greater the freight cost. Obviously, the cost of a pound of nails will vary from location to location even within the same retail chain. Further, these products are not high-profit products, which makes it difficult for the manufacturer to absorb the freight costs.

Example Two

A pharmaceutical manufacturer produces pet vaccines for sale to veterinarians. These products are packaged in two sizes: vials of ten doses and vials of fifty doses. The vials are packed in cases with twelve vials per box. The vaccines that are held for an extended period of time must be stored in a refrigerator to maintain potency, but they are shipped by prepaid air express to distributors who provide refrigerated storage as well as refrigerated delivery to veterinarians.

In this example, the freight factor is insignificant compared to the cost of the product, yet special refrigerated storage and fast handling in transit are an essential service. Distributors who cannot (1) receive air freight, (2) provide refrigerated storage, and (3) obtain refrigerated delivery service would not satisfy the manufacturer's physical distribution needs or those of the marketing channel. In this example, the freight cost (air express) is added into the selling price and is not a separate charge to the wholesaler. *The product is priced the same to all, on a delivered basis, whether it is shipped one mile or three thousand.* This product is not freight-intensive. It is probably a low-cost and high-profit item. The freight cost is insignificant to the profit earned and the price charged.

Freight Equalization

For products that are freight-intensive, freight equalization becomes a necessary consideration. This is more a marketing consideration than one of physical distribution, but since it has some physical distribution implications, it is included here.

Freight equalization is *always* prompted by a marketing disadvantage. The disadvantage is created when one of two competing manufacturers has a higher freight cost to reach the same market with a similar product.

Usually, the higher cost is the result of having to transport the product over a longer distance. The freight cost disadvantage may also result from the difference in freight rates and available freight carriers. Rail rates are normally lower than truck rates, and barge rates are lower than rail. If one manufacturer can ship by rail and the other must use trucks, the one using trucks is at a marketing disadvantage because of the higher freight cost. By employing a freight equalization marketing policy, the cost disadvantage is eliminated. The choice is a reduction in profit to improve the company's competitiveness in a market.

As an illustration, consider a manufacturer shipping bagged cement by truck and competing with a manufacturer shipping by rail. The freight-equalizing action is to adopt a policy of charging rail cost for truck delivery. This equalizes the freight charge with the least-cost carrier employed by the competitor.

Another situation may occur between two companies shipping from different locations. The company with a longer distance to ship with the same freight cost per mile simply states that it will equalize freight with its competitor's shipping location. In practice, this is applying the same freight charge for a longer haul. Applying the same freight charge equalizes the distance over which the freight charge is calculated.

It may be necessary to equalize freight costs with more than one competitor in the same market. The equalizing factor is always with the competitor that has the least cost charged for freight. Equalization is a marketing program option that deals with a differential competitive disadvantage. It is not related to the satisfaction of physical distribution.

Manufacturer's Marketing Programs and Physical Distribution

The marketing programs of manufacturers and their competition can greatly influence the physical distribution services needed and provided. Marketing programs can reflect unique market characteristics such as product use patterns, weather influence, and specific competitive disadvantages. These unique factors impose special physical distribution requirements on the marketing channel. Consider the following examples.

Example A

Manufacturers or producers of products that are sold seasonally or that have extremely short use seasons face unique marketing problems. Products such as snow blowers, nursery plants, swimwear, and lawn fertilizers fit into this profile. Physical distribution services for these products require them to be in the market, ready for use, in the quantity, size, style, or type wanted, when they are needed. Warehousing at the market level (wholesalers or retailers) and rapid shipment to the channel intermediaries is essential to satisfy the physical distribution needs.

Marketing programs will be used to encourage wholesalers and retailers to stock the products before the use season begins. In addition, marketing programs that *pull through* the products from the wholesaler to the retailer and from the retailer to the user will be used to deplete the shelves of the seasonal stock before the season ends.

Example B

The physical distribution of perishable products also presents some unique inventory-handling and product-shipping needs. In most cases these will be food products shipped from the grower to the market. Products such as chickens, lettuce, fruit, and other fresh perishables demand physical distribution services quite different than those required for nails. The selection of channel members who can provide these unique requirements for physical distribution is essential for the effective management of the marketing channel.

Marketing programs for these special situations relate to rapid delivery and temperature control to ensure freshness during transit. The retailer will also reduce prices on these products as they age. These products must be sold before they lose their appeal to the consumers, or if they are dated, before the dating expires.

Review of Physical Distribution

From the discussion and examples provided, it is easy to understand that physical distribution is a major concern in marketing channel management. Some marketers consider the subject of marketing channels primarily as a study of distribution. This text separates the physical distribution function in marketing channel management from the marketing channel considerations because physical distribution is only one element of the marketing mix. Physical distribution is important, but in its basic market function, it is only a facilitating activity for product marketing. However, a breakdown in physical distribution can nullify any good accomplished by all other marketing endeavors. Physical distribution alone cannot provide all the needs of a marketing channel.

Physical distribution serves the manufacturer and the channel members as well. Usually this function is performed by wholesalers and retailers, although manufacturers can also operate from public warehouses in the channel and provide most of the physical distribution function with facilitating agencies. This method of distribution provides some extended control over channel activities, but it also carries a cost to the manufacturer that must be passed on to wholesalers, retailers, and users.

Branches in the physical distribution channel or channel structure help reduce these costs.

Special problems need to be resolved for freight-intensive products. Freight equalization is one way to overcome a marketing disadvantage caused by freight inequality between competing channel members. Special problems relating to the season or perishability of products also challenge the physical distribution channel to be sufficiently flexible to utilize marketing programs designed to negate these problems.

QUESTIONS AND DISCUSSION

1. Is it possible for a company that does not manufacture a product to be considered a product source? Explain.

2. Name the four essential functions in the structure of a marketing channel.

3. Where should a manufacturer first look for a suitable channel structure to market its products?

4. List all six of the factors affecting channel length.

5. What distinction is made between market size and market volume?

6. Name at least four of the most commonly needed services in physical distribution.

7. What one element of marketing is also essential in the physical distribution system?

8. Why don't more manufacturers bypass the wholesaler and ship their products directly to the retailer?

9. Explain what makes a product freight-intensive.

10. When should marketing programs include freight equalization as a necessary element?

FOUR

Market Characteristics and Channel Management

The characteristics of a market may be measured in seven general dimensions: by the (1) geographic area, (2) product mix, (3) market size, (4) market volume, (5) market density, (6) market activity cycles, and (7) channel selectivity reference. From the standpoint of channel management, these seven market characteristics should be studied and analyzed to generate a *market profile statement*—the preamble to the development of management policy and marketing strategies for the market and marketing channel planning. This statement outlines in a few words the market dynamics created by the emphasis and balance among the seven dimensional characteristics in the marketing channel detailed in this chapter.

The identification of market characteristics is essential to create a standard reference to the market that is acceptable and understood by all. For most markets, there will be predominant characteristics as well as those that modify the market description. For some markets, a specialized terminology will be applied that may be common usage to a specific industry but not in use by the general public.

MARKET CHARACTERISTICS

The market designation recognized by the industry is the one that will be applied to markets for products and services, regardless of what a company may wish to call its product. The market for *blue jeans*, for example, includes many products that individual manufacturers would like to designate by their brand names. Notwithstanding, collectively all brands of "jeans" are a part of one market designated as the "blue jeans market." The area in which jeans are sold, the sizes and styles, and other of the seven market characteristics may be combined to further define the jeans market for considerations of channel management.

Geographic Market Designations

Most markets can easily be identified by geographic boundaries, "the eleven western states," "the state of California," "mid-Atlantic states," "U.S. & Canada," "South America," and similar designations. Geographic identification of a market serves primarily to evaluate the magnitude of the physical distribution job and the extent of the channel structure that will be required to serve the total market.

The sources of geographic data that apply to physical distribution may be found in national and local governmental agencies, trade organizations, freight handlers, banks, export-import agencies, advertising and public relations agencies, and many other groups. One may even need to provide a special market survey or audit to determine specific physical distribution needs such as refrigerated or heated storage facilities, containerized product handling, and regulations affecting the storage and shipment of toxic substances. In general, the data representing a market's geographic profile should contain the following topics:

- physical boundaries of the total geographic market
- freight carriers to ship the company's products
- storage facility requirements and availability
- special regulations affecting storage and shipment

The physical size of the market area may also affect channel structure. A large geographic market usually indicates a great number of intermediaries to provide the services that are needed. These services are related mostly to physical distribution and are a part of the channel structure considerations mentioned in chapter 3.

Market Designation by Product Mix

Many companies acquire their market definition by the product or product lines in the market. A milk processor may refer to a specific market as the *whole milk market* or the *skim milk* market. Each of these

Table 4.1
Product Characteristics in Market Definition (motor oil example)

Product type:	Motor oil for automobiles
Product name:	Texaco
Product size or packaging:	12 quarts per case, English labels
Product mix in the market:	SAE 50, SAE 40, SAE 30, SAE 20
Market profile statement:	The U.S. market for Texaco summer-weight oils packaged in cases of quarts

references point to specific product characteristics that are used to define the market.

Even when using a product characteristic to define the market, it is logical to first start with the geographic designation and then add the product characteristics. An example would be the U.S. chemical market, further defined by product characteristics as the U.S. petroleum oil market for automobiles.

Companies with diversified product lines will find that the geographic market consists of several different product characteristics, the *product mix*. The product mix for a company selling clothing in the southern states may be much different than the mix of products sold in the northern states. Although both areas may use the same basic products, one can easily understand that there is no market for sheepskin-lined caps in southern Florida.

Manufacturers of petroleum solvents know the big markets for their products are those where the large chemical producers can be found. Manufacturers of motor oil want their markets to include the large metropolitan areas where there are many automobile owners; thus the geographic designation coupled with product characteristics serves well.

The impact of product characteristics and types on the market designation may be highly significant. Most companies will define product characteristics by product type and product name, such as *Texaco SAE 10-40 motor oil*. The Texaco company may define a market by product characteristics such as the market for winter or summer grade oils.

The general product characteristics that may contribute to market definition are shown in Table 4.1. Remember, the reason channel managers need to accurately define the market for their company's products is to ensure that the channel structure will satisfy both the physical distribution and the marketing needs in the channel. Consider Table 4.1: The product type defines the product as a motor oil for automobiles, not trucks or heavy equipment. The name is Texaco, which identifies the brand rather than a specific product. The product size in the example indicates twelve quarts per case, rather than barrels of oil. One would conclude that this package is for the consumer products group. The importance of the product mix characteristics are to provide information to those doing the market planning and to facilitate physical distribution. The application of product mix characteristics to define the market are consolidated into the market profile statement, which concludes the list in Table 4.1.

Managing Product Type Characteristics. For companies who market in highly selective markets, or those with products identified by very specific characteristics, the product type and market characteristics are dominant considerations in channel management. Products with an ethnic appeal, or those needing special handling, would possess these characteristics. Consider a milk-processing company that produces and packages milk in several sizes and with different fat content. The market information for whole milk versus skim milk in specific markets would be as important to this producer as the total market for milk. In addition, product handling and the availability of refrigerated storage are vital for physical distribution planning. Knowledge of the special product characteristics in a market make channel management possible. The product characteristics that are important for marketing planning should be mentioned in the market profile statement. The motor oil product characteristics and market definition shown in Table 4.1 indicate the areas where information to aid channel structure planning or make management decisions may be needed.

Market Size

Our reference to market size is consistently and specifically applied to the actual or potential total *number of product users* located within the specified geographic market area. When the product is bread, everyone is a potential user and the market size is the total population within the marketing area. In some situations, the *number of units* of the product sold will relate to the market size rather than the actual number of users. The number of units sold will relate to both market size and volume when the consumers of specific products cannot be identified. The following illustrates this situation: For a company selling products to the equine market in the United States, it is important to know there are approximately 11 million horses in this market. The number of horses, *not* the number of horse owners, is the market size. The horses, not the horse owners, use or consume the products marketed. The number of units of various products sold may also indicate the size of the market for products. However, the number of units more often denotes the volume rather than the size of a market.

For manufacturers of automobile waxes and polishes, the number of automobile owners would indicate the total number of potential buyers. We know some owners never wax their cars. Many potential buyers own more than one car and will buy waxes, cleaners, and other related items several times each year. For car waxes and polishes, the total market is not expressed in terms of either the number of car owners or the number of cars in the market. The number of cars is irrelevant to the volume of waxes and polishes used because of the many variables relating to geographic location, the age of cars, and the owner's habits related to waxing. When there is little correlation between product use and the number of potential users in a market, the market size is measured as the number of product *units* sold the previous year. In the horse product example, there is a close correlation between the number of horses and the products used.

Market size may also be modified by *product type and use characteristics*. Automobile waxes come in liquids and pastes. Commercial use of auto waxes includes spray and foam applications by drive-through carwashes. These are examples of product type and use application that segment the market size. For auto waxes, the market segments would be designated as consumer and commercial markets. This subject is covered with specific details in chapter 9.

For products that are used up, or consumed, several times each year, such as computer paper, the product use rate adds another dimension to the market size. Although there are millions of computer printers using the same type of paper, each operator will use paper at a different rate. Knowing the number of printers (product users) in the market provides little information of value related to market size. The computer paper manufacturer must know how much of each type of paper is used annually within the geographical market area. This figure must then be broken down into figures for monthly usage, paper type, and segment of the market's geographical area. In order to tie the paper usage to computer printer sales (a useful reference), for example, the paper company will need to know the average usage of each type of paper by market per 1,000 computer printers in the market. This information provides a market size reference that is useful to the paper manufacturer in planning the channel structure needed and calculating the marketing cycles (monthly use data) that can be expected within each major market.

All the market characteristics thus far mentioned are useful to channel development and management. The basic information needed when considering market size is shown in Table 4.2. Application of the three market size characteristics is quite simple. In the following example, we are looking at what a paint manufacturer may need to include in calculating market size.

Table 4.2
Market Size Characteristics

1. *Number of market units or users.*	People, horses, cars, cases, etc.
2. *Percentage of using units in the market.*	10%, 25%, 50%, 100%
3. *Purchasing frequency for the product.*	Once per year, twice per year, five times per year, etc.

Example: Application of Market Size Characteristics

Our manufacturer produces many different types of paint but is entering a market new to the company: the latex outdoor house paint market.

Market Size Characteristics. For this example, the outline for market size characteristics presented on Table 4.2 provides the following:

1. *Number of market units or users.* In the paint company example, this variable relates both to the number of users and to the number of units in the market. There are two types of *units* and two types of *users.* One market size measurement is based on the number of new houses built each year (units) that are painted commercially (users). The other measurement is the number of homes (units) five years old or older that are painted either commercially or by the owner (users).

   Market research shows that there are 50,000 new housing units built in the market each year. There are also 1.5 million homes five years old or older in the marketing area. This indicates that the total *potential* market size is 1.55 million housing units. Since the houses consume the paint, they must be considered as the consumers. However, the buyer is identified as either a homeowner or a commercial painter.

2. *Percentage of using units in the market.* This is known to be 100% of the new housing units that are painted upon completion and 10% of the homes five years or older. With this information, the 1,550,000 potential users are identified as 200,000 expected users in the market (50,000 new + 150,000 old).

3. *Purchasing frequency for the product.* This entails two types of buyers: the commercial painters and the homeowners who paint their own houses. Commercial painters purchase paint on an average of fifteen times per year. Homeowners who paint their own houses purchase once every five years. This statistic reveals to the manufacturer that the commercial market purchases paint seventy-five times (15 × 5) for every one time by homeowners. Commercial painters will paint 100% of the new units annually (50,000) and also paint 75% (112,500) of the repainted units for a total of 162,500 units. The total homeowner market is 37,500 housing units in the market area. The only important remaining statistic is the number of units that will use a latex base house paint. For our example, we assume the total market will use latex base exterior paint.

By using this information on market size, the paint manufacturer can plan its marketing channel structure, product mix, and marketing management programs to reach the market segments important to the company. *If marketing channel managers make serious errors in determining the market size for their specific products, almost nothing else they try can produce the results expected.*

Market Density

Market density pinpoints where the market size (buyers or units) is concentrated. Market density may play an important part when developing marketing programs and channel structure. Specific market and product designations are made because the product needs are different in dissimilar areas and the market activity cycles are specific for each market segment. The following example involving the production of apples provides a look at the significance of market density.

Example. According to U.S. Department of Agriculture (USDA) market statistics, there are approximately 9 million pounds of commercially grown apples produced and used each year. The state of Washington produces about one-third of the total apples, while New York and Michigan each produce about one-third of what is produced in Washington. This indicates that the Washington market for products used in producing, packing, and shipping apples represents three times the density of that of New York or Michigan. Pennsylvania and California are next in production, but each of these states represents only about half the market size of New York. Together the top five states produce approximately 70% of the total apple crop. It is difficult to find markets where such a high percentage of the total production or product use is so concentrated, but these statistics provide a good example of market density.

On the surface, one would think the use of automobile tires would be directly proportional to the density of a metropolitan population. On closer scrutiny, we come to realize that public transportation, such as is available in New York City, Chicago, and other major cities, as well as the driving distance from home to office, has a dramatic impact on the usage of the automobile and tire wear. Channel managers need to challenge the data they receive to be assured they are applicable to their needs and present all the needed detail.

Market density influences channel length and the structure of the physical distribution system. Marketing programs are also significantly influenced by market density factors. Remember, market density is only one of the influencing factors. There are several more factors that affect channel length. Table 4.3 indicates the effects of market density on channel length.

Table 4.3
Market Density and Channel Length

	Long	Medium	Short
High Density	Seldom	Sometimes	Frequent
Moderate Density	No effect	No effect	No effect
Diversified	Frequently	Sometimes	Seldom

Other market factors may have a greater effect on channel length than market density alone. The marketing activity cycle, the buying frequency and the number of buyers in a market may well have a greater influence on channel length than the density of buyers. If there are few buyers in a high-density market, the channel length very likely will be short. If there are many buyers in a high-density market, the channel may be longer. The greater the requirement for product availability, created by a large number of buyers, the greater the pressure for a large number of retail outlets. This situation results in a longer channel.

Other important demographics of market density are directly related to the market itself. Channel managers must look beyond the number of buyers or units sold in a market as the only indication of market density. The following is an excellent example from agribusiness.

Wisconsin is the largest milk-producing state in the United States with about 1.8 million head of dairy cows. California ranks second with a little over a million, and third place belongs to the state of New York with about 950,000 head of milking cows. If we include Minnesota's 915,000 and Pennsylvania's approximately 750,000 head, these five states make up over half of the milk cows in the United States. This is a high-density market for those who would sell products to dairy farmers, milk processors, and milk product marketers. Although this is true, if a company serving this industry adopts the same physical distribution structure and marketing programs for Wisconsin and California, it would be in trouble.

Looking carefully at the internal characteristics of the market density, we find Wisconsin averages about forty cows per dairy herd, New York has about fifty cows per dairy herd, and California has about 160 head per herd. These statistics show the California market to be four times as concentrated as the Wisconsin market even though it is just a little over half the size in total market units. Wisconsin has about 45,000 dairy farms, whereas California has only about 5,600. The impact of these density characteristics would indicate the need for a short channel in California and a longer one in Wisconsin and New York. Companies who supply dairy farm products, milk-processing equipment, milk-packaging equipment, bulk and consumer product containers, or any product in the milk production and consumption marketing channel should know these market density figures concerning production. The density of dairy farmers who make up the product source for milk will indicate the channel structure that is needed and the type of marketing programs required to be competitive.

Market Volume

There are two ways to express the volume of business in a market. The first, and the most used, is the total dollar volume of the product sold. The second way is by the total number of product units sold. *Market volume refers to the amount of a specific product that the market can or does consume (or use) in a specific time period.* Dollars are the most universal measurement of product used or consumed. Most marketers, however, will need to use both dollars and units to express the volume of their markets. The need to use dollars in expressing volume is to provide the price per unit for the specific time period. The actual units used show consumption without giving price any weight in the equation. For many products, the price of purchase will vary during the marketing period. For this reason only the unit consumption numbers can show true market volume. In addition, the price of the product may significantly affect the volume used or purchased in a specific time period.

Market Volume Example. Coca-Cola and Pepsi Cola have been fighting to be the market leader in cola drinks for years. Using these two companies in an example related to market volume, let us assume that in the target market for cola drinks there are 10 million units (one unit is 12 oz.) of cola drinks consumed every day. We will also assume the market is split, with Coca-Cola the leader, with 35% of the market. Pepsi holds 30% of the market and all other colas, including private label brands, make up the rest of the market at 35% market share. Remember, in this example the market share figures represent units sold rather than dollars. The market size is characterized as 10 million units purchased and consumed per day. Coca-Cola sells 3.5 million units, Pepsi 3.0 million, and all others 3.5 million.

Pepsi Cola, in an attempt to take market share leadership, reduces the price of its product to consumers for a time period that is twice the normal promotional period and with 50% more discount than in the previous selling period. In short, Pepsi is offering consumers a double discount and double the time to take advantage of the discount. Pepsi also increased advertising by 35% in media expenditures during the promotional period. Coca-Cola matched the price cuts and the promotional time period, but not the other market-stimulating actions linked to advertising. The result was that Pepsi increased sales from 3 million to 4 million units for the selling period. Did Pepsi reach its goal as market leader? Unfortunately, the answer was no. All the market stimulation increased consumption to 11 million units per day, and Coca-Cola increased its sales from 3.5 million units to 4.3 million units sold. The All Other category suffered a loss of market share by 0.8 million units per day because the price differential between the "premium" brands and the others disappeared.

During this selling period, the promotional pricing reduced the *dollar volume* of each unit sold to the extent of nullifying any increase in revenue. The unit sales increased by a million while the dollar volume in the market stayed the same.

The lesson of this example is easily seen. To accurately measure the market volume, the channel manager must take into consideration all the market actions implicated during the period measured. To consider the dollar volume alone would lead one to the conclusion that the promotional program did not create the new and increased volume of business expected. Actually, a million more units of cola drinks were sold than would have occurred without the promotion. The shifting of consumer purchases from one brand to the other was from the All Other category to both Pepsi and Coke—not from Coke to Pepsi, as was expected by the Pepsi Cola Company. The promotion created new business for Coke and Pepsi in the amount of 1.8 million units. Pepsi received 1 million of this business and Coke 800,000 units. Since Pepsi started out 500,000 behind Coke, the 200,000-unit gain was not enough to take market leadership away from Coke.

Market Activity Cycles

By market activity, we refer to two basic influences on the market that create buying activity. Normal recurring *seasonal cycles* are the most important to many marketers. The Christmas season is a good illustration. The other type of cycle that stimulates purchasing is the *scheduled promotional incentives* that are intended to create a cycle of buying that would not otherwise occur. Mother's Day promotions would illustrate this type of market stimulation. For most markets there are several activity cycles that are repeated every year.

Seasonal Cycles. Seasonal cycles are predictable and recur annually. They may relate to spring house cleaning, summer vacations, tax refunds, planting and harvesting, school year, new model introductions, holidays, vacation time, or any number of activities. For channel structure and management of the physical distribution system, these cycles indicate inventory building, shipping, storage, and product-handling actions to suit the seasonal cycle demands. We look at seasonal cycles as normal market-generating cycles. They will occur whether or not companies in the market plan do something special to accommodate or stimulate the normal cycle of business.

Promotional Cycles and Marketing Programs. The second type of market cycle that will affect the management of physical distribution is the action induced by marketing programs and promotions. Some companies will routinely or periodically stimulate customers with promotional programs to do something they would not normally do.

Many traditional promotional cycles are tied to holidays, to post-holiday periods, and to seasonal changes. Special programs for the sale of winter clothes, snow tires, sporting goods, summer swimwear, and the like are typical of seasonal promotions.

Marketing Channel Selectivity References

Managing the competitive environment in a channel is not usually an option for a single company. The competitive environment, to which we make reference in the context of market characteristics, is centered on creating a channel environment that is either *selective, inclusive,* or *exclusive* in the competitive structure of the channel. It is not related to a product or a competitive program but incorporates the consideration of a complete market environment. The company can select from several options in the creation of their marketing channel structure. It also has an obligation to produce a channel that will not create conflict among channel members.

To be an effective and competitive participant in a marketing channel, a marketer is dependent on how the other channel members (wholesalers and retailers) view their opportunities in working with them. Most wholesalers have a choice of representing two or more manufacturers of similar product lines. To attract and secure the services of the most effective wholesalers and retailers, the marketer must provide a channel environment that is either competitive or preferential to those of competing manufacturers. The best wholesalers are provided with the most-preferred working relationships.

Types of Channel Competition

Competition in the marketing channel may be segregated into three types:

1. *Channel structure to channel structure* is competition between two parallel channels operating within different channel structures.
2. *Manufacturer to manufacturer* is direct competition between two manufacturers or marketers that use the *same* marketing channel.

3. *Channel member to channel member* is the competitive relationship established between all channel intermediaries: wholesaler to wholesaler, retailer to retailer, or wholesaler to retailer in the *same* marketing channel.

The realities of the competitive marketplace seldom allow companies to make unilateral decisions in creating a business environment. The degree of dependency of one channel member upon another and on the manufacturer will greatly influence the options available. Companies that market one-of-a-kind products that are in high demand and are protected by a patent can act quite independently in establishing their channel relationships. For the three competitive environments listed, the channel-to-channel competition is the least disruptive to channel members. Usually two different channels develop because they are needed. The manufacturer-to-manufacturer competition is the type with which most companies will become involved. Although it usually does not occur, this type of competition can cross channel lines. Internal competition between channel members at different levels, such as wholesaler to retailer, are not common. The troublesome relationships are more often between channel members at the same level: wholesaler to wholesaler and retailer to retailer. The creation of selective, inclusive, or exclusive marketing channel relationships between manufacturers and channel members is the way most manufacturers try to control the channel environment without conflict.

The extremes in product control lead to extremes in channel relationships. A company with an exclusive product that is frequently purchased will probably try to develop a completely inclusive market. If the exclusive product is infrequently purchased, the channel may be developed as one with exclusive relationships. The degree of selectivity a manufacturer seeks will be determined by the product characteristics and the channel options available.

EXCLUSIVE, SELECTIVE, OR INCLUSIVE MARKETING CHANNELS

The channel manager must determine which of the three types of channel competition (or cooperation) will strategically be the most effective in reaching the company's goals. The objectives of the company, or company unit, will lead to developing a marketing channel based on an exclusive, selective, or inclusive relationship within the channel. This decision may also be influenced by wholesalers and the retailers. Some channel members will decide for themselves if they need or want an exclusive, selective, or inclusive relationship with their suppliers. Table 4.4 profiles these relationships in the marketing channel. This table offers two separate points of view: how wholesaler and retailer channel members view their commitment to the marketers and how the marketers view their commitment to

Table 4.4
Exclusive, Selective, and Inclusive Channel Profile

Channel Member Position	Exclusive	Selective	Inclusive
Carries Competitive Lines	No	Limited	Unlimited
Assigned Geographic Territory	Yes	Yes	No
Uses Supplier Programs	Yes	Some	By choice
Provides Customer Services	Yes	Yes	By choice

Marketer or Manufacturer's Position	Exclusive	Selective	Inclusive
Competitive Channel Members	None	Limited	Unlimited
Assigned Geographic Territory	Yes	Yes	Unlimited
Follows Supplier Programs	All	Some	By choice
Provides Customer Services	All	Yes	Encouraged

the channel intermediaries. The marketer must be vigilant to prevent channel conflicts where differences of opinion occur.

It is not difficult to understand the characteristics of a market that is exclusive, inclusive, or selective. Two central factors will consistently result in market exclusivity or foretell the need for a more inclusive market. The first factor is *product cost*. The second factor is *frequency of purchase*. If a product is very high in cost, such as an industrial lathe or pleasure power boat, the actual need for exclusive representation in a specific geographic area is based on several realities. The high cost of a Hatteras power boat relates to fewer potential buyers in a geographic area than for products such as leather work gloves or rubber boots. The market for power boats is not dense, but it is geographically located where there is water suitable for boating. In order to be productive, the Hatteras dealer should have an exclusive territory in which to market the product.

There will be competition from other brands in an exclusive channel, but the market exclusivity for each brand is maintained. As noted in chapter 3 (see especially Table 3.2), when product cost is high and the number of potential users and the frequency of purchase is low, a short marketing channel is indicated. These same factors significantly contribute to the selection of exclusivity as a channel structure. These characteristics may also indicate that a retailer may be a company branch operation.

Frequency of purchase, the second major contributing factor to exclusivity, is also a reliable indicator. The relationship between purchase price and frequency of purchase should be considered. Very frequently purchased products are usually low in cost and prompt an all-inclusive marketing channel. In short, let everyone who can qualify market the product and participate in the channel activity. The buyers of products such as motor oil, caps, gloves, and maintenance items purchased as needed may be prompted to buy more than necessary with a favorable price, but convenience of product availability is the governing factor. Product availability requires that products be found in every reasonable outlet the buyer may frequent. This is an inclusive market characteristic, which is the opposite of that leading to exclusivity, wherein buyers seek out a retailer for exclusive products that are infrequently purchased.

Also consider the cost factor. Users may shop for the best price that leads to a more selective buying decision. A certain brand, or stores that stock a desired brand, will be selectively sought out by users of specific products. Selectivity occurs at both the retail and wholesale level, but there is usually less selectivity at the retail level than at the wholesale level. This is true because the wholesaler, much more frequently than the manufacturer, will determine who retails the products it offers. Wholesalers cannot easily dictate what retailers will carry in their stores, but when wholesalers offer most of the needed brands, offer credit, and provide services, they often successfully keep competitive products out of the retail stores to which they sell.

A good example of selective channel building is the Science Pet Food line. The manufacturer of this line initially sold only to wholesalers who sold to veterinarians. This selectivity at the wholesale level tried to ensure that the Science Pet Food line would not be sold to pet stores or supermarkets, but only through "vets." This high degree of selectivity favored their product, which was more expensive than many store brands. It also ensured the support and recommendation of small-animal veterinarians—authority figures.

Since the policy of Science was a bit too exclusive for some suburban and rural areas, the company included kennels as retail outlets for the Science brand. The wholesalers selling to kennels also sold to pet stores, so there was some bootlegging of the Science brand into these specialty retailers.

When the manufacturer of the Science brand of pet foods tried to expand product availability, it lost some control over the management of the marketing channel. Science products are now found in mass retail stores to ensure optimum availability to pet owners. The selectivity option ended in favor of an inclusive marketing program. Science lost the support of veterinarians but gained a larger total market share.

Basic guidelines based on the general characteristics of an exclusive, selective, or inclusive market may be applied to managing markets and marketing channels. Although only guidelines, they will show the direction of channel management under these specific market characteristics.

Table 4.5
Selective versus Inclusive Channel Characteristics

If the channel requires:	The structure will be:
1. Special customer service.	Selective
2. Reliable product availability.	Selective
3. Convenient product availability.	Inclusive
4. Control over marketing programs.	Selective
5. A high level of product knowledge.	Selective
6. Dealing with competitive marketing programs.	Either
7. Special storage or handling.	Selective
8. Pricing to be consistently competitive.	Inclusive

Managing the Exclusive Channel

Channel managers must consider two variations of exclusivity: *mutual exclusivity* and *selective exclusivity*. Mutual exclusivity is an agreement by the manufacturer not to sell to a competing channel member, with the channel member mutually agreeing to represent no other competitive brand. As an illustration, the manufacturer of Stetson hats may agree to sell only to one wholesaler in a specific geographic market as long as that wholesaler sells no other line of western hats. The wholesaler may sell boots, shirts, belts, and other western paraphernalia but will have a mutual and exclusive relationship with Stetson for western hats.

It is unlikely that a wholesaler can find retailers who will agree to sell only Stetson hats. Thus, the exclusivity is mutually restrictive between the manufacturer and the wholesaler. Wholesalers do not usually provide a mutually exclusive arrangement to retailers. Channel selectivity is a manufacturer's program, not one created by the wholesaler.

If Stetson embraces a selectively exclusive agreement with wholesalers, however, it may allow the exclusive wholesaler in a geographic market to carry another line of hats. In most selectively exclusive arrangements, the wholesaler will be required to carry only lines of hats that are not directly competitive to Stetson. Usually this means hats of a substantially different price and quality than those of Stetson.

Manufacturers who seek to develop exclusive marketing channel relationships must assume significant responsibilities to their channel members. Table 4.5 offers a list of the most common responsibilities of manufacturers, wholesalers, and retailers.

Responsibilities in the Exclusive Marketing Channel

Manufacturer's Responsibilities to Wholesalers and Retailers

1. Maintain a high level of product recognition by the user.
2. Offer competitive marketing programs.
3. Provide necessary credit.
4. Provide training and support to intermediaries.
5. Maintain a reliable and acceptable profit margin for wholesalers and retailers.
6. Maintain product quality and ample inventory to fill orders as needed.

Wholesaler's and Retailer's Responsibilities to the Manufacturer

1. Provide satisfactory market coverage of available retailers or users.
2. Accept and follow all marketing programs of the manufacturer.
3. Provide the required customer services.
4. Maintain a trained and competent sales staff.
5. Support company product guarantees and follow up on performance complaints.
6. Provide the manufacturer with up-to-date market information on competitive products and lines.

Managing the Selective Marketing Channel

The selective marketing channel is similar to the exclusive channel. The first question that must be answered is, "How selective should the company be in channel development?" The most selective channel is one where only two channel intermediaries are competing at the same level (wholesale or retail) in the same geographic market. Less than two competing companies is an exclusive market. More than two dilutes the degree of selectivity. The question then becomes, "At what point does a selective marketing channel become inclusive?" The answer is contained in the reason a company chooses to develop a selective channel rather than make its brand available to everyone. Some of the reasons for seeking a selective channel in preference to an inclusive one are listed in Table 4.5.

One of the most critical criteria for developing the parameters of selectivity is the need for the manufacturer to maintain control over the intermediaries in the marketing channel. Many manufacturers believe that if there are more than two competing intermediaries in the same market, the maintenance of control is severely compromised. With three or more companies seeking the same business from retailers or users, one of the three will always be the underdog. This situation results in price degradation, selective account service, and inside deals. The marketing channel quickly develops into an arena of conflict. The most effective intermediaries may then lose interest in providing market support and representation for the manufacturer who has not kept selectivity under control.

Selective marketing channels require more management of conflict issues than either exclusive or inclusive channels. For this reason, a high degree of selectivity in channel design is difficult to manage and maintain over a long period of time. Some marketers have developed a system of modified selectivity that works quite well for their situations.

Modified Selectivity

To make modified selectivity work, it is necessary for the manufacturer to clearly identify both the primary and the secondary market coverage responsibilities of the intermediaries. These responsibilities will have a geographic designation.

Primary and Secondary Market Coverage. There are several forms of modified selectivity, but all embrace the same basic marketing philosophy. This philosophy is to design a geographic coverage for wholesalers that will provide both an area of primary responsibility and an area of secondary responsibility. Selection of the intermediaries, wholesalers in this example, will be on the basis of their ability to naturally dominate the business in their primary market while providing a backup position in the secondary markets. This modification suggests that all markets will have only one primary supplier, but always one or more secondary suppliers for the same brand.

Wholesalers Size and Influence. A second modification for selective channel development is based on the size and influence of the wholesalers involved. Using this method of selectivity, a manufacturer may name three large regional wholesalers to cover the entire geographic market they serve. Then, inside of the regional wholesalers' territories (primary markets), several smaller wholesalers may be selected to cover market segments in which they play a *dominant*, but local, influencing role. In these local markets, the large regional wholesaler will act as the backup company and will consider these areas as secondary market segments. This method of selectivity is commonly used where a few markets of high density may be identified by the manufacturer within a large regional market structure. The very dense market segments will usually have retailers who are loyal to local strong wholesalers that provide exceptional service.

Product-Oriented Selectivity. The third most-used modification for channel selectivity is product oriented. A manufacturer may have one wholesaler in a market who represents all its products. The same manufacturer

Table 4.6
Inclusive Market Characteristics

1.   All *qualifying* channel intermediaries may buy the product line.

2.   The manufacturer determines participant qualifications.
    • Wholesalers and retailers must have the ability to buy in the minimum order size established as well as the ability and willingness to pay according to terms.

    • All channel intermediaries must have the ability to store products properly.

    • Retailers must be willing to buy at specific SKU levels.

    • Channel intermediaries who are willing to follow the manufacturer's suggested marketing programs will not deviate from the programs.

3.   Legal and regulatory restrictions, if they exist, must be followed as a condition of purchasing.

may also select product groups, identified by their use characteristics, to be sold by specialty wholesalers in the market. As an example consider a sporting goods manufacturer that offers all types of sporting goods for baseball, basketball, skating, golf, hockey, tennis, skiing, and many other sports. It has a clothing line for each sport as well as equipment. In the Northwest market, it has one large regional wholesaler of sporting goods equipment and another that handles only clothing and uniform products for all sports. In addition, there is one specialty wholesaler for skiing equipment and clothing, another for golf equipment and clothing, and another that handles team sports equipment and uniforms. With this segmentation and selectivity at the wholesale level, the manufacturer has developed excellent representation for its products in all primary and secondary markets throughout the region.

Inclusive Channel Characteristics

Development of the all-inclusive marketing channel is not simply to say everyone and anyone can have the products. The inclusive channel is a structure that must meet the marketing objectives of the manufacturer or marketer and still provide for channel management flexibility. The primary objective of an inclusive channel is to have the product line readily available to all users of the manufacturer's products. This does not mean every possible retailer will be solicited to stock the line.

There may be qualifying criteria, related to line representation, for both the wholesale and retail levels in the channel (see Table 4.6). Minimum stock-keeping unit (SKU) levels may be one measurement. Regulatory or storage requirements may also provide specific selectivity criteria. Order size, participation in marketing programs, and the ability to perform customer services are the most important tests for channel members. Moreover, it is important that the channel members have established credit or financial stability suitable to the manufacturer. The basic qualifiers, established by the marketing company using the inclusive channel, will apply uniformly to all channel members at each channel level. The qualifiers may be different for wholesalers and retailers. In general, the inclusive marketing channel will not try to restrict product availability to either wholesalers or retailers. The practical business policy restrictions, such as good credit, may be the only generally imposed qualification by some manufacturers.

The lists of inclusive market characteristics, which are included in Table 4.4 and Table 4.6, are intended to be representative of what only some manufacturers or marketers may require of the inclusive channel members. These restrictions are not necessarily typical of all manufacturers. The more qualifications imposed, the less inclusive the marketing channel will become.

Market Profile Statement

At the beginning of this chapter, reference was made to writing a market profile statement. After considering all applicable market characteristics, the market profile statement can now be written. We will use carpeting as an example.

Example: Marketing Profile Statement

The company in this example produces carpeting from one plant location and sells its product in all fifty of the United States. Two separate product lines have been produced for two different markets. One product line is designated for commercial use in offices and other commercial buildings. The other line is for consumer use in private homes. The following market profile statement applies to this company.

Market Profile Statement. The markets served by the carpet company include all fifty of the United States (geographic designation). There are two separate markets identified by product use: commercial carpeting markets and consumer carpeting markets (user designations). The company's marketing channel for the commercial products will be characterized as direct sales to users of commercial carpeting through channel intermediaries designated as manufacturer's representatives. The commercial market representatives will handle the company's line as their only and exclusive carpet line for commercial users. These representatives will usually carry or offer complementary lines of floor coverings such as wood or tile products but no other carpet products. Market size is expressed in two dimensions: (1) the number of commercial carpeting buyers in each major market area and (2) the number of square yards of commercial carpeting sold in the market area. These buyers may be commercial contractors or interior design companies. Market density is centered in the major metropolitan cities and is expressed as the number of commercial buildings as well as the square footage of office space represented. The market volume is expressed in both dollars and square yards of carpeting sold by all competing manufacturers in the previous year. As a reference, figures are also available concerning the total number of square yards of floor coverings of all types as well as the total dollars of annual purchases in the market.

This channel will be developed as a mutually exclusive channel, employing only direct factory representatives who will work in an exclusive and protected geographic territory. There are two variables in determining market size: the replacement carpet market and the new construction market. The market size figures include all competitive floor-covering products. Products are purchased according to the natural use and need of the market (market activity cycles). Marketing programs for the commercial market stimulate product education and application techniques rather than merchandising, pricing, and buying programs. Pricing is established by quotation on a job-by-job basis.

The consumer market includes the fifty states. For the consumer products market, selling is directed to large regional distributors by the factory's own sales force. Specific wholesalers specializing in floor coverings and related products are established for high-density market segments. All consumer products are available to all wholesalers. The market size is expressed as the number of homes in the regional market areas as well as the number of square yards of total consumer carpets sold in the market. Building intentions for housing units is factored into market size for forecasting future sales. Market density is centered in the suburban concentration adjacent to large metropolitan areas. Market volume is calculated by product sales from previous years and is expressed as square yards of specific grades of carpet types as well as the dollar volume of each type sold. Market activity cycles indicate normal usage patterns for new and replacement purchasing. The consumer market is stimulated by many marketing programs, mostly centered on price deals, that are advertised directly to consumers through the media. Competition is keen and includes not only other carpet manufacturers but also all floor-covering choices for the consumer. Markets are stimulated by buying and selling programs within local markets in the channel. These programs are offered by competitors as well as our own company.

Discussion of Market Profile Statement

The writing of a market profile statement is intended to bring together a general picture of the channel that will be managed, or developed and managed. This statement can be very specific and detailed. It can also be general and only point the direction for the managers involved with marketing channel management. The market profile statement should cover all seven of the market characteristics: geographic market area, products in the market, market size, market density, market volume, market activity cycles, and the market selectivity reference.

QUESTIONS AND DISCUSSION

1. List the seven market characteristics used to develop the market profile statement.
2. What are the four basic geographic characteristics of a market?
3. In what way can product characteristics influence market definition?
4. What distinction is made between market size and market volume?
5. What element of channel structure is most affected by market density?
6. What are the primary differences between natural market cycles and those that are the result of marketing programs?
7. What are the three types of channel selectivity?
8. Profile a channel that is mutually exclusive.
9. There are three basic modifications to selective channel development. They relate to primary and secondary market responsibilities. Explain the differences of each:
   - dominant wholesalers
   - wholesaler size and market density
   - orientation to product or product group selectivity
10. What qualifications are usually required to establish an inclusive channel orientation?

PART II

Product and Market Management Actions and Options

FIVE

Organizing to Manage the Marketing Channel

In this text, many references have been made to channel management actions as well as to those who manage these channel actions. Channel management, whether by one manager or a group of managers, follows a process that is not a specific management function. Moreover, seldom will a company have complete control over a marketing channel. The only controllable channels are those that consist of company employees selling directly to the users of the company's products.

The marketing process that we call channel management is forever changing as a company introduces new products into its line or as the current products and markets mature. Policies, programs, products, prices, and even people change frequently in the marketing channel. This ever-evolving environment requires managers to constantly evaluate what the changes mean and how they will affect the marketing objectives of the company.

Prices are seldom stable, and marketing programs with buying and selling programs can change quickly. The key to effective management of a company's marketing channel is not only to know what is going on in the channel but also how to plan marketing actions that will be successful with the company's channel members.

The first step is to recognize what elements of the marketing channel can be managed. These manageable elements are known as the *marketing mix*. Channel managers must manage products, prices, programs, physical distribution, and people in their marketing channel and follow a specific plan to reach the company's marketing objectives. This can be a complex task involving many people in the marketing and sales departments as well as manufacturing, research, product development, and human resources; it may involve the channel members as well. Eventually every area of the company and the marketing organizations of channel members will become involved in the actions of managing the channel.

The day-to-day tasks fall to marketing and sales managers—the people who are face to face with the channel members and the company's competitors. It is the marketing and sales people who know where to find current information in the market that is so critical to management decision making. This chapter deals with the organization of crucial elements in channel management. Subsequent chapters will deal with the specific actions related to product management, pricing management, marketing programs, and those management activities intended to motivate people in the channel.

WHAT CAN BE MANAGED?

Only those elements we find in the marketing mix can be included in a management system. Although one may influence competition or governmental regulations and legal elements, these areas cannot be managed day to day.

Organizing to manage the marketing channel starts with the gathering of critical information. Considerable factual data are needed to write an accurate and detailed market profile statement (see chapter 4), which is the place to start. With this evaluation in hand, managers will become familiar with the impact of management decisions on the channel and be better equipped to make projections and provide successful marketing plans.

The Market Profile and Channel Organization

The elements of the market profile that relate to channel management and organization are geography, people, products, pricing, and marketing programs. Geography is added to the marketing mix, whereas physical distribution is eliminated. It is assumed that physical distribution is not managed day to day but represents a more stable organization and function. The basic market characteristics identified in the market profile statement in chapter 4 are coupled in this chapter with organizational considerations leading to management action.

Organizational Questions
1. What geographic area is to be managed?
2. Which products are involved in each market area?

3. What pricing actions will the organization need to follow?

4. What is the size of the market to be managed?

5. What are the volume dimensions for which one must plan to provide products, people, and suitable budgets?

6. Do market density characteristics require organizational variations in the channel?

7. What type of marketing programs are needed to motivate market activity cycles and to maintain a competitive market position.?

8. Do the relationships in the channel tend to be selective, exclusive, or inclusive?

Organizing to manage a marketing channel will not usually involve new organizational structuring or hiring of specialists to perform specific functions. The job is to create an organization that can function logically. Existing departments and staff can usually extend their activities to include the requirements of a new marketing channel. To anyone who has worked in a business of any size, it becomes obvious that the management tasks are allocated and shared by many individuals at various levels of responsibility. In general, most corporations have specific management tasks reserved or designated for specific levels of management. Channel managers are normally involved at the division level, sometimes at department level, where they hold various staff positions such as director of marketing, marketing manager, product manager, or market research manager.

Table 5.1 provides a description of management titles for the organization of a departmentalized company. There are also field-level positions not shown that refer to geographic designations such as area sales manager, region manager, district manager, and territory manager. These titles may vary, but whatever the title, the functions attributable to each will need to be performed in channel management. Several jobs will be combined in smaller companies. In larger companies, the positions may be even further divided.

ORGANIZING TO MANAGE PRODUCTS AND MARKETS

The allocation of management tasks related to products is very different from company to company and from company type to company type. Some companies define their markets by product type or category. With this orientation, for example, a company may define a market as the market for *concentrated, frozen* orange juice. When defining its market, another company may include *all types* of orange juice, whether from fresh or frozen sources. This designation may be further refined to state whether the product is packaged for commercial or consumer use. This

Table 5.1
Internal and Field Channel Management Positions (for a departmentalized company)

1.   Marketing and Sales Department: Top Management Level

   •   President or Vice-President, Marketing and Sales

   •   Director of Marketing (Marketing Director)

   •   Director of Sales (General Sales Manager)

2.   Staff Management Level (Marketing)

   •   Marketing Manager (specific markets or product areas)

   •   Group Product Manager

   •   Product Manager

   •   Marketing Research Manager

   •   Advertising & Sales Promotion Manager

   •   Training Manager (Human resources)

   •   Technical Services Manager

   •   Manager Customer Relations

   •   Manager, Marketing Information Services

   •   Distribution Manager (inventory, traffic, shipping, warehousing, order entry)

   •   Credit Manager (staff position)

3.   Field Management Level

   •   Branch Managers

   •   Field Sales Managers (Region, District, Territory)

   •   Sales Promotion & Merchandising

   •   Order Processing, Shipping, Inventory control

   •   Customer & Technical Services

   •   Field Research (Market & Marketing)

designation is a *user definition* that can relate to either products or markets.

Another example of a user market reference might be for a manufacturer of vitamin A who sells its products in both the human market and the animal market. This company may identify its product groups as vitamin A for humans and vitamin A as a feed additive for livestock. Organizing to manage the two marketing channels represented in this illustration will obviously require specific market knowledge and very different marketing mix decisions for each market. One obvious difference is in the geographic orientation. The agribusiness markets are rural, whereas the consumer markets are metropolitan. A different internal and external management system is needed for each market.

The type of organization that is developed is usually influenced by the company's product groups as well as the product and market similarities and differences. Product managers, or market managers, may have to manage a single product or a whole line of many products. In consumer product management, such as is found with Procter & Gamble, the product management task is split first by product brand and then into individual products or markets that are assigned for product and market management. For example, there may be a product brand manager for Tide itself and individual product or market managers for the different products or markets involved with the Tide brand.

For industrial products and markets, several different possibilities exist for organizational orientation. The objective is to organize product groups in order to simplify the management task and limit the personnel to the least number of people with the fewest number of management levels.

Organizing to manage products in the marketing channel requires a systematic approach to ensure that the job is performed with the greatest ease for the marketing company and with the greatest clarity, efficiency, and effectiveness for the channel members. Table 5.2 can be helpful in identifying the correct organizational positioning for product or market orientation. This table lists six potential designations that refer to the relationship between products and markets.

Generally, a product or market will fit into one of the six designations found in Table 5.2, which comments on each designation individually. Keep in mind, however, that even though some designations may utilize more than one point of reference, there is still only one of two selections for organizational orientation: either *product* orientation or *market* orientation.

Example: Company A—Product and Market Management Organization

Company A is a manufacturer of industrial chemicals. It has three product groups, designated as (1) lubricants, (2) solvents, and (3) cleansers. The company sells in two major markets. The Company A brand of products is sold to industrial users. In addition, the company sells prod-

Table 5.2
Product and Market Reference

1. *Product Category*	Product group, product name, product type, or packaging.
2. *Market Type*	Commercial, consumer, industrial, institutional, or governmental.
3. *User Category*	Consumer or actual user of the company's products.
4. *Distribution Type*	Markets segmented by specific different types of distribution (generic or prescription).
5. *Buyer Category*	Market defined by the type of buyer a catchall category (automotive wholesaler, grocery retailer).
6. *Geographical Area*	Product differences by geographic area (Southern fried chicken, Canadian bacon, Irish linen)

ucts as a private label or contract manufacturer to companies who market their own brands. The industrial users buy all three of the Company A brand products from merchant wholesalers. The private label buyers purchase the same or similar products directly from Company A. These private label products are sold in many different markets in a variety of package sizes and for many different uses.

Organization of the product management function for Company A involves selecting the best option between *product* or *market* orientation. The industrial users are product *consumers* who actually use Company A branded products as supplies to maintain machinery and facilitate production in their own manufacturing plants. The market for private label products represents formulations and product designations selected by Company A private label customers, who are *marketers*.

Company A decided it needed product management (channel management) to be market oriented rather than product oriented, even though the company's internal organization preferred product orientation. One product manager was assigned to the industrial markets and another to the private label markets. The designation *product manager* was retained, as the managers would be involved with product development planning, production scheduling, and the marketing and sales actions defined as the tasks related to managing the marketing mix. For Company A's internal organization, these are all product-oriented activities relating to the manufacturer's own products as well as to those they produce and package for their customers in the private label markets.

Had the manufacturer decided to organize according to the three product groups, at least three product managers would have been needed, one each for lubricants, solvents, and cleansers. For Company *A* and its customers, market orientation is the most efficient product management organization. Study Table 5.3 to compare market-oriented organization and product-oriented organization.

Consider the problems that would occur should the manufacturer decide to organize according to product group rather than by market. The duplication of effort will be substantial. Each of the three product managers will have to develop market information for his or her specific product group in *both* markets. Customers of the company will be even more confused, as they will have to deal with three different product group managers and will probably have to buy from three different sales organizations from the same supplier. Imagine a private label marketer buying lubricants, solvents, and cleansing materials from this manufacturer and having to place orders with three different people in the same company. This situation is prevented by good organizational planning at the product management level. Even if product orientation seems logical to the manufacturer for internal management, the marketing tasks involving three separate product groups will be unnecessarily complicated.

When it is easy to do business with a company, a strong bond between supplier and buyer is established. The most significant marketing advantage to the manufacturer is the ability to present unified marketing programs to each of the markets in which the company wishes to participate.

In marketing channel management, the product factors to consider are those that are most proprietary to the manufacturer or marketer. These are the products with which the company brand or name is associated. For this reason, companies like to use a market reference that includes their company name, brand, or product name. When the product is truly proprietary—that is, unique or patented—the company can create a market reference to the product name. Kleenex is a good example. All brands of tissue are frequently called Kleenex. These kinds of products are rare. In addition, the costs related to establishing a brand name market are very high.

Product Category Orientation

In the example of Company *A*, a product rather than market reference to a specific broad product category, such as lubricants, solvents, or cleansers, would be an acceptable, though not preferred, designation. The product orientation may produce a workable organization if the programs of the managers are consolidated under market orientation for

Table 5.3
Market and Product Organization

Market-Oriented Organization

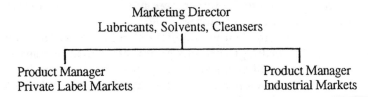

Marketing Director
Lubricants, Solvents, Cleansers

Product Manager   Product Manager
Private Label Markets   Industrial Markets

Product-Oriented Organization

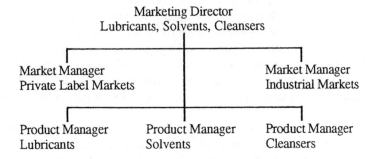

Marketing Director
Lubricants, Solvents, Cleansers

Market Manager   Market Manager
Private Label Markets   Industrial Markets

Product Manager   Product Manager   Product Manager
Lubricants   Solvents   Cleansers

channel management. Product orientation would *not* produce an efficient organization, however, because in addition to one additional product manager, two market managers would also be needed. The point is that at some level, the company will need to bring its product management under a market orientation. Keeping the market orientation at the product management level obviates the need for one additional product manager and two market managers. Thus, three positions and one level of management are unnecessary, as shown in Table 5.3.

Market Type Orientation

By organizing the product management function under two markets, industrial and private label, the orientation to market type is established. Any current and future products developed by the company for these markets could easily be included in this established market orientation. In the event that the company discovers or develops products for a different market, such as the consumer market, another product or market manager could be added for the new market without the need for further organizational change.

Distribution Type Orientation

In practical application, the Company A orientation to markets is also separated by distribution differences. Since the industrial products are sold as Company A's brand products whereas the private label products are manufactured for other companies to be sold as their brands, there is a split in distribution as well as by market. The industrial products are distributed by the wholesalers in the Company A channel, whereas the private label products are sold under a manufacturing contract and distributed directly to the marketing company, with no channel intermediaries. This represents two different channels.

User Category

Products that have a reference by user category are identified as the groups of people who buy or use the products. In our example for Company A, there are only two categories of users: industrial and private label. There are potentially additional market and user designations. It is likely that the company will have further designations for industrial users that may establish *user categories*, such as automotive manufacturing users, or users who are manufacturers of nuts, bolts, and screws. The company could also use a type of manufacturing equipment as a user category. This designation would list industrial lathe operators and injection mold operators as categories of *users*. Such information may be useful in planning marketing programs, creating convenient packaging, and organizing physical distribution to these market segments.

Organizing to manage products for a user category would relate product management to the identified user. For example, a company that recognizes this reference may identify its business as a manufacturer of products for private label marketers of lubricants, solvents, and/or cleansers. It is recognized that the actual user is not the private label marketer. The term *marketer* is substituted for *user* in this situation. As far as the manufacturer is concerned, its customer, the private label marketer, *uses* the products it buys for its own brand marketing. This reference could then be modified to geographic area, type of business in which the private label company is involved, and product categories represented by the private label brand. Consider the progression of market reference shown in Table 5.4, noting in particular *geographic area*.

Buyer Category

Buyer category is a catchall product reference that works when a more specific reference is not applicable. Specialty product manufacturers may refer to buyers of their products as *institutional buyers, commercial buyers,*

Table 5.4
Progression of Market Reference (Company *A* example for the industrial products market)

Product category.	Lubricants, solvents, and cleansing agents.
Market type.	Industrial markets and manufacturing.
Distribution type.	Merchant wholesalers of specialty chemicals.
User category.	Automotive parts and machine manufacturers.
Buyer category.	Not applicable for Company *A*.
Geographical area.	The U.S. and Canadian markets. The reference is to reflect pricing and product labeling differences related to the two geographic areas.

or *private brand buyers*. Other buyer groups may be defined by the type of organization they represent, such as cooperatives, governmental agencies, or exporters.

For some of these buyer markets, the supplier may need to perform a regulatory function, such as product identification or dating, for which the marketers of these products are held responsible. The contract supplier or manufacturer may need to satisfy these requirements for its customers and may wish to identify them by a customer designation or category.

Geographic Area

Product reference and management by geographic area is becoming less common as markets grow and companies merge to gain competitive advantages. Geographic references may be very broad, or they may define a small market segment. References such as the following are common: *Pacific Northwest* Apple Growers, *Southeastern* Poultry Producers, *Texas* Cattlemen, *Mid-South* Cotton Growers, *Eastern States* Bankers, or *North Central* Auto Dealers. A pure geography reference may designate Southern States, Pacific Rim, Latin America, United States and Canada, or European Countries.

When all the products sold by a company in a geographic area are grouped together in a geographic market designation, they are usually products that cannot be identified as specific to one manufacturer. Unique products will make their own markets and need specific management action. The organizational task for geographically identified markets is to manage the total business in the market area rather than by the product or product groups in the market. Market orientation is the only way this can work. Strong channel management and marketing programs are required in geographically designated markets.

The Progression of Product and Market Reference

For any product or market reference, there is usually a progression of specific designations that segment the market or more clearly define the market as it relates to the company's products. The progression usually starts with the most broadly applied designation and then will proceed to the specific. In Table 5.4 we see the application of the progression of references as applied to Company A. For the industrial market of Company A, not all the references in Table 5.4 are applicable to the market designations.

ORGANIZING TO MANAGE PRICING

Since chapter 10 deals with pricing strategies, little needs to be said about pricing management at this point. Organizing to manage prices is much like organizing to manage products: the day-to-day job of managing prices belongs to the product and market manager in cooperation with the sales group. Establishing pricing strategies and actual price numbers may be done at a higher level.

Communication is the key to managing prices. Everyone involved must be in the communication's loop to prevent errors when initiating the necessary plans for price changes. Three areas of decision making are related to pricing: product cost, profit objective, and competitive pricing. Those involved in making these decisions must establish an organized communication system for all three areas.

Product Cost

The relationship that involves product cost and profit objectives is an inseparable one. The product cost plus the profit cost equals the selling price. Thus it is extremely important that those who make pricing decisions know at all times what is happening to product costs. If costs go up, prices must also go up in order to maintain a consistent profit margin. Likewise, if a major competitor lowers its price and you must follow the market action with a compensating price reduction, your profit margin will go down. The key is to know what is going on at the market level as well as in the manufacturing area. This is accomplished by organizing a complete communication loop for all information that may affect product cost and profits as well as any competitive pricing activity. Table 5.5 shows who controls the actions in these three cost- and profit-

Table 5.5
Cost-Related Sources and Actions

Product Costs	Profit Objectives	Competitive Area
Manufacturing Dept.	Marketing & Sales	Marketing & Sales
• Production	• Profit target	• Competitive prices
• Handling	• Program costs	• Competitive programs
• Shipping & storage	• Adv. & promotion	• Channel actions
• Regulatory	• Sales projections	• Sales costs
Marketing Dept.		Market Research Dept.
• Packaging type		• Marketing trends
• Graphic design		• Cost trends
Purchasing Dept.		
• Raw material		
• Supplies		

sensitive areas. These areas are also communication's sources for cost and profit information.

The organization of a communication network may start with the field sales area. For price-sensitive products, first gather competitive pricing information to provide target numbers for a selling price. Knowing the price at which a product must compete in the market can provide pricing planners with upper and lower limits for the competitive selling price. The information that comes from field sales people or from channel members may be a monthly report or an action-activated report. A report is activated when something changes. What one does with the information is covered in later chapters.

Reports for competitive product pricing and marketing programs can be structured with standard forms. The most important aspects of channel-generated reports is that they must be timely and accurate. Competitive-price reporting must contain the basic information listed in Table 5.6.

The form outlined in Table 5.6 is for the external organization to use in communicating with the marketing department at the home office or wherever product management takes place. A similar form is used for

Table 5.6
Elements of Competitive-Price Reporting

Product(s) name _____

Product manufacturer _____

Product size/quantity/quality _____

Normal price $ _____Price change date _____

New price $ _____Date effective _____Termination date _____

Volume discount qualifications _____

Special terms _____

Other _____

Customer name & location _____

Action recommended _____

Product ordered ____Yes ____No Inventory in stock _____

Plan to order _____Yes _____No Will not order because_____

_____Reported by _____

Attach printed official price quotation, price change sheet, or other
documentation concerning the above price change.

Report sent to _____ Date _____

Note: This is a price change report for a field sales person or a channel
intermediary to send to the product source (manufacturer). The price changes
reported may be increases or declines. This report may also note changes in
terms or discount qualifications.

internal communications that affect either the cost of products or the
profit objective for a specific product or product group. The design of
the form used internally would be specific to the company involved and
will not be graphically displayed here. The information that is necessary
and that should be communicated to the marketing control area involved
with pricing decisions includes the following:

1. Title of the form (Cost and/or Profit Change Notice); date the form is issued
2. Department issuing the report; the person issuing the report
3. Product or product group involved in the cost or profit objective change
4. Reason for the change
5. Effects of the change on cost or profit
6. Date the change will take place
7. Inventory implications

The departments likely to be involved with issuing product cost changes are manufacturing, shipping, handling, and purchasing. The areas that will evaluate the effect of these changes on profits include financial, marketing, sales, legal and regulatory departments. It is up to marketing management to determine the appropriate pricing action to be taken and when it should take place. Those marketing people involved in pricing decisions *must* organize to collect all the information needed to make the right decisions. This will include consideration of the internal and the external channel organizations.

ORGANIZING TO MANAGE MARKETING PROGRAMS

The responsibility for managing marketing programs in the channel is shared by several groups within the company. It is also a task that is shared with channel members. Thus internal marketing managers and appropriate channel members work together to manage marketing programs. The communication loop must include all who will play a part in initiating and managing the action.

Organization of Internal Resources

Nearly all marketing programs will require the establishment of a budget, program development, knowledge of what is happening in the market, and a schedule of events to launch the program. Budget needs are detailed by marketing managers and sent to top management for approval. Program development comes from marketing resources. The competitive conditions in the environment in which the program must operate must be gathered from all available resources. The most important resource is the company's sales force. This is the group that will make the program a success or failure. Finally, the actual planning of the program must include commitments from production or manufacturing sources to be sure that products will be available as needed, when needed, and in the proper amounts at the designated locations. The following is a useful checklist of the four areas in the organization that must be involved with managing marketing programs. Note the responsibilities of each area:

Marketing Program Development. Marketing planning and product management, marketing information services, sales management for forecasting and training, financial services to provide costs and budget information, facilitating agencies such as sales promotion, advertising, and public relations for program introduction.

Top Management. Budget approval, program approval, and establishment of priorities and participation authority for other departments.

Field Management. Market research, sales managers, and all other resources that can provide competitive market information and establish personnel actions.

Manufacturing. Planning for production preparation, materials availability, packaging, inventory control, shipping and storage, and cost estimates; scheduling actual production.

Organizing to Motivate Channel Members

Motivating channel members is a continuous marketing action in the channel. It should start at the time a manufacturer or marketer is recruiting intermediaries for channel participation. Selecting the most effective wholesalers and/or retailers in the beginning is important for the motivation of all channel members. Most channel intermediaries like to work together and are motivated by the association with other top companies in the marketing channel.

Motivating the best intermediaries to become part of your channel organization, as well as providing marketing program support, may be promoted by the motivational enticements shown in Table 5.7. Using the marketing mix elements as a guide for motivating channel intermediaries, we find that motivating factors related to product focus on product quality and product guarantees. Pricing issues are centered on high profits, competitive pricing policies, and the availability of credit programs. Marketing programs represent the largest category of interest and involvement for channel intermediaries. In this area advertising, product promotions, communications, training, market building, channel selectivity consideration, and market research provide current and accurate information concerning the market. Physical distribution is involved in determining an effective channel selectivity reference even though this is a marketing policy decision. Providing necessary customer services and maintaining a high order completion percentage will have a direct bearing on customer motivation.

The final element of the marketing mix, people, is involved in every step of the marketing process. People can make any organizational orientation a success or a failure. (In later chapters we discuss the motiva-

Table 5.7
Motivational Incentives for Channel Members

1.	High profits	8.	Selective distribution
2.	Quality products	9.	Product guarantees
3.	Product promotion	10.	Advertising
4.	Credit programs	11.	Rapid, accurate communications
5.	Market research	12.	Market development programs
6.	Training programs	13.	Competitive pricing policy
7.	Customer services	14.	High order completion percentage

tion of people in the company as well as of people in the channel and their contribution to channel management.) So far as the involvement of people in any marketing program is concerned, the most motivational action management can take is to be sure that everyone is kept informed of what is planned to take place. It is especially important that the company's own sales force be kept well informed of plans that involve them and their customers in the channel.

SUMMARY

The organizational task for channel management starts with establishing a complete and supportive internal organization. Coupled with an external organization (the marketing channel) that is both capable and compatible and with a physical distribution system that serves all channel levels, the internal organization enables the company to participate effectively in the day-to-day tasks entailed in managing the marketing mix.

Only the elements of the marketing mix can be managed on a day-to-day basis. The development of an efficient and compatible internal and external organization is the result of knowing what needs to be done and how it can best be accomplished. The allocation of management tasks must be coupled to channel member capabilities.

Identification of the market demographics is focused on market geographic location, size, volume, density, product and market orientation, pricing, and the channel selectivity reference. Creating marketing programs that will accomplish the company's objectives, while at the same time supporting those of the channel intermediaries, is the mark of good planning, effective communications, and enlightened managers both in the company and in the marketing channel.

QUESTIONS FOR DISCUSSION

1. What marketing elements can be managed in the marketing channel?
2. Give an example of a product-oriented market reference and a market-oriented reference.
3. Give an example for each product-market reference below:
   a. Product Category
   b. Market Type
   c. User Category
   d. Distribution Type
   e. Buyer Category
   f. Geographical Area
4. Managing prices involves three areas of decision making. These are (1) product cost, (2) profit objective, and (3) competitive pricing in the channel. Explain briefly how each of these factors is related to pricing and profits.
5. What departments or groups in the internal organizations are involved with the establishment and maintenance of product cost, profits, and evaluation of the competitive environment?
6. Why is it important to have written reports on competitive price changes?
7. Make a list of at least six motivational incentives that manufacturers can offer to channel intermediaries.
8. Why is it necessary for the channel manager to be in constant touch with sales people when it comes to price management?
9. What three motivational incentives are related to physical distribution?
10. The marketing channel is managed by an internal organization and an external organization. Briefly state the major functions of each in channel management.

SIX

Effective Responsibility without Authority

Many staff positions that involve channel management are structured with considerable responsibility but possess little authority. Managers in these staff positions are dependent upon the cooperation of many others, called *resource people*, for the success of their activities. Resource people are found in both the internal channel organization and the external channel organization. Although some channel managers have specific areas of authority, most do not have enough to use the power of their position to influence others to provide what they need.

RESOURCE MANAGEMENT

Product managers represent the ultimate commitment to responsibility with little authority to accomplish the goals of their position. The product management function declares by its name that it is a position oriented more toward objects and activities than to people. Product managers are dependent upon the information provided by many people in different departments of the company. Because the resource people are mostly outside of the marketing department, it is difficult for management to provide product managers with direct supervisory authority over those who are crucial to the success of their work.

This chapter has only one objective: to provide channel managers with management techniques that will, when properly applied, make them effective managers even though their position has limited vested authority.

The channel manager's resources are those individuals who develop information, produce data, and provide services for the whole corporation, including channel managers. To manage these resource people, the product manager's authority would need to be applied across departmental lines, which is organizationally impossible. The channel manager cannot possess the authority to go to the financial group to demand statistical information. Nor can the legal, manufacturing, personnel, or sales department be subject to the authority of a staff manager to produce information or perform services on demand. Thus, facing the need to influence these various groups to perform and lacking the authority to demand results, what other tactics can product managers use? We have collected these characteristics into what we have termed the "authority profile." This is the profile of an effective manager who knows how to get things done through influence and persuasion rather than by demand.

The authority profile achieves its effectiveness more through method than personal dynamics. Not everyone has the charisma to influence people to do things simply by asking them. It is the objective of the authority profile to encourage cooperation from others by enabling them to be responsive. This responsiveness is generated by the prudent use of the four *P*'s of the product manager's authority profile: precision, perception, persuasion, and persistence. These four *P*'s provide managers who need authority with a means of being as effective as if they had authority. But product managers have the authority to ask only for information, yet they are held directly responsible to get it. Thus, product managers, as well as any other channel managers, must "look like authority, sound like authority," and produce results as though doing so were a vested part of their jobs. This is accomplished by using the tools of influence and persuasion—the four *P*'s—as a power base for staff management effectiveness.

THE AUTHORITY PROFILE

Develop the ability to be precise, perceptive, persuasive, and persistent whenever you need authority but lack it in your job description. Staff managers who must manage the marketing channel, particularly product managers, have a great deal of responsibility. Consider the word *responsibility* literally. It implies that to be significantly *responsive* one must display the *ability* to be so. Responsibility is further complicated for marketing channel managers because theirs is both a give and a take responsibility. Channel managers may not have the authority to make others take responsibility, but they surely have the need to bestow it.

Thus marketing channel managers must be able to get responses to their requests and be capable of responding to the questions of fellow workers upon whose cooperation they depend.

PRECISION

The first P demands that the manager be *precise*. In order for resource people to respond to requests, they must clearly understand what is expected of them. To make clear what a manager expects in response, the request, whether written or verbal, must be precise. Following is an illustration of what can happen when precision is ignored. In this situation a marketing channel manager is writing to the credit manager for needed information.

Request Memo (to Sam Paine the Credit Manager)

Sam,
I'm working on a promotion for our Number One line of products. The promotion requires that we "load in" our wholesalers almost twice the normal order size. This promotion may put a strain on some of our best customers' credit lines. Can you advise me the total credit limits for all of our wholesale customers who buy this line?
Thanks,
Bob

Reply Memo to Bob Dunkin (the Marketing Channel Manager)

Bob,
Last year our credit limits for customers buying the Number One line totaled $5 million. The previous year, we had a total of $5.5 million. This year we have about $4.8 million total in extended credit limits now established.
Glad to help,
Sam

Let's take a look at what Bob Dunkin, the channel manager, really needed to know. It is quite different than what he got from Sam, the credit manager. The information needed was to support a promotional plan that called for extended terms to facilitate a request for orders that would approximate twice the normal order size for most accounts. The extended terms would allow the accounts to keep their credit current (paid on time), but the order size would elevate many accounts over their normal credit limit. This channel manager was obviously not trained to be precise in his communications. Although the information received provided more than what was asked for, it was not what was needed.

What Bob Actually Needed to Know

1. What is the current line of credit extended for *each* customer buying the Number One product line?
2. What is the usual amount of credit tied up (in use) by each account?
3. Which accounts show sufficient credit worthiness to have their credit limits raised and by what amount?
4. By using extended credit terms, could an account be shipped an order that would put the account over their credit limit?
5. Can this information be provided by the fifteenth of next month?

Communications that are not precise invite not only incomplete responses but also the wrong information. What will the credit manager think when Bob comes back to get the information he really needs to know? What has happened to the time schedule for the project and who is in control? Would it have been helpful for Bob to provide a specific list of the customers involved? (The answers to these questions have obvious implications.)

Precise Communications

Managers must consider how to communicate with great precision, but not in great detail. The key is to make sure the resources who are to respond may do so with all of the needed information. Their *ability* to *respond* (responsibility) is tied directly to the precise request received.

Since marketing channel managers are always working against deadlines, they should never allow poor communication to be a reason for a resource person to delay a response. If there is any doubt, written requests may be tested on a colleague to see if what you are seeking is clearly expressed by what you have written. Always leave a copy of your written request with a date indicating the time an answer is expected. Confirm the resource's ability to respond in the time frame you have suggested. Either get agreement or reset the time expectation to one that is mutually acceptable.

Not every manager can naturally or easily develop precise communication. For this reason, using the following Checklist for Precision will be helpful for many managers in establishing their *ability* to be precise.

Checklist for Precision

1. Provide a detailed written request.
2. Confirm a mutual understanding of the request and the ability to respond.

3. Confirm the agreed time for completion.
4. Obtain a written commitment.
5. Stress the importance of your request and the value of the information.

When managers communicate in precise terms, they will save time for everyone involved. Of even greater importance to the managers, a precise request tells those involved that the manager who is making the request knows what is needed and is in control.

A professional trainer in a large corporation (with whom I worked in training employees to use the four *P*'s of the authority profile) has developed a useful example for precise communication. He gives instructions for participation in this exercise by asking the trainees to use all five of the elements in the Checklist for Precision. This trainer uses a customized example, tailored to his company, which is similar to the following example.

Example: Precise Statement Exercise

Participants are asked to write a precise statement to the financial services manager requesting the effect on profits of a $10-per-unit price reduction (to meet competition) for a product selling fifty units per week. Marketing action of some type may be taken to meet competition and the channel manager needs precise information to help in making decisions. Participants may make any assumptions necessary to write the memo.

Precise Statement Exercise Answer (Memo to the Financial Services Manager)

Bill,
Competition is cutting prices by $10 per unit on a product competitive to our product number 7117, which we manufacture. If we meet this price reduction, what effect will it have on our profit per unit? I need to make a decision whether it is better to meet it or wait out the competition's price deal. The next selling period starts in about thirty days. Therefore, I will need this critical information within the next ten days in order to have sufficient lead time to react if that is indicated. We must meet our profit projections even in a competitive environment and your information will help greatly in our evaluation of lost units of sales compared to lost profits per unit. If you can respond by the time requested, give me a yes or no on the attached memo and fire it back to me. I really appreciate your timely help.
Roy

The trainer asks the question, "Does this memo have all five items listed in the Checklist for Precision?" It does provide a detailed written request (item one). The second item is covered by communicating the need for information to be supplied within ten days. The third and fourth items, asking for confirmation and agreement of the time in writing, are combined with a request to reply on the attached copy of the memo. Good reasons are also given for the importance of the information (the fifth item). By following the five items in the Checklist for Precision, you can expect a good response.

PERCEPTION

The second *P* stands for being *perceptive*. Managers must perceive whether a commitment has been made. To be certain one should make a face-to-face contact. Some people are astute listeners and may be able to "read" the voice tone and sincerity of a phone call. Most of us need facial expressions and body language, as well as voice inflection, to tell us if someone intends to perform as agreed. If the resource has difficulty making an appointment to review the commitment, that is a good clue for a lack of willingness or ability to respond to the request. Perceptive managers will ascertain the reasons for reluctance or responsiveness as soon as possible and take the appropriate action. They will also provide encouragement to those who give positive responses.

Look for the clues that will tell you whether a commitment has truly been accepted after it has been precisely communicated. Managers should ask questions if they perceive that clarification or more information is needed to facilitate a response. Resources must also be impressed with the urgency and seriousness of the request.

The marketing channel manager's perceptive evaluation is most critical in the first progress check on the agreed-upon commitment. It is necessary to check on progress long before the due date of the request. Checking on progress is highly important early in the overall exchange because a lack of progress in fulfilling a need may lead to a compensatory change in the request.

The requesting manager must be the one to perceptively ask questions and follow up on the request. Managers should not expect resource people to voluntarily admit they lack the ability to provide what is asked of them. *Most people avoid making themselves look incompetent.* Managers must set up a reminder file and use it sufficiently in advance of the due date to allow a response: This is facilitating the ability to respond.

Be perceptive by making your sixth sense one of *common sense*. Assuming that others will spontaneously respond isn't good enough. You must be precisely perceptive of what to expect. Focus on two points regarding perception: First, know that the most critical determination of a resource's ability or willingness to respond is the first time the resource is contacted to determine progress. Second, if the resource person contacted cannot keep the agreed-upon date, you must ask, "What can I do to help get this project on track?" This requires a two-part answer:

1. Determine why the information will not be available and what may be done to facilitate the process.
2. Set a new date, if that is needed, and confirm an agreement in writing for the new date. This is both a precise and a perceptive communication that will result in a new commitment to provide the information.

PERSUASION

The third *P* has to do with being *persuasive*. Managers must be sure that the precise message they have communicated, and perceived as accepted, is also being acted upon in a timely manner. A person's persuasion, directed to influence a resource's performance, should result in the action needed that will keep the project on track. Since the manager cannot exercise authority, his or her persuasiveness should ensure acceptance of the needed commitment and the cooperation to complete it. Remember, persuasion can be more effective than the power of authority. People tend to do first what they want to do or are persuaded to do, not what they must do or are told to do. What is demanded of them always has a lower priority.

Key Elements of Persuasion

The most important element in being persuasive is to be absolutely correct (precise) in your statements. Always check your records to verify dates and the types of action requested. Confirm in whose court the ball is currently bouncing before you make a persuasive followup to facilitate action. The second most critical element in persuasion is to establish— or reestablish—the importance of your request and the part played by the resource person in its accomplishment. Look at the Persuasion Checklist to identify the necessary actions to be persuasive.

Persuasion Checklist

1. Be correct in your facts.
2. Establish the importance of your action.
3. Be pleasant.
4. Show your appreciation before it is earned.
5. Give credit to resources for their contribution.
6. Make sure that resource people know that what they do is important.

Some of the items in this checklist overlap or may be performed at one time. However, they are identified individually to provide easy recognition of each point.

You have communicated a need *precisely*. You have *perceived* that the commitment is accepted. You have checked back and *persuasively* kept everything on track. It is time to show the *persistence* that will result in accomplishment.

PERSISTENCE

Don't make this *P* into *pest*, but do be persistent in making sure that the commitment is kept. Managers who are reliable instill the same quality in others.

A note of caution is needed: Persistence must produce results to be effective. When managers couple the persuasion with persistence, they are more likely to produce the results. It is also necessary that managers know it isn't enough to ask if the work is ready or if the task is progressing. Be precise in communicating your expectations. Ask about specific aspects of the assignment critical to its success. Determine if everyone still has the same targets and is expecting the actions that are planned in the anticipated progress. Here are four checkpoints for the persistent manager to use.

Checkpoints for Persistent Managers

1. Be *precise* when you ask about specific progress.
2. Be *perceptive* to the fact that the obligation to perform remains a high priority.
3. Use *persuasion* by offering assistance.
4. Be *persistent* in reminding the resource of the importance of the commitment.

Managers who master these four *P*'s will successfully assume the profile and effectiveness of authority without trying to exercise it. Remember, effective managers are precise in their communications, perceptive to the response and acceptance of a commitment, persuasive in getting a "want to" priority set for their requests, and persistent enough to be sure everything gets on track and stays there to produce the expected results.

THE FIFTH *P* IS PASS

Since everyone must eventually deal in the realities of the actual work environment, where there are many priorities and real authority with which to deal, we must recognize that there will be times when even the four *P*'s properly applied will fail to get results. In these cases, we must create a fifth *P*, *pass*. To do this, think of yourself as a running back on a football team with your boss as the quarterback. (Your boss must be the quarterback because he or she is always handing you the ball, asking you to run with the ball, telling you to get on the ball or keep on the ball, and reminding you not to drop the ball.) When the four *P*'s fail and you still have a commitment to score, hand the ball back to the boss and call for the fifth *P*: *pass*.

The channel manager should request his or her boss to throw the ball over the head of the resource person who keeps stopping progress. Have your boss pass directly to the superior of the unresponsive resource person. Since most channel managers do not have the authority to go over heads, they must borrow or enlist the authority from a person who does have it. Then employ the pass with finesse. We suggest a soft pass, not a "bullet." Staff managers should not get their resource people in serious trouble with their supervisors.

Caution should always be employed in calling for the pass play. Make sure it is necessary! Confirm that there are no other moves you can successfully make to accomplish your objective. Passes are visible. They indicate a situation that calls for risk and so should not be used if anything else will work. However, even with the risk, the pass can be a necessary play. Learn how to use it well, in case it is needed, but do not use it too often. In so doing you risk being intercepted. When someone else has the ball, you lose all control of the action.

The Pass Plan

Effective channel managers, and especially product managers, know how to run with the ball without blockers. These managers have found a way to get things done quietly, efficiently, and effectively with their own manner of applying the principle of the authority profile. But even the best of these managers must sometimes call for a pass. They also know that not every successful action can be accomplished by one's own effort. Sometimes a pass is the only move possible. If a pass is unavoidable, follow this procedure to set up the play.

The Successful Pass. Go to the person with the authority—your boss—and show documentation of your need. This will include your follow-up communications with the resource person blocking your progress. Point out that your documented efforts have failed to get results. Present the action plan you would like the person with authority to use, and be precise in the description of this action.

Outline the Play. Get a commitment from the boss to have the pass executed along with the time or date by which the person with authority will take action. At times it may be expedient for the channel manager to put the pass play into action by borrowing the authority to do so from your boss. This is done only with permission *in that person's name.*

An example of how the pass plan may be used is borrowed from the Precise Communications exercise presented earlier involving Sam the Credit Manager and Bob the Channel Manager. This example concerns the need for extended credit to initiate a product promotion that you as the channel manager are planning.

Pass Plan Example. You have been planning a preseason promotion that incorporates a "load in" feature. In order for you to reach your commitment and sales goal, customers will be required to order twice the amount of products they normally order. Because an order of this size will push many customers beyond their approved credit limit, you have requested the credit manager to approve a plan to provide extended terms—a longer payment schedule—by using delayed billing for that part of the order that is over the credit limit. You have presented the following logic for this maneuver: Since the billing has not taken place (you are operating under a delayed billing plan), the customer's accounts payable will remain current within the company's terms and at the same time not exceed the approved credit limit. Your request for approval of this plan has not been acted upon even though you have applied the authority profile as skillfully as you know how. The deadline for action has come and gone, and now you must ask your boss for a "pass" to Sam's boss, who is the controller.

You have followed the procedure for initiation of the pass plan as follows: You have presented to your boss all the documentation necessary to show that your considerable efforts have been unsuccessful in getting the needed information (Step One: Go to authority). You have also prepared the memo, which follows, as a suggestion of what needs to be communicated (Step Two: Present an action plan). You have asked if your boss agrees that the memo needs to be sent to the controller immediately (Step Three: Get agreement and a timetable). You have suggested that if your superior is too busy to take immediate action, you will, with approval to do so, send the memo in your boss's name (Step Four: Put the pass plan into action).

Request Memo (to the Controller)

Dear Peter,
Our marketing channel manager, Bob Dunkin, has created a product promotion on which we are placing great importance in helping us to reach our first quarter sales goals. Without this promotion we will fall short of our profit projections for the period. Bob has been working with your credit manager, Sam Paine, to gain approval of extended credit terms, a critical part of the program. I'm sure you know we would not proceed without your approval. I would appreciate it

if you would look into what is holding up the completion of this work on your end. I am keeping "feet to the fire" on my end. Sam and Bob agreed to have these credit approvals by 11/20, a date which has come and gone. Please give me a call on extension 2123. Thanks for your help, Peter. It is always appreciated. Edward

Marketing Director

Analysis. This memo (or pass) to the credit manager clearly reinforces the importance of the requested action. It states the consequences of failure. It directs attention to the one who is responsible for the action and remands the responsibility to the credit department. Then to soften the impact on Sam Paine, it indicates a shared responsibility by Sam and Bob. Finally, this pass asks for immediate action by suggesting a phone call response. The passer also offers appreciation for the assistance before it is earned.

The final action by the channel manager (Bob) is to express appreciation to his boss for such an excellent pass play. The truly effective channel manager will also thank the resource (Sam), who was prompted into action as though it resulted from his own initiative.

When the Pass Fails, Punt

It was clearly stated that the pass is a risky action to take. Because more people become involved in the situation, there is more chance for failure. If the pass plan fails, the channel manager must quickly take remedial action. First the channel manager must go to the resource person causing the problem to evaluate the situation face to face. The resource person (in our example, the credit manager) must be made to realize that because the pass failed, they (both Bob and Sam) have placed their superiors in a confrontational position. If a showdown occurs, both Bob and Sam stand to lose no matter what the outcome. The next step is one that will place the blame on whoever is holding up the progress of the request for approval or disapproval. Will the resource person want the boss to take the blame? Not likely. In your discussion with Sam, the resource person, make sure that he understands the magnitude of the situation and ask what he thinks it will take to get the action started to save face for everyone involved. If Sam cannot offer a logical solution to this problem, it is time to punt.

The Punt

Everyone knows that a punt is a kick. In this case, the kick will have to be placed where it will get action even if it is painful for someone. A conscientious channel manager will do everything possible to prevent a punt, but a boss who has been unsuccessful in a very visible action likes to kick something. A punt may offer the best choice. Unfortunately when a punt is in progress, someone wins and someone loses.

If it is sufficiently important to complete the course of action that is started, then a punt is the only answer. If, on the other hand, the channel manager can find an alternative way to successfully complete the marketing action, without the help of the reluctant resource person, this new avenue should be substituted for the punt. Whenever possible take another road to success, one that does not burn bridges or cause hurt feelings that will have to be dealt with sometime in the future.

There are many ways for an enterprising marketing channel manager to accomplish an objective. If one direction is blocked, it is sometimes better to try another and save the confrontation of either a pass or a punt. In the case of the reluctant credit manager, our channel manager decided to ignore the problems that may arise should accounts exceed their credit limit when placing double orders. The orders were placed, without the delayed billing feature, in the hope that the credit department, in its lethargy to action, would not hold up shipments. If it did hold them up, sales could try to get approval on an order-by-order basis, even though this would involve more work for everyone. Such action may lead to many small battles but will avoid a big one.

SUMMARY

Maintaining a high level of morale and enthusiasm in the ranks of channel and product managers is a difficult task. A lack of authority to perform one's responsibilities may lead to morale problems or open frustration. It has been the experience of this author that the proper integration of the authority profile into the skills of staff and middle managers in *all* departments can greatly improve management effectiveness and personal job satisfaction.

The four *P*'s of the authority profile are intended to provide managers with an organized method of consistently producing results, without the need for authority to be vested in their position. Managers will need to work hardest to perfect their own techniques of using persuasion and persistence, since these are the most difficult to use effectively and are more personal than being competently precise or perceptive.

The pass play is one that should be held in reserve for a critical action. Frequently asking for help reflects on one's ability to manage. Managers need to work out a pass plan carefully before going to the boss—bosses have very little tolerance for subordinates who lead them into an ambush.

QUESTIONS FOR DISCUSSION

1. Name the four P's of the authority profile.
2. Why is it impractical to give channel managers a significant amount of authority?
3. There are five points in the Checklist for Precision. Name them.
4. What is the most critical checkpoint on the progress of a resource to provide information?
5. List the six points of the Persuasion Checklist.
6. Which other P should be coupled with persistence to improve success?
7. The pass plan has four steps. The first is to go to the person in authority. What is taken to the person in authority?
8. What are the other three steps in the pass plan?
9. When one has successfully completed the pass plan, there are two people to thank. Who are these people?
10. When the pass does not work, what is the next action? Give an example.

SEVEN

Building the Marketing Database and Forecasting Sales

It is generally agreed that the most effective marketing executives manage by the numbers. Although this is a narrow point of view, there is no avoiding that the numbers can spell either success or failure for all marketing actions. Some business people believe marketing executives must be creative, inspirational, and take bold actions. In fact, the most successful marketing managers are analytical, careful in their evaluations, and quite conservative in their decisions unless the situation clearly calls for boldness. Although not the primary ones, creativity and inspirational leadership are always assets to those in marketing management.

Marketing actions are almost always preceded by exacting preparation based on many facts. Most of these facts are defined in terms of numbers. What has happened in the marketplace, as well as what is happening and what may happen, are events that are reported and forecasted in terms of numbers. Comparisons of historical data to current trends, along with projections of what specific marketing actions are expected to produce, provide much of the database for marketing managers. The starting place for planning marketing activities is numbers. They are also used to express the final results of what the plans produce. Statistical facts are used to define the market, evaluate products, construct prices, project profits, measure competitive activities, and evaluate the results of marketing programs. These numbers, which comprise the database, are necessary to forecast sales and the results of marketing programs. Since sales data make up much of the basic information in the marketing database, the actions and methods used to produce the sales forecast are included with the subject of building the database.

BUILD YOUR OWN DATABASE

In most companies there exists a considerable amount of data readily available from computer records. Usually the marketing data are gathered to report sales, gross and net profits, tax-related figures, and the revenue produced during the past business year or business period. In some companies, this information is compared to the previous year or to a group of past years. If a marketing plan was followed, actual sales and the results produced by marketing programs are compared to the expectations that were forecasted. Large companies provide data in minute detail for many departments of the company. In many mass merchandising retail operations, for example, the recording of individual sales by a cash register will also provide daily inventory updates for an assortment of products while at the same time providing the dollar volume of sales for the day.

The considerations of this text are directed primarily to industrial products and markets, but mass merchants will receive sufficient attention as well. The basic information required to build or update a database is similar for both areas, with primary differences related to the frequent updating of the basic data programs required by mass merchants.

Get the Right Numbers

Sales statistics supplied by the electronic data processing group, computer services, or whatever group collects data and produces computer reports are generated for use by the sales department and for financial analysis. The numbers prepared for the sales and financial areas will prove valuable to the channel manager. Both the *volume (units) of sales* and the *dollars of sales* are needed. In the unlikely circumstance that only dollars or units are available from both sources, marketing channel managers should request records to establish both the units and the dollars of sales. Sales departments will usually have dollar figures; but if only tons, pounds, gallons, cases, or some other volume measurement is historically kept, dollar sales figures should also be added.

The figures from the sales area will *not* always be consistent with what is available from the financial area. Sales numbers may be gross sales or transaction figures, rather than net sales. Remember that sales people are interested in the *gross* units or dollars sold, whereas the financial area is more interested in *net* dollars sold, in costs, contribution to profits, and other factors. In general, it is best for the channel manager to use the figures provided by the financial area rather than those from sales because the financial people will be dealing with net sales figures. The sales department numbers are not wrong, of course; however, they do not serve the same purpose for marketing and financial planning as they do for sales analysis. To the sales department, dollars may be looked upon as a unit or volume measurement. Since sales goals are usually set in gross dollars of sales, it is easy to understand why it is considered a unit by sales people.

When forecasting sales by territory or product group, the dollars generated are a projection from the *number of units* of each product and size forecasted. This is calculated from the selling price per unit supplied to the sales group by the channel manager.

Sales forecasts are figures channel managers *must* get from the sales department. It is very likely staff marketing managers will be responsible for producing the initial sales projections from these forecasts. Sales projections are provided by product, product size, and by geographic area. Based on the sales projection numbers, product costs are estimated as well as profit projections. Using the sales projections, the marketing channel managers will project production schedules, inventory levels, promotional program activity, and advertising budget estimates: *All start with the forecasts for sales provided by the sales department.* The most important projection of all is the budget projection that is initially based on the sales forecast figures. This budget projection must be supported by the sales figures. (The forecasting section of this chapter discusses the marketing channel manager's role in making these projections.)

Basic Data Needs of the Channel Manager

Most of the channel manager's basic needs for database information start with sales data. One could argue that product data, related to costs and pricing, should be the priority, but the volume of sales and the forecast of sales trends have a significant influence on product costs and prices. The marketing channel manager's thorough knowledge of statistical data relating to sales and marketing is required for successful channel management. Many of these statistical records are a compilation of sales statistics with an analysis of their relevance to various marketing programs, activities, and planning.

It is expected that marketing channel managers, charged with product and market responsibilities, must know more about the products and markets assigned to them than any other person either in sales or marketing. Market or marketing managers involved with channel management must also deal with many *sources* of statistical data. Much of this knowledge is collected in the form of *sales* statistics. Because these statistics will be used in many ways, it is critical to the performance of their job that marketing channel managers know which statistics to collect, how and where to obtain the right numbers, and how to analyze and present them. Companies that do not have formal marketing or product management positions involved in channel management will still have marketing functions and product and market actions to plan, execute, and manage. In many such situations, the sales area will provide those who perform the planning and management actions with much of the statistical data they will need.

Marketing channel managers, particularly product managers, should develop a special relationship with the sales department, for it is the sales group that develops and maintains a constant contact with channel members and reports on competitive situations. All the marketing programs presented in the channel are either introduced by sales people or managed by them in the channel. One can easily see that a channel manager's ability to perform as a member of the marketing staff and as a contributor to the actions and activities of the sales department depends upon a good and close relationship with those in the sales department.

> *Sales numbers are used to measure the success or failure for programs the channel manager plans, promotes, and puts into action. For this reason, much of the database will relate to sales figures.*

It is vital for marketing channel managers to know how sales figures are gathered, recorded, and analyzed. The sales group is primarily responsible for the number of units of product sold (sales volume). The success of marketing programs is determined by the profits generated from the sales volume. Sales will frequently report its figures on the basis of gross sales. Profits must always be expressed as related to the net sales numbers. Marketing channel managers must know the difference between net figures and gross figures as well as when to use both. Channel managers must also know which figures are used for sales forecasts prepared by the sales department and their intended purpose. Sometimes sales forecasts are made to justify adding new sales personnel or to cover expected increases in expenses. Channel managers must, in short, get the correct figures at all times.

Table 7.1 presents a list of the channel manager's basic data needs. This list includes all the areas from which information is required to build or maintain a workable marketing database. There are other areas from which useful data are available for specific needs; however, Table 7.1 is a good starting place for most channel managers.

Sales Numbers in the Database

From Table 7.1 we find that data must be gathered from three different areas: (1) sales performance numbers, (2) marketing program figures, and

Table 7.1
Channel Manager's Basic Data Needs

Sales Numbers	Marketing Programs	Market Demographics
• Gross & net sales	• Pricing data	• Size & volume
• Annual sales	• Profit calculations	• Geography areas
• Five-year sales	• Advertising	• Market share
• Geographic breakout	• Promotions	• Market trend data
• Product group data	• Competitive analysis	• Documentation
• By market segment	• Forecast analysis	• Density
• Historical document	• Historical document	

(3) market demographics. The tabulation and analysis of gross and net sales is the starting place for building a database. This activity is given special attention because everything that follows will refer to the sales numbers developed from the list in Table 7.1. Either gross or net sales dollars or units are recorded as the references for whatever calculations are made. The exception may be in listing some of the market demographics.

Gross and Net Sales. In some situations the channel manager needs to use both gross sales figures and net sales figures. The net sales statistics are by far the most important because they are used for basic financial analysis. We must always keep in mind that the most critical measurement for marketing programs is made by an analysis of the profits they produce. Profits come from net sales.

To calculate net sales, deduct the returns, discounts, allowances, and freight costs from gross sales. These calculations "net out" both dollars and units. There are few businesses where all sales are final. Sometimes products are ordered and then returned for credit. Sometimes products arrive damaged or are shipped incorrectly. These *returns* will be deducted from the gross sales report and will reduce the units sold as shown in the net sales statistics. The following is an example showing how profits and sales figures are affected by the calculations of net sales versus gross sales (see Table 7.2).

Analysis of the Net Sales versus Gross Sales Example. (1) The units are expressed as tons. Five thousand tons yield a million dollars of gross sales. This calculates to be $200 of gross dollars per ton. (2) Note the returns and the effect a reduction of 500 units has on gross sales. The net units of sales are 4,500 tons. (3) Discounts are now recognized, since

Table 7.2
Net Sales versus Gross Sales Example

	Units (tons)	Dollars	*Dollars/ton
• Gross Sales	5,000	$ 1,000,000	$ 200.00
• Returns	- 500	- 100,000	
• Discounts		- 25,000	
• Allowances		- 2,000	
• Freight		- 12,500	
Net Sales	4,500 tons	$ 860,500	$ 191.22 /ton

* Based on gross sales of 5,000 tons. Discounts are 5% on 50% of sales volume. Allowances are 2% cash on 10% of sales. Freight cost is $25/ton on 500 tons returned.

they reduce the gross dollars by $25,000. These discounts are the result of a 5% volume discount on 50% of the sales. It should also be noted that if some of the returns result in sales below the minimum for the volume discount given, the discount will have to be recovered; otherwise it will become a discount given, not earned. These situations increase the projected cost of marketing programs by allowing payment for performance that did not take place. (4) Observe the effect of allowances on dollars of sales. In the example, 10% of the sales have earned a 2% allowance for cash payments, which results in a $2,000 reduction in sales dollars. This situation is typical, even normal, for many marketing programs. (5) The freight factor is handled differently with diverse products or groups of products. Not all products are freight-intensive. In our example (Table 7.2), the company has had to pay the return freight on 500 tons, for a total of $12,500. This cost is charged against gross sales dollars.

In the net sales versus gross sales shown in Table 7.2, the sales dollars per unit are $200 per ton for gross sales. It is possible that the net sales figure represent more than one product. If this is the case, then a breakout of sales for each product represented in the 5,000 tons will have to be made. To gather significant statistics, one must know what contributes to their makeup and what they represent.

Why will the sales department want to express sales numbers in terms of gross sales volume rather than net sales volume? Gross sales figures provide the best possible interpretation of the sales effort. Also, sales must measure the effectiveness of the sales activity and not just the statistical results after all deductions. Sales performance and commissions may be calculated on a gross sales figure. In addition, gross sales numbers are the starting place to calculate the effect of each deduction and to determine net sales.

If sales figures are calculated and reported in dollar units rather than product units, will you usually find the dollars are net or gross numbers? If the figures come from the sales department and do not specifically state they are net sales, managers must assume they are gross sales. Usually, sales statistics from any source other than the sales department will be net sales. Channel managers must know the source of the figures they use.

Annual Sales Figures. Annual sales numbers are the most-used sales calculations. Some companies prefer to report their data by sales or marketing period. Even so, annual figures including sales are universally used in financial documents. Annual sales are so important because they represent the productivity of the total effort of the company. It matters not whether manufacturing, research, legal, or any other department of the company performs with distinction, if the sales department is not successful, all will eventually fail together. Many actions and much cooperation from all departments are necessary to ensure success. In the end, the annual net sales figures are used to calculate profits. Profits provide the figures upon which budgets are calculated for the coming year's operations.

The annual sales figures also provide the basis upon which marketing and sales managers can measure the success of their operations against their forecasts. Annual sales dollars and units are forecasted and product costs are projected based on these sales expectations. The marketing and sales budgets are also requested based on expectations of forecasted net sales and profits. Usually there is a projection of current or the past year's sales that is compared to the forecast year expectations. Increases or decreases in sales and market share are based on these annual sales and forecast projections.

Reporting the net annual sales figures must be done so that all who read them can easily relate to the significance of the figures. To channel managers, actual dollar figures or units sold for the year are significant. To the chief executive officer (the CEO), they mean nothing. But everyone can understand figures expressed as *percentages*. Percentages give universal understanding to all statistics. Using percentages to show sales increases or decreases can provide all who review the record an easy and quickly recognized situation analysis.

Percentages are used for another reason. For dollar figures to produce the same percentages from year to year, even with the same volume,

Table 7.3
Five-Year Sales for Product A

	Unit Sales	Annual unit Change	Annual % Change	Variance to Base Year
Base year	50,000	Base	Base	Base
Year.....1	57,000	7,000	+ 14%	+ 14.0%
Year.....2	98,000	+41,000	+ 72%	+ 96.0%
Year.....3	60,000	- 38,000	- 39%	+ 20.0%
Year.....4	61,854	+ 1,854	+ 3%	+ 3.7%
Total		276,854 units *excluding base year* (four years of sales)		

would be very unusual. Unplanned changes in product costs and selling prices produce this situation. In addition, the use of marketing programs, which affect prices for a short period of time, will change the average selling price per unit from one selling period to another. Although percentages are excellent for overview analysis, when relating one year to another, they tell very little of what is happening in the current market. The product manager needs to know specific product- and market-related statistics in order to know which management actions are appropriate. However, top management, who direct actions based on numbers, *can* derive critical information from percentage comparisons. Marketing management *cannot* use percentages for critical analysis that will provide data for day-to-day management of the channel.

Five-Year Sales History. By using historical records from the financial area, channel managers can build a five-year history of net sales and unit costs for every product in their area of responsibility. In addition, basic product cost data, which may be available from manufacturing and marketing records, should provide information upon which one can calculate unit sales figures leading to market share information. With these data, one has a good start in building a database.

Shown in Table 7.3 are statistics covering five years of sales for Product A. These data show a base year and four consecutive years of sales performance. The base year may well be the beginning of five consecutive years of sales, but it is not always the case. The base year reference is used by many companies to represent the level of sales that is significant to profits or market maintenance. The base year may be a competitive share benchmark or perhaps represent the market share level that the company wishes to maintain. Since the sales figures are given in product units rather than dollar units, it would be easy to calculate the market share figure if the total market units were given, but they are not. The market share is not given in the table, since it is probably not the factor upon which the base year is founded. For this example, assume that the base year sales volume represents a level of manufacturing *production* that projects a favorable and consistent product cost resulting from efficient utilization of the production facility. If the assumption is correct, then the numbers represent a manufacturing company.

In Table 7.3, another statistical assumption is made regarding the second year of sales. In the second year, units sold* rose 72% to show an abnormality in the five-year sales trend. This example is included to show the effect of statistical inconsistencies or aberrations from the norm. There is no explanation provided in the example for the unusual sales increase in year 2 of this table, but it was probably due to a marketing program designed to accomplish this result.

Analysis of Five-Year Sales History (Four Years of Current Sales)

1. Four-year sales total 276,854 units ÷ 4 = 69,214 units per year average.
2. Three-year sales total (exclude year 2) 178,854 units ÷ 3 = 59,618 units per year average. Year 2 is an abnormality and should not be used in the average annual sales.
3. *Conclusion*: Unit sales can be substantially increased in one year without significantly affecting sales in the next year. The market for this product shows considerable elasticity.
4. The very important measurement provided by the Variance to Base Year calculations show that steady growth continues in year 3 and year 4.

Dealing with Abnormalities in Sales Statistics

If the second-year sales increase, shown on Table 7.3, had a significant effect on sales for the following year, what should the channel manager be looking for? When a big increase in one year takes sales from the next year, the channel manager would have to consider several alternatives. First, an analysis of the costs involved in moving the business from one sales period to another would have to be made. Comparing these costs with the benefits derived from the program would indicate whether the benefits exceed the cost. The benefits of preemptive selling are higher immediate cash flow, less inventory to carry, less exposure to competitive selling, and the creation of pressure on wholesalers and retailers to resell the product. These are very attractive benefits to the marketer.

The analysis of this situation would be to compare a normal year's volume, costs, and profits to that of the average for the normal year and the abnormal year combined. If the benefit is commensurate with the cost, the marketing program that created the increase in sales was a good move. The channel manager must also look at the negatives, however. There may be a negative effect upon customers who have to deal with a higher-than-normal investment in the inventory of the company's products. The result may be retaliation in the form of lower new orders when their inventory is reduced to the point of reordering. This may explain part of the return to normal purchasing levels in the year following the increase. The increase in sales for year 2 may also have created a strain on credit for channel members at both the wholesale level and the retail level.

For many products and product groups, it is normal to offer selling programs and promotions that move sales from one period to another. For seasonal products or those that are weather related, it is a favored marketing strategy. These programs are usually planned, executed, and measured for a shorter cycle than one year. The key to evaluating the negatives concerned with a preemptive sales program is to look for retaliation from customers and competitors.

Review of the Base Year Method for Sales Analysis

Selection of the base year method of sales analysis is normally made by using one of four criteria. Remember the base year selected need not be concurrent to the years for which it is acting as the point of comparison. One or all of the following criteria may be involved in establishing base year statistics.

Manufacturing Efficiency. For manufacturing companies, the base year is usually established on an optimum level of output to attain production efficiency. The period may not be as long as a year, but the number of units will be for a fixed period of time or for a production "run" to produce a fixed number of units. This statistic can then be extrapolated for the establishment of the base year.

Return on Marketing Investment. A second method for establishing a base year is used primarily by marketing companies. These companies are interested in maintaining a market share at a level high enough to support their investment in marketing programs. The required market share is expressed as units of sales and used as the base year benchmark. Dollars are also recorded and may be used in market share calculations, but seldom are they used independently of unit sales to express market share.

Product Gross Margin. The third method used for the establishment of a base year figure is the product gross margin analysis. This method requires that annual sales be maintained at a level that will result in an efficient cost of production and sufficient marketing cost absorption (by profits) to achieve a fixed minimum gross margin for sales of the product. This method assumes that available capital can be invested by the corporation in a variety of profitable projects. A minimum profitability is set to qualify for the investment support. The product gross margin method is used primarily by research- and technology-oriented companies that may also manufacture the products.

Variance to Base Year Analysis. In Table 7.3 we have calculated the annual percent change or variance to the base year as one of the most critical evaluations of sales performance. The unit sales are down 38,000 units from the previous year; this is the annual unit change. The annual percent change records a drop of 39%. This would appear to be alarming were it not for the figures shown in the Variance to Base Year column noting a 20% *increase* over the base year. Progress is still on target even with a drop in sales from the previous year. Year 3 actually shows a greater increase over the base year than Year 1 sales, which produced only a 14% improvement over the base year.

Geographic Breakout. Recording information in the database must reflect the requirements of specific channel managers. Not all managers will need a geographic breakout showing sales from every territory, district, region, or area. However, since the sales department will rely on the geographic breakout figures to evaluate sales personnel as well as customer performance, it may be important for the channel manager to have this information in his or her files. Another reason to obtain geographic breakout data is its usefulness in the event a specific geographic promotion becomes necessary. District and regional programs for seasonal products are essential. Channel managers should determine the geographical segmentation necessary for their data requirements. The use of cyclical marketing programs and natural use cycles for products in the market will indicate logical geographical segmentation.

Product Group Data. Most channel managers will require sales data relating to individual products. Product forecasting and planning is necessary for each product in a product group. However, market share data is not always available on a direct product-to-product comparison. Market research will more than likely be able to acquire data on product groups such as canned soups of a popular size. Sales data for the individual types of soup such as tomato, chicken noodle, and bean may be more difficult to obtain even though the product manufacturers will surely have this specific data. Figures should be gathered by product group when the products logically fit into a group and such figures are available.

Market Segment Data. The market segments into which a company sells its products will naturally segregate sales figures into the markets where they belong. Our example for the pharmaceutical industry shows products segmented into "over-the-counter" (OTC) and prescription market segments. The market segments we identified in earlier chapters mention the commercial, industrial, governmental, consumer, and agribusiness segments, among others. Sales data must be kept and utilized for each important market segment if a channel manager is to have the data upon which enlightened marketing decisions will be based.

Historical Documentation. The need for historical documentation is cited for all three of the channel manager's basic data needs: sales numbers, marketing action figures, and market demographics. When available, a history of five years is required to provide basic data. Why five years rather than three or less? A longer view is necessary because of the incidence of abnormalities in data based on a year-to-year evaluation. It would, for example, have been impossible to explain the effect of year 2 in Table 7.3 on the statistical probabilities for future sales without the additional years of history. A comparison of the first two years may lead one to think that the market was growing rapidly, which was not the reason for the growth.

A three-year comparison may provide a *trend line* representing growth or decline of sales. A comparison of the years 1 through 3 for Table 7.3 shows a growth trend even with the severe decline from year 2 to year 3. When year 4 and the base year are added to the analysis, the sales trend is established and a measurement of magnitude is provided. Data of less than five years provide only a trend line that is not sufficiently reliable for marketing channel managers to use as base data. This applies not only to all sales numbers but to marketing action figures and market demographics as well.

Marketing Program Figures

The figures designated as relating to marketing programs are tied to managing the marketing mix. Managing actions that are related to changes in product packaging, product line development, and product maintenance, as well a competitive analysis, are the product data issues. The programs related to pricing must clearly be reflected in the database whether or not the pricing action is one prompted by competitive promotions or a basic pricing adjustment. Profit calculations are closely tied to pricing. Programs that have been utilized in the past as well as in present promotions and marketing initiatives are all part of the data needs of the channel manager. Even if these programs do not change pricing, they always increase the marketing costs for the period and are usually tied to an increase in the sales figures as a result of the marketing program. The need for data related to marketing actions will vary significantly from company to company and in relation to different product types. It is the channel manager's job to identify the requirements of his or her position. Managers can look in the following areas for significant data that relate to marketing actions.

Pricing Data. Recording price information is one data requirement that cannot be overemphasized. To determine the selling price, the product costs and profit cost must be established. The elements that make up a product's selling price should be listed in the database for each product. These elements will reflect the cost of materials, manufacturing charges, packaging, shipping, if applicable, and profits. The profit is expressed as gross profit for this calculation. Most products will be assigned a standard price or *list price*—the price listed in the catalog and in the statistical records as the official price for a product. Standard pricing is used for most statistical evaluations. Prices that do not match the standard are noted as deviations from the standard price.

Forecasting is tied to standard pricing, as are profit calculations. Whenever a price change takes place, for whatever reason, it must be recorded and become part of the pricing database. At the year's end, it is necessary for channel managers to have collected data showing how many units of sales were made for each product at specific prices.

The channel manager's responsibility in pricing contributes significantly to the marketability of the products involved. Prices must reflect a realistic competitive position, and they must result in a volume of sales that will support production estimates for manufacturing costs.

Profit Calculations. Profit calculations needed for the database are similar to those for pricing; that is, the profit calculations will be for standard profit objectives, which assume that all costs and prices will remain as recorded in the base data. This situation seldom occurs, however. There are always changes in costs and prices over a year. For this reason, the profit calculations used for the database are given as percentages. Profits are expressed as either a percent markup from product costs or the margin of profit as a percentage of the selling price. These percentages will first represent gross profits. After the total gross profit is calculated for all sales of the product, marketing costs and selling costs are subtracted to reach the net sales revenue figure. From this figure all allocated overhead is deducted to provide the net before-tax profit figure. See Table 7.4 for these calculations. After the fact, the channel manager should calculate the actual profit percentages and compare them with what was expected.

In general, the gross margin of profit is viewed as profits on sales. Manufacturing companies sometimes refer to the gross profit margin as an operating profit. Marketing companies will frequently deduct all marketing expenses from net sales to arrive at a figure presented as the

Table 7.4
Net Profit Calculation

Selling price	$ 100.00	
Gross profit (margin)	$ 45.00	45 % margin of profit
Less marketing costs	$ 11.25	25 % of gross profit
Less selling costs	$ 6.75	15 % of gross profit
Equals net marketing profit	$ 27.00	27 % of selling price
Less total allocated overheads	$ 2.25	5 % of gross profit
Equals net before tax profits	$ 24.75	24.75 % of selling price

marketing profit. After the deduction of all allocated overhead, what remains is the net before-tax profit. There may be other deductions from
the operating profit to establish the net before-tax profitability. These
deductions will relate to corporate activity and such things as tax credits
and depreciation not known to the marketing group. Dividends are fig-
ured from the net after-tax profitability of the corporation. This makes
the corporate deductions from profits an important figure, but is not one
with which the channel manager should be concerned.

From chapter 3 we saw the calculations for gross profit. The calculation
for *gross profit markup* is found by multiplying the product cost by the
markup percentage and then adding the result to the product cost. The
gross margin of profit, calculated from the selling price, entails deducting
the product cost from the selling price and then dividing this profit figure by the selling price to reach the margin percentage. The result, as
shown in Table 7.4, is the gross margin of profit. Before a calculation for
net profits can be made, the gross profit must be known.

Channel managers have the responsibility of calculating expected net
profits and then using these numbers to make a forecast. The channel
manager's influence on product costs and profits is found in four different areas: establishing the selling price, calculating the cost of advertising, determining the cost of product promotion, and forecasting product
needs for production planning. The selling price, you will recall, is calculated by tabulating the products cost and then adding in freight and
a profit figure. Multiplying the product costs by the markup percentage
provides the selling price. The gross profit figure that results by sub-
tracting product costs from the selling price is evaluated in view of the
competitive conditions in the market, and only then can an actual selling price can be determined. If one wishes to use the margin-of-profit
calculation rather than the markup method, the starting place is the
established selling price. An evaluation of the market prices and the

prevailing competitive situation will indicate what selling price is acceptable.

The channel manager's responsibilities to net profits are linked directly to the control of marketing costs such as advertising and product promotion and indirectly to influencing the selling costs. Developing marketing programs that are easily presented by the sales people will help keep selling costs down, as discussed next, under Advertising and Promotions Data. Obviously, someone must advise the production people, and those in materials purchasing, what products to produce, the sizes and types needed, how much to make, and when it will be needed. Forecasting inventory needs and advising those who must know them are obligations of the channel manager. Long production runs and purchasing in large quantities usually mean greater efficiency and lower production costs. Packaging types that are "friendly" to existing equipment will also add to manufacturing efficiency. Carefully planned scheduling of production and materials purchases can result in a lower product cost. The schedules are established from product forecasts made by the channel managers. Working with those in manufacturing and purchasing who can advise the most cost favorable manufacturing circumstances and buying conditions will help to achieve the lowest possible production costs.

Advertising and Promotions Data. Advertising and promotions are listed separately in Table 7.1, but they are closely related. The data needed for advertising and product promotion are tied to the budgets allocated for these marketing activities. It is more important to know the exact advertising and promotional costs of a program, and the results it produced, than how the program was constructed. These database figures should include the budgeted expenses, the actual expenses, the forecasted results, and the actual results of the marketing program.

The O. M. Scott Company in Marysville, Ohio, provides an example of the need for good documentation of marketing program numbers. Reviewing the past performance of a spring promotion for one specific product showed an increase in sales of 25% over the selling period for the previous year. The historical documentation noted that a "price off" promotion was used to achieve these results. There was no mention of the size of the price reduction or how much money was spent to develop, advertise, and engage in the promotional actions. These data were useless. All that was learned was that a mystery surrounded the notation of a 25% increase in sales for the period.

Obviously, channel managers must document the needed figures to make marketing program data usable for evaluations related to the costs and the results achieved. If other information is pertinent to the success of the program, it may also be documented. Relating costs to results will take the cooperation of all those who contribute to bringing the marketing program together. This will include advertising people, sales personnel, and all those associated with product promotion.

Included in this area are the selling programs created by channel managers concerning the terms of sale, product guarantees, and customer services. Costs related to all these programs must be included in the historical documentation.

Forecast Analysis. Channel managers are involved with the development and analysis of all forecasts related to sales figures, marketing figures, and market projections as well. The need for forecast numbers in the basic data is found in two areas. The first involves forecasting assumptions used by marketing people and provided to the sales department for their forecasting activities. These assumptions are usually related to economic influences related to costs, prices, profits, and market growth or decline projections.

The second area of activity for the channel manager is the analysis of performance against forecast. Many companies who critically analyze sales numbers will not record how well the marketing-related forecasts—costs, prices, profits, and market numbers—are related to actualities. Not a "head in the sand" situation, this simply reflects the ever-changing environment in which marketing occurs alongside actions employed in reaction to changes as they occur. It is the opinion of the author that marketing forecast data should be scrutinized the same way as sales forecasts, and someone should always be held responsible for the reliability of the forecasts.

Market Demographics

Channel managers are well aware that markets are not static. Markets will undergo changes in size, volume, and user density. Market share data will change throughout the selling period. Even the geographic designations of a market can change from year to year with the addition of new customers and new sales territories requiring changes in geographic boundaries. Channel managers must be vigilant to be sure the figures for sales from one year to the next represent the same geographic areas or the changes that have taken place. In many cases, the channel manager will need to ask sales managers whether any territory, district, or regional boundaries have been changed during the year. When preparing a database, remember that measurements should represent the same conditions from year to year so that reliable comparisons can be made.

Size, Volume, and Density. The need for basic data on the size, volume, and density of a market is of high priority. Changing prices along with product deletions and additions will significantly influence market size and volume figures. Density changes take place more slowly as the population adjusts to the growth and decline of market areas.

Geographic Areas. The opening comments on this subject reflect the channel manager's need to know geographic changes in the market. Changes caused by the addition of new customers may have a significant influence on the area covered—a situation over which the channel manager has no control. The need to know specific information must be coupled with the channel manager's ability to ask for the correct data and get them.

Market Share and Market Share Trend Data. Bringing together market share and market share trend, two topics listed separately in Table 7.1, is a logical extension of how these data are used. Market share data can be compiled year to year. This information may be expressed either as dollar figures or units of sale. Units are employed to express the market share when dollar figures do not represent a measurable or meaningful share position. The automobile market, for example, is described as the number of cars sold or purchased during the year, not the number of people who bought cars or the dollars spent in purchasing them. A manufacturer's market share is calculated as the number of cars of all types the company sold during the year. In this situation, the dollars would not relate to a meaningful expression for market share calculations. It is the number of actual automobiles bought that is the common denominator, not how much money is spent to buy them.

The market share trend data, required by channel managers for their database, reflects the position of the marketer and its major competitors in the market. The changes in share position over a five-year period (or even a three-year period) can provide trend data that shows which companies are becoming stronger competitors as well as those that will be the easiest from which to capture new market share. This proposition is detailed in the next chapter under the topic Competitive Market Share Analysis.

Summary for Building the Database

Managers involved with marketing channel management have many jobs to perform. The channel manager is expected to be the expert on company products and markets. Channel managers are also expected to know the history of what has happened to their products and markets and what is planned to take place in the future. Management of the marketing channel is possible only if the managers involved will learn to use sales and marketing statistics as a common language in all they do. Every department in the company communicates through the language of numbers. The numbers critical to channel managers are those concerning sales and marketing statistics. Channel managers will do well to keep in mind that the only manageable elements in the channel are products, prices, marketing programs, physical distribution, and people.

A thorough knowledge of the numbers involving these subjects will provide channel managers with the basic data they need to manage the marketing channel.

FORECASTING SALES

In addition to dealing with historical statistics, channel managers must deal with current and forecasted sales and marketing statistics. The current numbers for sales and market share are usually compared to a past period, such as the previous year, for evaluation of performance. The database numbers are valuable in this exercise. Also, current numbers become a part of the database for future use. Evaluations of current figures related to sales, market share, and of the company's competitive market position are necessary to help in making day-to-day channel management decisions. The projection of expectations from management actions are tied to sales promotion, advertising, and other marketing programs.

Projections and Forecasts

Marketing channel managers are expected to project the expected results of marketing activities on a continuing basis. Expectations related to product costs, pricing actions, product promotions, and sales are calculated monthly. To accomplish this, the channel manager must be provided access to the computer reports covering these subjects. The channel managers are also provided with significant data from projections that come from the market research group, financial group, marketing information services, sales department, manufacturing sources, advertising department, product research, technical services, and those involved with regulatory affairs.

Forecasts will come from sales as well as those from areas involved with product cost calculations and marketing planning. Managers will need to know if packaging cost will be increased, if materials needed for production are available, if regulatory actions are expected, if strikes are anticipated, if advertising rates will hold, if products can be produced according to the proposed schedule, and if the requested budgets are realistic for the projected sales.

What is the difference between a forecast and a projection? *Forecasts* are based on historical data, current market conditions, and plans that have been accepted for the coming year or sales period. *Projections* are based on up-to-date monthly data and provide a statement of anticipated results based on what is currently happening. Projections may relate to the forecast by projecting expectations for reaching the forecasted results based on current progress, current plans, and knowledge of what is expected to occur. Competitive data also become a part of the evaluation for projections made for expected sales results.

Projecting expectations for budget performance and profitability are key areas in which channel managers must become involved. Budgets are usually finalized in the marketing planning area. The channel manager will project cost figures for all activities planned in his or her product area. This includes the cost of promotional discounts, terms, and planned price reductions.

Forecasting and Projecting Budgets and Profits

An important part of channel management is in providing the statistical background information for budget preparation. Accuracy is a must in these projections. All figures must be checked before submission. This is especially true when using sales forecasts. Managers must be sure that the forecasts are based on the same cost criteria and selling prices that were used in plan preparation.

Profit projections are a separate item related to budgets. The use of profit figures in budget projections is essential. The channel manager will be expected to provide cost details and the assumptions upon which they are based for all planned marketing actions (advertising, promotions, etc.) that affect forecasts. Projecting profits for budget development is quite different than projecting profits for product profitability. One may use percentages in projecting profits for budget needs. The percentages may be projected as a percentage of sales or as a percentage of gross profits before marketing costs are applied. Usually the profit plan will be based on net sales forecast for each product.

FORECASTING METHODS

Since so many marketing actions center on the sales forecast, and since channel managers are deeply involved with forecasts, it is essential that they understand how sales forecasts are put together. There are many forecasting procedures employing a variety of computer programs. Just about every company will have its own variation. Basically, there are only three types of forecasts: the plus factor (or historical) method, the top-down method, and the bottom-up method. The plus-factor forecasting method may be used for forecasting everything from sales to material costs for production. This is the most common forecasting method. Top-down forecasting is almost exclusively applied to sales. Sometimes it is used to forecast profits for a product line or a whole marketing group. Bottom-up forecasting is also used primarily for sales. This is a buildup forecast that starts at the territorial level and collects those numbers relating to districts, regions, areas, and then the total market.

Sales forecast numbers are the most used and the most changeable. They are segregated into geographic areas, product groups, and product sizes. Forecasts are projected for sales planning, production planning, marketing planning, and financial planning. The channel manager will interface with all the departments where these resources are found. The method of forecasting will dictate the kind of data and the necessity for specific data to complete the forecasting activity.

Plus Factor Forecasting (Historical)

The preferred designation for historical forecasting is *plus factor*. Why? One does not *forecast* history; it is recorded. We try to accurately record historical data and then apply them to the forecasting assumptions and objectives. The preferred name reflects the effects of the *plus factors* that control the outcome of the forecast. Plus factors are those objectives or actions that we add to what has happened in order to forecast what we expect to happen because of the added factor.

Since the channel manager plays such a large part in plus factor forecasting, we will look at this method in some detail. This forecasting method functions as its name implies. Starting with what is known, the forecaster will add what is needed or wanted and then forecast the results. What is consistently known, of course, is history. Past sales figures would include sales volume, geographical distribution of sales, cost and budget factors, profits, and significant competitive statistics. This is where plus factor forecasting starts. The historical database should include all pertinent facts upon which the plus factors will be added. The plus factors are determined by the channel manager. They must be consistent with the marketing and sales strategies that have been approved as a part of the marketing plan.

Adding the plus factor to historical figures may be as simple as assigning a fixed percentage of sales growth as an across-the-board increase in sales volume (units or dollars). The factors may also be as complicated as imposing various economic, price, cost, and competitive assumptions on the forecasting model. It is vitally important to forecast the expected changes in the marketing channel demographics for the forecast period. This would include population shifts (density), growth or decline of product users in the market, and an assessment of the competitive situation. If one of the plus factors is the recognition of a new major competitor, market share figures will be sure to change even if sales numbers stay constant. Should the plus factor be an increase in sales of 5% across the board, the forecast detail will include how the increase in sales is to be accomplished.

The plus factor forecasting method depends on accurate historical data. The forecaster then needs accurate current information upon which to base the plus factors indicated by the forecasting strategy. The Plus Factor Database Checklist will help channel managers to be sure to include all the necessary information.

Plus Factor Database Checklist

1. Last year's (or last sales period's) sales in units and dollars.*
2. Growth factors for the forecast year expressed as product units.
3. New product additions in units and dollars.
4. Product deletions in units and dollars.
5. Economic factors and market factors affecting the forecast period:

   • Costs (+ or −) expressed as a percentage of the previous year.
   • Selling prices (+ or −) expressed as percentages of the previous year.
   • Competitive impact expressed in terms of market share.
   • Other significant factors.

*The historical period upon which the plus factors are added may not be the previous year. It may be a base year established for specific reasons as mentioned earlier in this chapter. For the following discussion, we are assuming the historical base are the sales numbers recorded for the previous year.

Last Year's Sales. Recall that both units and dollars are necessary for this tabulation. Why are both needed? Because when prices change, the dollars do not provide an accurate measurement for the number of units sold. Channel managers must forecast units in order to provide production figures and receive pertinent cost figures, based on specific volume numbers. By knowing both units and dollars, one can project the average selling price at which the indicated volume will be sold during the forecast period.

Growth Factors. If there is a growth factor included in the marketing strategy, it must be expressed as units for the initial forecast. The cost of the products for the volume and for the forecast period may change between the time the forecast was originally projected and the time the approved forecast is issued. By forecasting growth as units, all appropriate costs may be applied as they are confirmed. If the growth factor is presented as dollars, projections for product cost related to the growth will have to be estimated for the profit forecast.

New Product Additions. Forecasts must reflect both units and dollars for new product additions. The historical forecast is made in both units and dollars; thus the same measurements must apply to new products in order to make the historical reference. The channel manager will need to refer to both units and dollars sold, measured against the previous forecast.

Product Deletions. Product deletions planned for in the forecast year can have a significant impact on the sales of the products left in the line. Deletions also have a strong dollar impact on income and the cost of disposing of products not sold. The final outcome of product deletions must be taken into account in the forecast.

Economic Factors and Market Factors. All marketing plan assumptions that affect product costs and prices will influence the forecast. Any reduction or increase in programs used to stimulate the market may change the product's competitive position, resulting in either a lower or a higher volume of sales. Assumptions may also be made on the market economy, regulatory concerns, and other uncontrollable cost factors such as freight, ingredients or raw materials costs, energy, labor, and other costs. The channel manager must recognize all the assumptions that affect his or her product area and include these assumptions as they affect the sales forecast. How assumptions are handled is discussed following the discussions of forecasting methods.

Top-Down Method

The top-down forecasting method serves only as a guide for channel managers to use during the forecasting process. This is not a true forecasting method. Surely it is not a method for forecasting sales. It is usually a list of targets issued by top management calculated to produce fixed and inflexible objectives. Usually these are objectives related to reaching specific financial goals. They may also be related to production or volume objectives depending upon the type of company involved. Top-down forecasts are frequently tied to one of the other two methods.

By its name, one can tell that top-down is a forecast inspired by management objectives. Many companies have developed computer models and/or systems that accept a wide variety of statistical assumptions, many which we have discussed. Based on figures calculated from these assumptions, a forecast estimate, or forecast target, is produced. Corporate goals for the coming year are frequently expressed in terms of a growth percentage for the company. This goal is then divided into objectives for the operating divisions or the marketing department as guideline objectives for forecasting. There are four objectives where the top-down impact is typically directed: *growth; profit; cost cutting,* also known as budgeting; and *management-mandated actions,* such as a reduction in personnel. In some cases, the guideline is arbitrary and developed without consultation with marketing management. When this is the case, managers try to negotiate the problem areas.

When top management wishes to communicate acceptable growth objectives, there may be a request for forecasts reflecting an across-the-board increase of a specific percentage in the volume of sales or market share. If the objective is tied to increased profits, the top management may ask for a fixed percentage of improvement in net before-tax profits. This would leave all options for achieving profit improvement open to marketing management. It would not be unusual for top management to ask for specific profit-enhancing actions, such as reductions in the cost of production, marketing expenses, or sales expenses. Top management may also ask for increases in selling prices. In the area of management action, one may have to deal with the decision to close a plant or to restructure a sales group. Whatever the action, top management will communicate with marketing and to channel managers as a strategic consideration in planning the sales and marketing forecasts. Forecasts that do not meet the top-down objectives need not be submitted.

The channel manager's job is to accept the top-down objectives and then analyze the implications and effects of the indicated targets. Should the channel manager not agree with what top management has handed down, he or she may challenge these objectives with alternative suggestions and try to influence necessary changes in the targets. Whatever is agreed to must be developed into an actual product and market forecast that is acceptable.

In many companies, corporate planning is done on a financial base. Therefore, top-down forecasting is the preliminary profit plan. The profit expectations are assigned to operating divisions based upon their historical contribution to the financial performance of the company. The top-down forecast prepared by corporate planners will not provide details on how the targets are to be reached. If doing so is critical to the target requested, top management may provide information concerning increased operating costs, new facilities, new products, legal or regulatory problems, and budget limitations. The top-down forecast is usually an internal document communicated to the operating divisions to provide direction and guidance in the preparation of all operating budgets and forecasts. Before preparing the profit plan, the product manager should determine if there are to be top-down targets or planning guidelines.

Bottom-Up Forecasting Method

The bottom-up method tends to be employed when the company directly controls its selling activities with its own sales force. This forecast is initially prepared by the sales group. It is based on established selling prices, product additions or deletions, packaging sizes, and historical information. All this information is provided to the sales department by the channel manager. Sometimes this is called the *field sales forecast*. It starts in the field with each sales representative forecasting each product he or she sells by size and by month or selling period. The sales representative will be supplied with forecasting forms which have the selling price for each product size already set for the forecast period. This is a *rolling forecast*.

In some companies, the bottom-up sales forecast is provided for four or six quarters and will be revised monthly or quarterly as the year progresses. A quarter is dropped when completed, and a new one is added at the end of the forecast period.

Strangely, the bottom-up forecast that is produced by sales people tends to be overly optimistic. Why would we expect otherwise? Sales people are by nature optimistic and tend to forecast the best possible results from their efforts.

The final bottom-up forecast is a compilation of all territories and sales areas with sales management adjustments made along the way. Once the official bottom-up forecast is completed, it is time for the channel manager to determine what assumptions he or she will use for developing the forecast produced for upper management.

Sales Forecast Assumptions

It is normally best to start with assumptions that affect product costs. Consult with the manufacturing group (materials handling and/or purchasing) for cost factors affecting product materials and packaging costs. Let this resource know in advance, in writing, what information you will need and when you will need it. Apply the four *P*'s of your winning channel manager's personality and you will be successful. Manufacturing managers must also make forecasts. They will be concerned not only with material costs but also with the cost of energy and labor. The one thing manufacturing managers will need to know from the channel manager before they can project costs for the forecast year is the sales volume or number of product units they must produce.

In addition to having data on the physical aspects of manufacturing, channel managers will need to know if there is a union contract to be negotiated. If so, be aware of the timing and the expected outcome, since this may greatly affect inventory decisions. You may have warehouses to supply in support of marketing action plans. The amount of inventory to be placed in strategic warehouses may be affected by these factors. Once the cost assumption is established, go next to selling price assumptions.

Field sales people will forecast the volume they believe they can produce at the price indicated. If this forecast results in a volume figure lower than the one used to project units for production planning, then the channel manager must go back to manufacturing to determine whether the cost per unit will hold or increase. The figures agreed upon become a part of the documented assumptions for sales volume.

Major Forecasting Assumptions

As listed earlier in this chapter, the database will provide figures for all the marketing mix elements. The same holds true for marketing assumptions. Assumptions are usually made on each of the following topics:

1. *Products.* Channel managers must get the essential information regarding product assumptions for each product within their area of responsibility.

2. *Units.* Since price changes may affect volume or incorrectly reflect the volume projected, it is essential to project unit sales.

3. *Prices.* Assumptions on price changes do not always hold. Competitive situations will frequently prevent price increases originally assumed as possible.

4. *Costs.* Cost change assumptions are critical to both profit and volume projections. Channel managers must note any expected changes in costs as early in the forecasting activity as possible.

5. *Plan Year Selling Prices.* It is important to note that the competitive selling price relationship of the product has been addressed in the channel manager's marketing plan.

6. *Changes in Unit Sales.* Whenever unit sales changes are assumed to take place, the reason for the change must accompany the forecast. Increases and decreases will be dependent upon specific market factors. These factors must be covered in the forecast if it assumed that a change in units sold will come during the forecast period. The channel manager should become familiar with all the forecast assumptions from *every resource* who contributes to the forecasting database.

Example: Assumptions Checklist

A typical checklist for making assumptions covering the forecasting process should include most of the topics in the following:

√ Units are expressed as tons (2,000 pounds). Units will increase 10% in the plan year.

√ Dollar increases will be 20% in the plan year, 10% from volume and 10% from price increases. The volume increases will be from *new* business.

√ Unit costs will increase 5% in the plan year as a result of material and labor cost increases.

√ Prices will increase 10% in the plan year. Plan year selling prices will be competitive.

√ Gross profits will be up 5% as a result of price increases of 5% above cost increases for each unit of sales.

√ Sales will reach or exceed the forecast of units sold.

√ The market will increase 5% in units purchased. Our increase will be 10%, represented by 5% increase in market growth and 5% business taken away from competition.

√ Marketing channel changes reflect the addition of a new sales district and seven new sales representatives. It is expected that our customer list will expand by 5%. No significant new competition will enter the market. New users of our product will provide growth.

√ The cost of marketing services to the channel will remain constant as a percentage of gross sales.

The assumptions we have used in this example are projected to apply to all products in the group. This, of course, will not be the case in a real working situation. As an example, if one product was forecasted to greatly increase in cost, then the price would probably increase more than 10% and the volume increase of 10% would probably be less. Also, in the case of a second-year product, which is just beginning to reach its sales potential, the growth target would more than likely represent a 25% to 30% increase rather than 10%, as in this example. Also, since volume is going up dramatically, the channel manager may not wish to open the door to competitors with a price increase. In any event, the assumptions must be applied realistically to *each* product.

Forecast Assumptions Discussion. Do forecast assumptions apply in the same way to all products listed? Not necessarily! Forecast assumptions for products may be very specific concerning price or cost issues. Assumptions covering broad economic situations—energy, labor, or freight, for example—may apply to all products. The channel manager should always note which assumptions will be used for each of the products or product groups.

There are a significant number of uncontrollable economic factors that should be covered in the assumption's statement. Among them are broad economic variables, legal questions, governmental regulations, environmental issues, inflation, the cost or availability of raw materials, labor contracts, freight and tariff rates, and new competitive products. These are all uncontrollable factors that will have an impact upon the economic evaluation of products and markets.

When forecasting sales volume, remember that the selling price at which a product is forecasted to sell will have the greatest influence on the volume that is sold. If the price goes up, the volume may go down. If the price goes down, the volume may go up. The reason the price change is made will have a great bearing on whether the selling price change will affect the volume sold. If the reason for the new price is to pass on an increase in production costs, the effect is different than if considering a new and competitively acceptable selling price. There is usually no choice but to accept an increase in production cost, along with its effect on profits. If the market can assimilate an increase in the selling price without a negative competitive impact, there are no cost considerations, only profit improvement.

When forecasting the number of units to be sold, channel managers must consider the possibility that an increase in the forecast may result in a longer production run, resulting in cost savings. Requests for increases in the amount of product produced may also cause costs to increase if increased production leads to overtime labor costs. Decreases in units forecasted almost always result in an increase in product cost.

Forecast Checkpoints. The value of the comparison between units sold and units forecasted is a "must know" number. If forecasts are on target, the assumptions can be validated. If there is an unexpected increase or decrease in sales, the channel manager must determine why the change took place and how the assumptions should be adjusted to allow for the deviation from the numbers expected. One must always have dollar figures to calculate profits and compare to the historical profit contributions. In some cases, usually when the product is a service, dollars are used not only as the financial measurement but also as the number of units sold. As an example, the cost of an insurance policy does not change with the number of policies sold. Additionally, reporting the number of policies sold has little value as a measurement of productivity. The dollar value for the total policies sold does provide a measurable unit of productivity.

The gross profit per unit, another critical calculation, must be a part of the database for each product to allow comparisons between products. Budgets should be directed to support the most profitable products. The channel manager must also consider the total dollars of gross profit that each product contributes to sales and profits. This calculation can indicate the importance of a product in offsetting costs and making direct contributions to profits. High unit sales of products producing a large amount of revenue, even with a modest profit per unit, may be more important than those that have a high gross profit per unit of sale, but with relatively few units sold.

Most managers will be required to evaluate the accuracy of their forecasts. Actual sales, not the forecasted figures, must apply to historical reference as well as to ongoing sales performance. Keeping monthly records for the volume of sales is important. This comparison can tell whether or not inventory levels will be sufficient to accommodate sales that are significantly higher than those forecasted. The contrary situation would result in the inventory being too high because of sales lower than forecasted.

Forecasting market trends relates to the size of the market, the direction it is going, what the competition is doing, and the effects of the channel manager's efforts in comparison to the market trends. If the market is growing faster than the channel manager's product share percentage, this loss must be noted and explained.

Sources of Competitive Information for Forecasting

More than any other group, the field sales people are one of the major sources of information on competition. Sales people are constantly face to face with the competition and their programs. However, the field sales force is not the only source of competitive information. Information that comes from the sales area should not be relied upon as complete and accurate. Including field sales, there are at least six sources to be contacted to solicit competitive information:

Field Sales People. The sales force can provide information on prices, promotions, product acceptance, field inventories, and customer relations. The information provided by field sales people will usually be an opinion, not always fact, and should be treated as such.

Sales Management. Sales management may be located in the field as well as at the home office. These managers can provide information on competitive credit polices, product information and technical support, customer training programs, guarantees, the strength and size of the competitive sales force, selling programs, and management relations with mutual customers.

Market Research. Competitive information generated by market research would be printed information available to the Market Research Department from trade reports or as the result of specific research provided by request from the marketing area. Market research can measure sales trends by major product groups and the volume of advertising and promotional activities for major competitive companies; as well, it can provide sales trend data for competitors and their products.

Customers. Customers are not always a reliable resource for competitive information. However, they can provide needed information on many subjects. Look to customers for information that can be verified by other customers. Information one would seek from customers includes the terms of sale, buying programs, contract conditions, product promotions, cooperative advertising deals, training programs, pricing policies, purchasing allowances and volume discounts, guarantees, and sales aids such as literature.

Product Development. Product development people in the company as well as independent researchers, universities, and governmental agencies may be able to provide information on new products that are being tested. Specific information related to forecasting would be directed to significant product improvements or new product introductions expected in the forecast year.

Manufacturing. Do not discount the potential for a significant contribution of information from manufacturing, materials handling, or the purchasing area. The development of new processes and the significance of new facilities related to cost improvements can be critical. Also, the availability and purchasing of strategic materials or the existence of trade relations and upcoming union contracts for competitive companies, for example, may provide very important information for the channel manager.

SUMMARY

The need for documentation that supports all the recommendations for forecasting and planning cannot be overemphasized. The channel manager's need for specific data will depend on the company, its products, and the markets involved. The product manager's documentation list shows four basic areas where documentation is available. This information should be a part of the channel manager's files in order to support the rationale used in establishing forecast assumptions.

Channel Manager's Documentation

1. Documentation starts with the available historical records. When looking at historical records, managers will find out *what* happened in the past. If the data are complete, one should also learn *why* the results occurred. Look for abnormalities in the historical documentation, then find out why it took place.

2. Forecast assumptions are identified as the second most important area of documentation. Be thorough in listing assumptions and making changes as they occur.

3. Current computer reports are expected by channel managers. Make sure that whoever supplies these numbers is aware of the importance of these data.

4. The final area of documentation is the forecast itself. Keep this documentation current with all changes.

Forecasting can be a difficult task whether for sales, profits, or the expectations of a marketing program. Channel managers will be able to forecast with reliability only to the degree that they have developed reliable sources of information and carefully compiled a database of relevant statistics. Resources must be carefully developed for the vital information that will be used in building the database as well as for forecasting. The channel manager's reputation is dependent on the reliability of the resources used and the thoroughness of the information gathered.

QUESTIONS FOR DISCUSSION

1. The three areas from which the channel manager should gather information for the database are sales figures, marketing program figures, and market demographics. Name at least three sources of data for each of these categories.

2. Net sales figures provide the most important source of data to the channel manager. What department supplies the net sales data?

3. The base year method of comparison for sales data is founded on three separate criteria. One of these is the volume of sales that will maintain an efficient production run and product cost. What are the other two base criteria?

4. The Variance to Base Year column is the most important comparison recorded for a five-year analysis of sales. Why is this information so important?

5. What is the difference between a forecast and a projection?

6. When the field sales forecast figures are reported below the volume projected by the channel manager, what is the first action that should taken?

7. Of the three forecasting methods discussed in this chapter, which one can more easily be used with the other two? Explain.

8. Why is it necessary to keep accurate market trend information? What group can provide data for these calculations?

9. When is it bad news to see an increase in your sales dollar volume?

10. When sales in one year show a significant increase, does this indicate that demand for the product has reached a new buying level? Explain your answer.

EIGHT

Calculating Market Share and the Competitive Share Analysis

Many companies will calculate market share information as rapidly as it can be gathered. Products that have a high turnover in the market require the collection of market action data much more rapidly than "slow turn" products. Marketing companies will make critical decisions regarding market stimulation activities, such as advertising and promotions, based on the market share and share trend analysis. In addition, it is logical to believe that those actions that influence a company's market share can just as easily be initiated by a competitor as by the company's own marketing programs. For these reasons, accurate and timely market information must be gathered not only for specific products but also for major competitive companies in the market. It is this information that provides current market demographic figures upon which market share calculations are founded.

The market research people, who are usually a part of the marketing department, are the ones who develop and provide current market data. Market research will analyze this information from several perspectives. The needs of the channel manager for specific data and analysis must be clearly presented to the market research group, or whoever is involved in gathering market data. Usually, only general product or product category data is gathered by market research. Specific information, tied to a single competitor, a single product, or specific market segments, will more than likely require the development of costly individual research programs.

Market Share

The need to calculate market share data will vary from company to company depending upon the importance of the product group and the marketing actions that are planned. There are three basic uses for market share figures, as follows:

The Company Compared to the Market. The company will wish to know how its products are performing by comparing the company's sales with those reported for the market as a whole. These data will provide the true market share for the time and period to which the information may be applied.

The Company Compared to Competition. More specific information will be needed in comparing the direct, or company-to-company, relationship with major competitors. These figures are needed to facilitate competitive marketing actions for specific products directed to specific competitors.

The Market Growth or Decline Trend. Information on the direction and magnitude of growth, or decline for the entire market, will provide trend data. The direction of the market in terms of growth or decline cannot easily be determined with information from only one year. Many possible market-stimulating or -depressing actions may take place that are extremely difficult to record, recognize, and measure for the short term. Five-year numbers are needed for accurate trend projections. However, trend *directions* may be recognized with statistics from three years if there is a *consistency* in the trend direction.

A fourth calculation, *competitive share analysis*, relates to changes in the market share *between* competitors. (Calculations for the competitive share analysis follow later in this chapter.)

Market Share Calculation Examples

Current Market Share Calculations. If it is important to keep current market share figures for a product, or category of products, one will need updated information on the market size and current marketing activities as well as the product or category to be measured. The current market share is calculated by dividing the current sales of the company's product by the total market sales for the same or competitive products. Since it is difficult and costly to gather specific data for individual products, the most usual comparisons are made for product categories.

Example 1. Numbers on the sales of small 1.5 volt dry cell batteries, as a category, are available quarterly from a market research company that sells its services to client customers. This information includes the total sales of the 1.5 volt batteries, including sizes from AAA to D, as a single dollar figure for the entire category. Updated information is requested by a member client so that new market share information may be calculated. The problem is that data provided by the market research company includes sales for AAA and AA size batteries, which the client company does not sell. To calculate the company's market share only for products it sells, the client company requested a special report that excludes the sales of AAA and AA batteries. The figures received are summarized as follows.

Example 1

Total sales for the 1.5 volt battery category	$15,300,000 (3rd quarter)
Deleted sales for the excluded products	$ 1,300,000 (3rd quarter)
Net product category sales (excluding AAA & AA sizes)	$14,000,000 (3rd quarter)
The company's current product sales	$ 2,800,000 (3rd quarter)

$2,800,000 ÷ 14,000,000 = .20 or 20% current market share

Annual Market Share Percentage. It is more likely that sales numbers will reflect a full year rather than shorter periods. Market figures will probably be segregated by the major products that contribute to the market numbers for the category. However, to receive the detailed data, companies will pay for a special market research report. In the next example, it is assumed that the specific product information needed is available and there are no excluded products.

Example 2

Annual sales for the total product category	$10,500,000
Annual sales for our product in the category	$ 2,000,000
Total sales of competitive products	$ 8,500,000

$2,000,000 ÷ $10,500,000 = .19 or 19% annual market share

Forecasting Market Share Trends

Forecasting the market share for a specific time period is risky business at best. One can never accurately predict what competition will do to change the basic market dynamics. A new competitive product introduced earlier than anticipated can spell disaster. Price reductions can drop profits below an acceptable level. Unexpected cost increases may require price increases that will reduce sales of the product. There are many reasons why forecasting market share can be a difficult task. Most of these reasons are tied to the unpredictability of the actions competitors may take that will significantly affect the market. Nevertheless, share forecasting is a necessary exercise for the channel manager. The only protection one can provide in share forecasting is to be careful in making the assumptions upon which the forecasting is based.

Forecasting the market share requires one to develop information in three areas:

1. historical data on market trends
2. historical company share trend
3. sales expectations for the forecast year projected as a share percentage for the product

Market Trend History. The first step is to obtain five years of historical data on the market for which one is forecasting the future share figures. Based upon these historical data, note the effects of various change factors on the market. Using assumptions about the change factors, project the market size for the forecast year. One may use dollars, units, or percent-of-base-year figures for this projection.

Market Trend History for the Company Product. The five years preceding the forecast year are normally used for historical figures related to the company product. For this historical sales projection, both dollars and units should be calculated as well as the market share for each year of history.

Projected Sales Expectations. Sales projections based upon the historical data are presented as the market share for the forecast year. Apply the forecast assumptions to the share trend projection and show the changes that occur because of these assumptions.

Forecasting Market Share Trends: Marketing Scenario

The Hose Company has been selling a ⅝-inch top-quality garden hose for ten years. During the past five years, the sales for garden hoses has climbed proportionally to the number of *new* homes sold annually. In addition to the new-home buyers, a base year figure set at 300,000 homes represents the replacement-hose market. Twenty-five percent of base year, 75,000 units, is considered to be the replacement-hose business. Market research indicates that we have a solid 25% of the

Table 8.1
Five-Year Market Share Comparisons (percentages)

	Base Year	Yr. 1	2	3	4	5	Forecast Project'n
Total Market Sales	100.0%	105.0	110.0	97.0	113.0	115.0	84.0%
Total Company Share	15.4%	15.2	15.1	15.4	15.1	15.0	16.0%
Product category Share							
Quality	20%	19.0	18.0	20.0	18.0	17.0	26.0%
Standard	55%	56.0	57.0	56.0	56.0	56.0	52.0%
Economy	25%	25.0	25.0	24.0	26.0	27.0	22.0%
Market Variance to Base Year		+5.0	+10.0	-3.0	+13.0	+5.0	-16.0%
Company Variance to Base Year		- 0.2	-0.3	0	- 0.3	-0.4	+0.6%

*Base year is 375,000 units (hoses), 300,000 new home sales + 75,000 (25%) replacement.
Market share for the company is based on 13% of the new home market and 25% of the replacement market, calculated to be 75,000 units annually.

replacement-hose business in our market, or about 18,750 units. With a one-year exception, new home sales have been steady for the past five years with about a 5% average growth per year. Our product represents 13% of the garden hose sales to new-home owners, and 25% of the replacement market. In the base year the *total market* reached 375,000 units and our combined market share was 15.4%. The following statistics are tabulated in Table 8.1.

The new-home sales market is expected to be very slow during the forecast year, down 60,000 homes or 16% from the previous year. The replacement market should continue to be 25% of the base year's sales. Based on our sales history, we would expect to sell 13% of the new-home sales figure (13% of 240,000), or 31,200 garden hoses, to new-home buyers. In addition, our sales to the replacement-hose market would be about 18,750 units (25% of 300,000 = 75,000 unit market × 25%, our market share, = 18,750). Our total unit sales for the forecast year are projected to be 49,950 garden hoses (31,200 + 18,750). This figure represents a decline of 7,800 hoses (13% of the 60,000 decline in new-home sales) from the previous year. However, because of our high position in the replacement-hose market (25% share), our share of total hose sales for the forecast year will increase. The hose market for the forecast year will be 240,000 hoses to the new-home market plus 75,000 units to the replacement market, for a total market of 315,000 units. We are predicting sales of about 50,000 units in a market of 315,000 units sold, or a combined market share projected to be 16%.

This example provides the opportunity to note the importance of accurate historical data in forecasting what may happen in the future. In addition, it is critical for future analysis to list *all* the assumptions made to support the forecast. A marketing strategy that will strongly support the company's strength in the replacement-hose market segment should be considered. The Hose Company needs to investigate its potential to improve its share of the new-home market.

Three Steps of the Market Share Forecasting Process

The process suggested for market share forecasting is completed in three steps. The example shown in Table 8.1 shows how this process may be expressed in a table of analysis for market share percentages applied to garden hoses. It should be noted that there is no provision for direct competitive share information. The competitive share applies only to the product categories in this example, not to the other companies. Market share forecasting considers the products and the markets. When a company manufactures only one product in a category, it is also useful to show the market share of other products in that same category. These data are needed in order to relate how well the company is doing in its own category as well as how the product is performing compared to the whole market.

The Quality Garden Hose Company has a dominant share of the quality garden hose market. It is not necessary to include a base year in the market share calculation unless there is a significant reason to do so. In the example, the base year is used because of the stability of the replacement-hose market related to the base year. The outline for the market share forecast process is as follows:

Step One. List the five-year market trend data. Apply the effects of the forecast assumptions to the historical trend projection for the forecast year. Project the market size for the forecast year by taking into consideration the effects of the assumptions.

Step Two. Show the company's five-year sales, market share, and historical trend projection for the forecast year. Apply the effects of the forecast assumptions and project the company share of the market based on these assumptions.

Step Three. Provide a market share analysis for all major products or product categories covering at least thee years; then apply the forecast assumptions to this analysis showing the resulting changes, if any.

CALCULATING THE COMPETITIVE MARKET SHARE

The competitive share shows the market share relationship of the company's product to each of its major competitors and to the market as a whole. One or several competitors may be included in the competitive share analysis. Most channel managers will track all competitors who have a significant share of the market. If the market is large, with many participating companies each with a small share, the manager should track only those companies that are direct competitors. The rest of the companies will be listed as the All Others category. As a rule of thumb, all companies with an equal or greater market share are major competitors and should be included in the analysis. The competitive market share trend reveals the relative strengths or weaknesses of the major market participants. It also indicates which companies are becoming more competitive as well as which are declining in their relationship to other companies in the market. This information is extremely valuable for forecasting future market share expectations.

The competitive share analysis is needed by the product manager to help direct marketing actions that target the most productive competitive areas. One can increase business and market share in only two ways: either new business must be created, which will increase the total market size, or market share must be taken away from a competitor. Knowing which competitor is the most vulnerable to attack from an aggressive marketing program is critical to the planning of successful marketing strategies. An up-to-date competitive share analysis is needed to provide this data.

The competitive share is calculated by making a market share comparison between the company's product or product group with each of the competitive products that maintains a significant share position in the market. The comparison measures the relative position of the company's product to that of its major competitors as well as to the changes in the total market.

Essential Competitive Share Trend Data

The market is a dynamic environment that is always changing. Most markets are comprised of several companies that compete for the business that exists in the market. These same competitors will attempt to capture the available business with marketing programs designed to provide them with an advantage over their competitors. As these actions take place in the market, trends develop that relate to the strengths and weaknesses of the competing companies. Trends in market growth or decline will also take place. It is the measurement of these trends and the identification of their impact on a company's business that provide data that can lead to successful competitive marketing programs. The two critical competitive trend lines that need to be charted follow.

Changes in Share Position Compared to Changes in Market Size. Changes in market size and market share may be expressed in actual dollars, units, or percent of change. This first trend line shows how the market is progressing compared to the market share for the company's product. Whenever possible, the market size should show both dollars and units of product sold. If the unit measurement (pounds, tons, gallons, etc.), cannot be equally applied to all products, it should not be used. All changes in market share are expressed in percentages.

Changes in Competitive Share Position. Each major competitive product as well as an All Others category must be included in this analysis. The changes in the share relationship between the company's product and those of its major competitors is the next calculation. The trend of a company to improve or to yield its share position to competitors provides direction when looking for new opportunities and for overcoming competitive problems. Here again, dollars as well as units should be shown if both are relevant. Dollars are important, since unit costs will change because of marketing promotions. In addition, some companies will position their products to sell for less whereas others will reach for the premium end of the market. If both the economy price and standard price products are in competition for the company's market share of premium products, then the dollar share percentage of the total market is relevant, as are calculations relating to the share trends for each product type in the category.

The Competitive Share Trend Chart, Table 8.2, gives an example of how these market measurements are used in calculating the competitive market share.

Example: Calculations for Competitive Market Share. In this example, you are Company *A* and your two main competitors are Companies *B* and *C*. The relationship between the companies shows that significant changes have taken place that must be explained because they affect the market share of the company's product. The effects of these changes will be explained in the analysis of the chart. The performance of your product and the products of your competitors must be compared to the market and also to each other.

Competitive Share Trend Analysis

The format for making the competitive share trend analysis may vary considerably depending upon the information needed by the channel manager and the company. The standard method of analysis is to start by making the comparison between the company's product and the mar-

Table 8.2
Competitive Share Trend Table

Company	Opening Share	Year One	Year Two	Year Three	% Change Cumulative Trend
A					
Annual Share	20%	20%	25%	28%	+ 40.0%
Market $	$ 19.60	$ 20.00	$ 26.25	S 30.80	+ 57.1%
B					
Annual Share	25%	25%	25%	25%	No change
Market $	$ 24.50	$ 25.00	$ 26.25	S 27.50	+ 12.2%
C					
Annual Share	17%	15%	13%	11%	- 35.3%
Market $	$ 16.70	$ 15.00	S 13.65	S 12.10	- 27.5%
All Others					
Annual Share	38%	40%	37%	36%	- 05.3%
Market $	$ 37.24	$ 40.00	$ 38.85	S 39.60	+ 06.3%
Total Market	$ 98.00	$100.00	$105.00	$110.00	+ 12.2%

Note: Year One is_____ ; dollars are in millions.

ket. This calculation provides the market share data and shows the product and market share trends.

Company B's Market Trend Analysis. In the three years for which the data are compared in Table 8.2, the total market figures show a cumulative 12.2% growth. The company grew 40% from its year 1 market share of 20%, to a 28% share of the market. This was a gain of 8 percentage points in the company's share of the market. The market grew by 12.2% in dollars while the company grew 57.1% in dollars over the three-year period. Both figures show the company to be growing significantly faster than the market in share rate and in growth rate. The $12 million market growth was nearly matched by the company's $11.2 million increase. The company's growth started in year 2 after new marketing programs were implemented late in year 1. Market share, which was static for the past two years, started to increase in response to the programs. The company is growing faster than the market and is increasing its competitive market share as well.

Analysis of Company B. Company B, the major competitor to Company A, maintained a constant market share of 25% for the three-year period. Although Company B did not increase its share percentage, it did grow in dollars at the same rate as the market growth of 12.2%. This would indicate Company B has a strong and loyal following that grows at about the same rate as the market. In year 2 of the trend chart, Company *A* matched the market share percentage and the dollar volume of Company *B*. Company *A* passed *B* in year 3 by three percentage points in market share and by $3.3 million in volume. Company *A* did not take any of its increase, in either market share or dollar volume, from Company *B*. In fact, Company *B* did not lose market share or its dollar position to any of its competitors or to the market growth. This is a strong competitor. Company *A* will not likely be able to shift business from Company *B*.

Analysis of Company C. Company *C* is a major participant in the market, but appears to have weak marketing programs and does not react well to competitive situations. It is vulnerable to the marketing programs of Company *A* as well as those of others. This is indicated by the ability of Company *A* to take two percentage points of market share from Company *C* in year 2 and three additional percentage points in year 3. The All Others category took two percentage points of market share from Company *C* in year 1. Company *C* lost 35.3% of its market share and 27.5% of its dollar volume with declines in every year in both market share and dollar sales. Company *C* still has a fairly high share with 11% of the market, but it is not a strong competitor.

Analysis of the All Others Category. The All Others category lost two percentage points of its market share during the three-year period. This amounted to a total of 5.3% for the three years. In year 1, All Others took two percentage points from Company *C* but lost three percentage points of market share in year 2 and another in year 3. This loss may have been due to Company *A*'s strong marketing program, which was capturing the market growth while the All Others category did not grow at the same rate as the market. The sales of All Others did increase 6.3% in dollar volume even with a declining market share. It looks as though the All Others category is collectively stronger than Company *C*; nevertheless, the All Others category is vulnerable to marketing programs and is not capable of keeping up with the strong upward trend in market growth.

Competitive Share Trend Analysis. The marketing program introduced by Company *A* for its product was competitively successful in accomplishing its objectives. It was able to improve market share by eight percentage points, which represented a 40% increase in its share of the market. The increase came from both market growth and Company *C*, which gave up six of the eight percentage points gained by Company *A*. The other 2% increase in market share came from the All Others category.

Although Company *A* did not make an impact on its major competitor (Company *B*), it did improve share position from five percentage points behind Company *B* to top them by three points in year 3. Company *A*'s dollar volume also exceeded Company *B*'s dollar volume for the first time. This makes Company A the new market leader. The dollar volume increase of $11.2 million from year 1 to year 3 consisted of $8.8 million from increased market share and $2.4 million in growth not related to market share improvement.

Company A's competitive share trend is very strong against all competitors, including Company B. Its overall competitive trend is also strong, showing a consistent 13.3% annualized increase in market share while still participating in the market growth from its beginning share position.

QUESTIONS FOR DISCUSSION

1. Why is it necessary to keep accurate market trend information?
2. When is it bad news to see an increase in your market share?
3. How much detail is needed in gathering market information for use in calculating share percentages?
4. When calculating the market share projection for a forecast period, keeping a list of assumptions made in preparing the forecast is considered highly important. Why is this such an important task?
5. When making a market share forecast, one does not project the competitive share percentages for other companies. What competitive calculations are made in this forecast?
6. Explain a competitive share analysis and how it may be used.
7. The competitive trend projections are based on the competitive share percentages. What does the competitive trend projection show?
8. Why not project a competitive share forecast from the competitive share analysis?
9. In what two areas can a company look to capture new market share?
10. Where a company is gaining market share in a competitive market, how does one determine where the increases in share are coming from?

NINE

Managing Products,
Managing Markets

Product and market management is the same job. Obviously, the market for specific products cannot be separated from the products. Products and markets are managed by the marketing channel managers. The actual title for these managers may be product manager, market manager, marketing manager, or some other designation. Since they are dealing with products and markets, these are the people referred to in this text as marketing channel managers. The title product or market manager does not imply that the title holder will manage only products or markets. When we refer to product manager, market manager, or channel manager in the text, always consider one reference interchangeable with the other.

There are several activities that do apply individually to products and markets. These activities will be considered in their relationship to each other and how they are managed. Even so, we will not try to separate the products from the markets into which they are to be marketed. When we do discuss market management, it will always be in reference to the management actions and activities regarding the products in those specific markets.

THE PRODUCT AND MARKET MANAGEMENT PROCESS

The process presented for the how-to tasks of product and market management is intended to facilitate the placement of all channel management actions into the proper sequence. This process considers the interactions of products and markets. The market position that a product has reached and the competitive relationships in a market are evaluated by considering appropriate marketing strategies to reach specific objectives. Following these analytical activities, the selection of realistically obtainable channel management objectives and appropriate product and market management actions are discussed under a variety of circumstances.

When taken in sequence, the steps of the product and market management process will provide the channel manager a way of (1) identifying the *current situation* in the market, (2) *evaluating the actions needed*, and (3) *managing the marketing channel* activities to reach the established objectives. Many activities are involved in the steps of the management process. Managing actions, however, are *not* planning activities. Although the information gathered to manage a channel can be helpful as a reference for annual marketing planning, the management process takes place daily. Chapter 11 presents the planning process used in the marketing channel. The product and market management process involves only four steps:

Step One. Complete the product and market phase evaluation.

Step Two. Write the product and market phase scenario.

Step Three. Perform an evaluation of product characteristics.

Step Four. Establish directional marketing management objectives.

The first task for the channel manager is to identify the current product and market phase for products of interest to the channel manager. Products and markets go through several phases during their lifetime. The channel manager will need to locate where the products and markets stand in their evolutionary phase before management actions can be considered. It should be obvious that unless we know where we are when we start, we cannot plan where we are going, how to get there, what it will cost, or even how long it will take. It is not too difficult to locate the current position of a product in a specific market, determine its market share, and identify competitive relationships with the aid of the checklist presented in Table 9.1.

Several activities are unique to products and also to markets. Although products and markets for the products cannot be separated, the uniqueness of each must be considered. For this reason, market management is discussed here in regard to the *market actions* involved and referenced to the *products* in the market.

Because this first step is important in managing products in the marketing channel, we have provided a "road map": the Product and Market

Table 9.1
Product and Market Phase Checklist

1. Discovery and development of marketable products.

2. Introduction and market education.

3. Establishment and development of major markets.

4. Establishment and development of secondary markets.

5. Exploitation of product modifications.

6. Exploitation of all established markets.

7. Diversification or consolidation.

8. Product and market decline leading to discontinuation.

Phase Checklist (Table 9.1). All products and markets go through some or all of these phases during their lifetime.

Step One: Product and Market Phase Evaluation

Discovery and Development of Marketable Products. The discovery and development of products may come in several different ways. They may come from scientific investigation, which we call *research* or *discovery*. Products may also be found by *searching*, rather than by researching. We may search in other companies, markets, or even countries. A common method is to buy products and further develop, modify, or incorporate them into a specific product line or channel.

Product Introduction. Once a new product is ready for marketing, it must be introduced or positioned for entry into the intended market. The market must be conditioned to accept the product through education in the form of training, promotion, demonstration, and advertising. A company cannot neglect making the necessary investment to develop the market for a new product. It is not uncommon for companies to spend millions of dollars on product research and discovery and then follow this with an insufficient effort in its introduction and market education.

Establishment of Major Markets. As one's first objective, it is a good channel management strategy to attain a reasonable share in the major markets in which the company intends to participate. To be successful in the long run, a new product must compete in the arena where the action takes place. Objectives in strategic marketing actions for the product should include market share goals for major markets. Not all companies will define market segments in the same way: A major market for one company may be a secondary segment for another. Channel managers must make their own judgments in defining a major market.

Secondary Market Objectives. Both primary and secondary markets should be identified in the strategic marketing channel development plan. To reach secondary markets may require further research, product development, or channel modifications. These markets may be too small for extensive investment to develop. Channel managers must consider both the ease of entering secondary markets and the effect on activities involving primary markets.

Exploitation of Product Modifications. Many products are improved by continued research or development activities. The improved versions can be strategically placed into markets to improve market share, increase profits, stimulate growth, or maintain a competitive position.

Exploitation of All Established Markets. Market exploitation does not include efforts to increase market share. Growth in market share usually takes place in the early phases of market development. Exploitation is a maintenance or survival tactic. Special pricing actions, deep discount promotions, challenge advertising, target market blitzes, and competitive exploitation are examples of market exploitation programs.

Diversification and Consolidation. *Diversification* may be a growth strategy as applied in the fourth step of the channel management process. When it follows market exploitation, diversification is a market maintenance or survival strategy. Diversification may include the introduction of generic or private label variations of a product already fully developed in the marketing channel. It may take the form of new product formulations for specific markets, such as powdered forms of products in one market and liquids in another, or metal products in a premium market and plastic versions in a competitive market.

Expansion into new or foreign markets, even by having other companies market your brand, is also an act of diversification. Normally diversification involves taking products to new markets, not just new geographic areas. In the food industry, for example, a company that decides to sell its products as store brands as well as under its own label is diversifying into a new market, since the market is for products sold as store brands. Even putting the same products under different labels on the same shelf in the supermarket is an act of market expansion. Companies may choose to diversify into new competitive markets by developing a new marketing channel or using an existing channel in active markets. A common illustration is the development of the generic drug market for products that had their beginning in the prescription drug marketing channel.

Consolidation is the opposite of diversification. A company may find the competitive situation in some markets, or market segments, too difficult to maintain profitably. This may lead to the withdrawal and abandonment of those markets. Consolidation is more a survival strategy than is diversification. Consolidation is a marketing channel alternative

Table 9.2
Product Life Cycle

1. *Introduction.*	The short period of time showing rapid increase in sales dollars.
2. *Growth.*	A steady increase in sales as the product is promoted and advertised.
3. *Maturity.*	That point of leveling off in growth and meeting competitive challenges.
4. *Maintenance.*	A share of market at which sales volume can be profitably maintained.
5. *Decline.*	Sales volume for the product drops rapidly and the needed market share is lost.
6. *Discontinuation.*	The sales volume drops below a level supporting marketing costs.

employed to defend and hold a strategic position (usually a specific minimum market share) in highly competitive markets. Consolidation also takes place in the final stages of the product life cycle.

Product and Market Decline, Survival, and Discontinuation. In the face of product decline in an otherwise healthy market, channel managers should consider specific tactics for either continued survival or discontinuation. Should the market for specific products decline or vanish, such as happens with advances in technology, alternative tactics or strategies are needed to survive or get out of a diminishing market.

The application of the Product and Market Phase Checklist will vary with different products and markets. All products and markets will go through some, if not all, of the phases listed. The marketing channel manager must identify both the market phase and the product phase for the company's products. It is helpful to consider the product and market life cycle as a starting place for product and market phase evaluation. This will result in the setting of channel management objectives.

Product and Market Life Cycle. Everyone who has become involved with marketing studies is familiar with the typical product life cycle bell-shaped curve representing the phases of a product's life. This curve is intended to portray what happens to a product after it is introduced into the marketplace. The usual points of reference are presented in Table 9.2.

In the Product Life Cycle list (Table 9.2), nothing is said about the market activity that occurs during the phases of the product's life. This is an unrealistic supposition. As this text emphasizes, markets and products must be considered together. The marketing life cycle presented in this text includes both product and market considerations. This is a marketing channel orientation to the developments that take place in the channel for both products and markets as they compete for their share of the market. To illustrate the combined product-market life cycle profile, the following scenario is presented.

Product and Market Life Cycle Scenario. A new unique product (perhaps a patented one) is discovered and developed for a market (*product discovery and development phase*) and is turned over to a marketing group. It is introduced to the market by educating potential buyers concerning the advantages and benefits of the new product over existing ones (*introduction and education phase*). Next are established the major markets (*development of major markets*) as well as the smaller secondary markets (*development of secondary markets*). At some point in the product's life, it is copied and a competitive version is introduced. In order to maintain or prolong some degree of product uniqueness, the product is modified (*product modification*). The product modification is intended to provide recognizable value benefits to provide several more years of advantage to the product's originator. Eventually, in reaction to market pressures, exploitation of the product and the market in which it is sold may become necessary through price reduction, promotion, extended distribution, and/or other marketing and channel actions calculated to maintain a reasonable market share and profitability (*exploitation of existing markets*).

In the event the product can easily be copied at little investment cost, the following is likely to take place: Several new products will be introduced into the market and will attempt to take a share of the existing market volume. The new competitors may even open new markets for the product (*diversification phase*) that the original producer excluded by plan. Severe price erosion is the next competitive expectation. With lower profits, a drop in product quality takes place to help cut production costs. A drop in quality is usually followed by a reduction in product effectiveness or usefulness. A decline in profits will also result in little market support through education, advertising, or promotion. A further decline in profitability will take place as the result of overproduction by too many producers, forcing prices even lower. Market neglect sets in and the marginal producers drop out (*consolidation phase*). Remaining manufacturers establish their position with reasonable profits and maintain the market for as long as the product is useful (*commodity or generic product maintenance phase*). New products from technological development will eventually replace the old ones (*discontinuation phase*).

For products that are difficult to copy or that require a high investment of capital to produce, only a few new producers may step in with the result that a degree of uniqueness for the product or for specific brands of the product may continue. Usually the competitive environment is stabilized, providing a good position for product quality, service, education, advertising, promotion, and other investments in maintaining the marketing channel. These market investments will be made for as long as the product satisfies a need in the market at a reasonable price (*competitive market maintenance*).

Product and Market Phase Checklist

By the illustration given, the channel manager should be able to easily see the importance of knowing where a product or product group is located in the Product and Market Phase Checklist. To make the checklist more usable, it is consolidated here into the five critical points of evaluation.

Checklist

√ *Product development and introduction phase.* A new product is developed and placed in the market supported by an introductory marketing program.

√ *Market development phase.* Both major and secondary markets are developed or have been included in channel development plans for future action.

√ *Product modifications or innovations.* Improvement in product benefits, development of new product forms, new packaging, or cost improvements that lead to price reductions and greater value are researched and implemented.

√ *Market actions.* Includes market exploitation, expansion, diversification or consolidation, and even the development of new marketing channels for the product.

√ *Product and market maintenance or survival.* Depending on the competitive climate, the product will move into either the commodity market maintenance or the competitive market maintenance phase.

Obviously, this checklist can be used to identify the current phase of products or markets. It may also be used to predict the future position of the product by the direction in which it is moving. Knowing the direction in which a product is moving allows the channel manager to use the checklist as a guide in planning future product and market activities. The market scenario that follows provides an opportunity to use the checklist for channel evaluation, management, and planning.

Step Two: Writing the Product and Market Phase Scenario

The Aero-Tec X Company is presented as a marketing situation to show how the Product and Market Phase Checklist is used. An evaluation is made of the information gathered for this company to determine the appropriate channel management actions. This example is based on a true market experience, but the details are fictitious, as is the company name.

The Aero-Tec X Situation. For twenty-five years the Aero-Tec X Company has been manufacturing its line of ten products and packaging them into highly refined aerosol containers. The company is the recognized leader in aerosol technology. It is also the price leader in its field, with high prices and high profits resulting from top-quality products packaged to perform with reliability. The products have been given cosmetic upgrading over the years, primarily related to packaging and labeling. In the past two years the Aero-Tec X Company has been losing market share to similar products packaged in upgraded versions of trigger-spray containers, which cost much less than aerosols. The Aero-Tec X product managers, who have the responsibility of marketing channel management, have been asked to present upper management with a plan to recover the lost market share and to maintain the improved share in the future.

Market Scenario Assumptions. We can assume the ten products were developed and introduced with excellent educational effort and success. The products are offered as top quality and are the price leaders. Since the company is also noted as the recognized leader in aerosol technology, we can assume it has developed all the primary and secondary markets in which it wishes to participate. By giving some products cosmetic upgrading, Aero-Tec X has provided some product modifications, but not many. We understand Aero-Tec X has been manufacturing its line of ten products for twenty-five years. Product innovation is now a necessity. Since the company has been losing market share for the past two years, it is obvious no market actions (such as market exploitation) have been taken.

Options Presented by the Channel Managers. The options developed follow the Product and Market Phase Checklist. It is obvious that the first two points on the checklist have long ago been accomplished—product and market development started twenty five years ago. What is needed follows:

1. Develop new aerosol products (product modification).

2. Develop new pump- or trigger-actuated products (new product development).

3. Develop new nonaerosol applications for existing products (product innovation).

4. Develop aggressive product promotions to negate the competitive price differential between the aerosols and trigger sprayers (market exploitation).

5. Consider diversification into the contract manufacturing business and offer other noncompetitive marketing companies the advanced aerosol technology.

This would ensure high production runs, volume purchasing of component ingredients, and low production costs (diversification).

6. Include a public relations program in any new-product introduction plan to substantially reduce environmental concerns by the public for aerosols.

7. An analysis of the company's position resulted in the following conclusions regarding current product maintenance and survival. The company is not as yet in a survival situation, but it needs to adopt some or all of the recommended strategies for regaining and maintaining its market share.

Developing a scenario for the product or market phase is accomplished by writing a narrative account of the product and market phase evolution. It is especially important for new product managers and channel managers to determine the product and market phase for both the products and the markets under their responsibility. If possible, marketing channel managers should provide information concerning how the product(s) got to its current phase and why the market is at its specific phase of development. All channel managers should write a short situation description for each of the products in their area. The report should review the products and markets history in relationship to the items enumerated on the Product and Market Phase Checklist. The scenario developed for Aero-Tec X would consider all five of the actions on the checklist. It should indicate which products were developed for introduction, how the major and secondary markets were developed, and what product innovations or modifications, if any, have been considered or tried, and with what success. The scenario may also provide a list of market actions, with the results expected and the results accomplished. Actions or plans related to market maintenance or survival strategies will also be a part of the evaluation, where appropriate.

The scenario does not need a lot of detail, but it does need a chronology of events showing when actions were taken, what was expected from them, and what actually occurred. Continuing with the example given for the Aero-Tec X Company, the following scenario was developed.

Product and Market Phase Scenario. The Aero-Tec X Company has been selling top-quality, top-priced aerosol products for twenty-five years. During the past two years the company has suffered a decline in market share due to competitive pressure from trigger-actuated nonaerosol products. The company's lead product, an aerosol ant and roach spray, has lost 5% points of market share, dropping from 35% to 30% market share. All the market growth during this period has been with the trigger and pump sprayers. Both competitive products are priced at 25% to 35% less than aerosols.

Analysis. Using the Product and Market Phase Checklist, the following analysis is presented for the Aero-Tec X Company.

- *Products developed and introduced*: The company has made no major changes in the product line in the past five years. The leading product is Ant & Roach Killer aerosol.

- *Market development*: Six years ago the company introduced some of its products for sale into the pet products area. New packaging and labels were developed and a new marketing channel developed for distribution into the pet products markets.

- *Product innovations or modifications*: There have been no product innovations or modifications since entry into the pet products marketing area.

- *Market actions*: Two years ago the company introduced its first program providing a discount for volume purchases. This program provided a 5% price reduction to customers who would commit to a 2,000-case "take or pay" commitment. The contract would have to be completed within six months.

- *Product and market maintenance or survival.* The company is unable to maintain its current market share of Ant & Roach Killer with its quality but high-priced aerosol product. During the past two years all the market growth is in the trigger- and pump-actuated spray products. Price differentials between aerosol and trigger-actuated products along with the adverse environmental image of aerosols have established problems that cannot be overcome with promotional programs. The company is not now in a survival situation, but to maintain its market position it must introduce new products that will participate in the area of market *growth* now being captured by the trigger- and pump-actuated spray products.

The final comment in this example, which is a recommendation to take specific action, is not truly a part of the product and market phase scenario, which should only state the current facts. The recommendation is, however, a logical conclusion and would probably be included as a comment in a real situation.

Step Three: Evaluation of Product Characteristics

The key to determining the right marketing strategies for a product or market is found not only in its market position but also in the individual product characteristics. These characteristics are a major factor in selecting product and market management objectives. They are analyzed and evaluated in order to help in the selection of the directional objectives for channel development and product and market management. Specific marketing objectives to be instigated by the channel managers would follow as a part of the marketing channel planning activity.

The following characteristics are those with which the marketing channel manager needs to be concerned. It is the balance of these product attributes coupled with the product market phase position that will determine the directional objectives that may be followed in channel plan-

Table 9.3
Product Characteristics Checklist

1.	*Controllability*:	Does the company still have control over the product's future.
2.	*Profitability*:	Will the product deliver satisfactory and predictable profits?
3.	*Desirability*:	Will the product still deliver expected benefits and satisfy wants?
4.	*Competitiveness*:	Is the product competitive in price and performance?
5.	*Market Share*:	Will the product's market share profitably support marketing programs?

A careful evaluation of these product characteristics will indicate the potential actions that may be taken by marketing channel managers.

ning. A careful evaluation of these product characteristics will indicate the potential actions that may be taken or should be avoided for marketing channel management. Use the Product Characteristics Checklist (Table 9.3) as a guide.

Determination of Product Characteristics

Product characteristics are used together with selected directional management objectives to plan channel actions. The directional objectives are growth, product and market maintenance, profit improvement, survival, and discontinuation. These objectives are discussed in detail in the fourth step. The five product characteristics—controllability, profitability, desirability, competitiveness, and market share—follow.

Controllability. Does the company still have control of the product's future in the major markets, or has competition forced planning to be defensive and reactive? Controllability does not mean the company can do anything it wishes in the market. It does mean that independent action may be taken. The company can follow its plans without too much worry about what the competition will do. If the company cannot control the marketing actions, the marketing channel manager cannot select growth or improved profit as a marketing objective. If the product or market actions are still controllable, however, planning may take any direction it wishes.

Profitability. A product that will produce satisfactory and predictable profits will allow the company to pursue market maintenance objectives.

Good profits are also needed to pursue growth objectives. To grow, a company must spend money in the form of marketing programs. If the product is both controllable and profitable, management action may include growth, improved profits, and maintenance objectives. Growth is not an appropriate marketing objective if profits are below standard or if the product faces a highly competitive market environment in which it is difficult to exercise control over the marketing programs.

Desirability. The desirability of a product is defined in terms of its ability to fill a need or satisfy a want in the market. Does the product provide the expected benefits, give the necessary value, or sufficiently satisfy a want for consumers? If the answer is yes, the product is still desirable. A yes answer allows the marketing channel manager the freedom to plan other appropriate market actions. If the product is losing its desirable characteristics, both growth and profit will decline, as will the ability to control the product's destiny. Declining desirability indicates that the company should consider a marketing strategy for product maintenance. If product modifications cannot restore the product's desirability, discontinuation or survival plans may be in the near future.

Competitiveness. Is the product competitive in performance and price, and does the buyer still think it provides the value expected for the price paid? Products must remain competitive to grow. Sometimes, with hard work, products with a deficiency in competitiveness can produce improved profits, but with less market share.

Market Share. A viable product must maintain a market share that is high enough to sustain the cost of good marketing programs. If the market share is declining, growth is not a logical objective. Improved profit can be an objective, but only for the short term. In general, if the share is declining, it is because of a deficiency in one of the four previously mentioned product characteristics. If market share is increasing, growth, improved profits, and further gains in market share may all be acceptable marketing objectives. Remember, market share is tied to product characteristics, *not* to the market phase.

A product's characteristics and market position will not be the same in all markets. It is therefore necessary for the channel manager to have information from several sources to determine product characteristics.

Table 9.4 provides a quick reference for the selection of logical marketing channel development objectives. This is accomplished by determining the product characteristics necessary to select a specific marketing objective. The selection of a directional objective must also be consistent with the market phase determined earlier. As an illustration, one would not usually pick growth as a logical directional option in a declining market even if the market share is high.

Table 9.4
Selecting Marketing Channel Directional Objectives

Objective	Product Characteristics
Growth	Controllable, profitable, desirable, competitive.
Product & Market Maintenance	Controllable, profitable, desirable, competitive, reasonable market share.
Improved Profit	High market share, profitable, desirable, competitive.
Survival	Desirable, competitive, reasonable profitability, or contributing to profits.
Discontinuation	Not possessing sufficient favorable characteristics to set reasonable objectives.

Step Four: Setting Directional Channel Management Objectives

Once the position of a company's product or product group has been identified in relationship to the Product and Market Phase Checklist, the channel manager must determine which basic marketing objectives or marketing actions would best fit current and future planning. The objective-setting comments should be brief and positioned as *directional objectives*, not as goals. Goal setting is a part of the planning process. Objectives must be compatible with the product and market phase scenario. The basic objectives may be selected from the list of five options that we refer to as product and market directional objectives. No other options are realistic, apart from combinations with options moving in the same direction.

The basic directional objectives may be selected from five options. There may be several compromise alternatives consisting of combinations or degrees of application of these options. How far one goes in the direction indicated by the objectives selected is a part of the detailed strategy for the product or market involved. The selection of a logical directional marketing objective from the five options available requires critical judgment. Channel managers must realize that all future detailed marketing channel planning and product and market actions will depend upon an accurate assessment of the objectives considered possible from the analysis of market phase positions and product characteristics.

Directional Product and Market Options

Each of the following options may become a marketing channel objective. There are two dimensions that must be evaluated together: the market phase and the product characteristics. Growth is the first option one may consider as a management objective for marketing channel development.

Growth. The growth option may be expressed and measured in several ways. Increased market share, increased total units or dollars sold, increased profits, more new customers, or even a move into new markets (diversification) may be considered growth. The addition of new product innovations or modifications may be considered growth of the product line. An important growth measurement for channel managers may be expressed as the competitive share trend. As discussed in the previous chapter, the competitive share trend shows the relative position of the company's product or product group, expressed as its market share, compared to the market share of major competitors.

Product and Market Maintenance. The maintenance channel objective usually has two considerations: First, the product must continue to be profitable. Second, the market share, expressed in units sold, must be cost effective in order to produce the product. In our example of Aero-Tec X, it is obvious both products and markets are in a maintenance phase. The products were developed and introduced. The major market was developed. Innovation or modification of the products was only cosmetic, so more could be done in this area. The market was not exploited with marketing action, and diversification was not mentioned. These are opportunities for growth and perhaps even improved profitability. Aero-Tec X has been satisfied to maintain its mature products and markets because, until recently, it has not lost a significant part of its market share.

Profit Improvement. Profit improvement is limited to making more profit *per unit of sale*. This is accomplished not by selling more total units and in so doing generating more total revenue with the same percentage of profit—that activity is labeled growth—but by increasing the profit made from each unit of sale. This is true profit improvement. Profit improvement may be achieved through a reduction in production costs, resulting in an increase in profits. One can also reduce the costs related to marketing the product. Raising prices may always be considered as a profit improvement option. Note that the selection of profit improvement as a directional objective is usually linked to other objectives such as growth, survival, or maintenance.

Survival. Survival is usually considered a directional objective for channel marketing action when some major event has taken place in the market. It may be a competitive factor, regulatory change, upward cost revision, or something as drastic as a strike or the loss of a major production facility. The introduction of a competitive product selling at 25% below the market standard price would be a good example of the need to consider survival tactics. The new product may also have significantly improved benefits over the company's product. To select survival as a directional objective is a very serious step that should be taken only after careful analysis of all other options.

Discontinuation. The successful discontinuation of a product currently sold in the market is one of the most difficult actions to be planned and correctly executed. If the product to be discontinued is being superseded by a better one, the task is not as difficult. It must nonetheless be done with careful planning of the management action. In some cases, a product that falls into the discontinuation category will be kept in the line to support sales of very profitable products. This may be done even if the product has all the negative characteristics in the checklist. Marketing channel members have different reasons for keeping a product in the line beyond its usefulness to the manufacturer. In some cases, there is still good market acceptance, but because of low profitability the product must be considered for elimination. When a product is still wanted in the channel but for some reason should be discontinued, it becomes essential to prepare marketing channel members for this action, just to prevent problems. Indeed, there are good reasons for discontinuing a product.

Products should be discontinued when:

- profits drop below an acceptable level
- total dollar sales become insignificant to the market and channel members
- the usefulness of the product no longer provides a reasonable cost-to-benefit ratio
- market share drops below the level that will support marketing costs based on the lower number of units sold
- competitive products offer substantial advantages

Listed are the most common reasons. A product possessing any one of these negative characteristics may be a candidate for discontinuation or replacement. Usually two or more negative product characteristics will be working together to create a significant problem. However, any one serious deficiency in favorable product characteristics may result in a discontinuation decision.

The decision to discontinue a product is always an emotional one. Also, product discontinuation may be costly. The discontinuation decision must take into consideration plant utilization or closedown costs, materials in inventories, channel inventories and returns, the market influence of the product, and the company's image as a result of the action. There is even the emotional impact on the sales force members who for years have been selling the virtues of the product to be discontinued.

For most companies, it is eventually necessary to discontinue products. Marketing management and an enlightened channel manager can minimize the negative effects. Usually, replacement of the declining product can be planned, and a transition from old to new can create a positive situation rather than a problem. In general, companies hold on to old products long past their value to the market or the company. In so doing, they may diminish the effect of the new product's introduction. This is done not from greed but primarily because there are many customers who still like and use the old product, and they may not easily convert to the new one. As with the survival objective, the actions necessary to discontinue a product must be carefully planned. See Table 9.4 for the options.

Selecting Directional Objectives

Table 9.4 covers the product characteristics and the directional objectives. This table provides channel managers with a quick reference for selection of logical marketing channel development and management objectives. Study this table with care and note the logical reliance of product characteristics in relation to market phase realities. After a directional objective has been selected, it is the channel manager's obligation to evaluate whether there are any market phase situations that would preclude or inhibit the selection made.

There is always a judgment to be made in the product characteristic's evaluation and the selection of an applicable directional objective. Sometimes channel managers have no choice but to follow upper managers' admonitions concerning which objectives to follow. When pursuing directional objectives that seem to be poor choices, channel managers should use Table 9.4 to get insights into what they may do to make changes in the product or market characteristic's profile to reach the established objectives.

Product and Market Analysis Statement

A product and market analysis statement is simply a narrative that starts with much of the information found in the product and market phase scenario. This information is supplemented by the evaluation of options for directional objectives and the product characteristics that support the product and market analysis statement. This statement should be written for each product or product group with which the channel manager is involved. It is used as a reference for how a market or product was evaluated at a specific time. In addition, the product and market analysis statement is useful in marketing channel planning and for documenting assumptions used in sales forecasting. This statement is also valuable in the analysis of data used to develop the current market share, market share trend forecasting, and competitive market share trend calculation.

Aero-Tec X Company Product and Market Analysis Statement. The Aero-Tec X Company has marketed a line of aerosol products for twenty-five years (market phase). The product line has not been substantially modified but has been upgraded with the advance of technology (product modification phase). The market for the company's products is mature and fully developed (market phase). The company can no longer control either the product or the market action (controllability). The product line is still reasonably profitable and desirable, and for the most part the products in the line are an excellent value for the benefits received. The product line is very competitive with other aerosol products and has a 30% market share (market share). The company has adopted a basic marketing objective to maintain the product's competitive position in the marketing channel and hold its market share position. All marketing channel actions will support these objectives.

The market for aerosol products is a mature market that is probably on the decline. Product innovations, such as containers with a trigger sprayer, have reduced the market share for aerosols. These products have become popular with the market segment that is looking for lower prices or has an environmental concern. Aero-Tec X has been less than aggressive in product and market development or market diversification. Neither has the company been active in the development of products that may be an alternative choice of purchase to aerosols. Aero-Tec X maintains a reasonable profitability for its product line because of low-cost manufacturing and a market share leadership position in aerosol sales. Current products are selling well and are widely accepted by the consumer as both utilitarian and with value for the price charged. Market share has dropped five percentage points during the past two years. The problem with a lower market share is that the manufacturing costs will increase as the units produced decrease. The reason for the drop in market share is that the market is now being defined to include nonaerosol products used for the same purpose as the aerosol products. Because these products are a substitute for aerosol purchases, they reduce the market available to aerosols, even though they do not directly compete product to product. The company should evaluate the potential for nonaerosols as a market diversification objective. It may also consider improving its aerosol market share or diversify into contract manufacturing in order to keep the production at a highly efficient level.

Product Documentation

The product and market analysis statement will need to be supported with detailed knowledge that goes beyond the statement itself. In short, channel managers must be sure to have the necessary documentation to support their statements and recommended action plans for objective implementation. Product documentation should at least cover the following four areas:

Product Introduction. Introduction of the product should include the history relating to the product's original development and introduction program. These data should provide information on the success of the introductory program. In addition, record which major markets have been entered, how the product was packaged, how pricing is structured, and what marketing programs were adopted to be competitive in the major and secondary markets.

Product Innovation or Modification. The second most important event in the life of a product is innovation and modification. The first time a product is modified, or when product innovations such as new sizes and new product claims are added, the market dynamics for the product and its ability to compete will change forever.

Product Maintenance. This activity includes all marketing and pricing actions taken in defense of the product and its position in the market. Maintenance of the market share position can be critical to costs and the ability to initiate supportive marketing programs. Channel managers should record actions for improved profit, market share, product replacement, product modifications, and competitive product actions. Three-year data are needed to establish market trend lines.

Competitive Action. When related to marketing programs, competitive actions should be included in the documentation data if they were used to support profits or market share or to compete with pricing programs related to volume discounts, product terms, marketing allowances, or direct price reductions.

Market Documentation

The documentation of market actions, like the recording of actions related to products, is a part of the channel manager's basic data. As pointed out, market development is not separated from product development. However, there are market development activities that are not directly related to specific products. In this category of activities, the channel manager must document the following:

1. the *market development actions* that are taken by the company to expand the market

2. *market exploitation actions* undertaken by using price reductions or other inducements

3. *market maintenance actions* taken to support education and recognition of the product's benefits through advertising and promotional programs

The planning related to market expansion, exploitation, and even maintenance actions may take place at levels above the channel managers. Channel managers should be aware of how the market-planning direction taken by others will affect them. Marketing channel managers are by necessity protective of their markets and products. They do not like "outside" marketing plans, such as for private label marketing, to affect their area. Nevertheless, it should be recognized that most products of value seldom reach all markets into which they can be sold. When channel managers participate in the planning for outside marketing, they may better control how it affects their products and markets.

THE CHANNEL MANAGER AND PRODUCT DEVELOPMENT

The topic of managing products and managing markets has thus far centered on the relationship between markets and products and the inseparability of the product-market relationship. Also, considerations that apply to markets without mentioning specific products in the process of planning or setting objectives have been covered. For the most part, channel management concerns are directed to products because they are more manageable than the market. In addition, the products belong to the company, whereas its markets are those of many companies.

There is one important area in which the marketing channel manager should be vitally active. This is broadly referred to as *product development*. Throughout the discussion of the product manager's functions and responsibilities, reference to the term *marketing needs* has been made. This reference is to products in use and those that need to be developed to satisfy market needs not now fulfilled. Because of the importance of this topic to channel managers, it is covered in considerable detail.

How involved marketing channel managers become in product development depends greatly on the type of company for which they are working. If it is a machinery or equipment manufacturer, the channel manager may be an engineer and would get involved early in the new-product development process. In this example, market knowledge rather than discovery research controls the product development activity. If it is a company heavy in basic research and product discovery, the product manager would not usually get involved prior to the beginning of product development for an entity already discovered. For a manufacturing company, where the focus is on production, the channel manager may actually initiate the product development activity. In this example, product needs start with the market. In seed companies or those working with genetics, for example, the product manager may have very little to do in the product development area. For technology companies, the activity of product development is in the hands of scientists. In service-related fields such as insurance and computer software, product development is usually an ongoing modification of products already being marketed. These areas may not have a separate product management function, and consequently the marketing channel managers may be more concerned with sales. Product development may also be considered a business development activity rather than product development.

For research-oriented companies, the regulatory impact is frequently a controlling factor in product development. In manufacturing companies, materials costs, manpower, and facility utilization become central considerations. For marketing companies, new products usually come from outside resources. Technology companies, such as research companies, develop their own products through discovery, research, and development. They develop markets *for* their products, rather than establish products for markets. However, they may make product modifications to suit specific markets.

The channel manager's influence on product development should be considerable. There is one tool channel managers may apply that will be of help in the product development area—the *marketing needs profile*. This is a product, market, and profits projection developed by product managers or other channel managers to be used in helping orient and direct product development in specific product areas where a need has been identified. The marketing needs profile also helps set priorities for product development and provides information to direct the allocation of resources toward potentially more lucrative products and more productive research areas.

The Origin of Product Development

In general, new products may be obtained in two ways. Products may be discovered through research and product development, or they may be developed from known sources through the application of what is known to what is needed. Some managers point to a third way to obtain products: purchasing what is needed from those who have it. This last way is acceptable, but for our discussion it is not considered product origination.

Product Discovery. The discovery or development of a product starts in one of two ways. Either the new product (or perhaps product modification) is the result of *research* (discovery) or it is the result of a specific product *search* (development).

The *discovered* product is the result of scientific investigation. In this case, a product or entity is discovered first, and sometime later a use for it is developed. To be aware of the practical applications of a discovery, the research people must know the marketing needs for the product's area of application. How can this be assured? It starts with the marketing channel manager's *marketing needs profile*. Once market information is known (the need), the discovery may be directed toward the development of a marketable product. In short, *discovery starts with a product*. The product has been discovered for whatever use to which it may be applied. Through refinement, testing, and modification, the product can be developed into a new marketable entity. Many companies call this the *R&D process* (research and development process).

Product Development. Unlike the discovered product, the *developed* product starts with the market rather than with the product itself. A product that is to be developed is conceived when developers know a specific product is needed in the market. A market need differs from a marketing need in that the requirement is for a product not currently found in the marketplace. A *marketing need*, in contrast, is the requirement for a product that the company does not now possess but that is currently available from competitive companies.

Once a specific market need is identified, the product development activity is to search for a specific product discovery (or product development) that can provide the product the market needs. It is important for the marketing channel manager to recognize that there may be a great difference in the origins of discovered products versus developed products. In many cases, the developed product will be one that is brought into the company from the outside. Usually, the discovered product is the result of research within the company's organization. To clarify the distinction between the two methods, think of the word *research* and its root *search*. When we know precisely what we are looking for, the necessary action is to *search* for it. When searchers do not know precisely what they are looking for, they must search and *re-search* again and again until something is found that fits or a use is found for the discovery. This is *research*.

In the case of the already discovered product, you know precisely what you are looking for. The task is to search for and find a product source. One searches for the known or researches for the unknown. Sometimes searching for the known also involves a development action similar to what may follow product discovery.

Market and Marketing Needs Profile

The market or marketing needs profile will identify the product requirement as a search or a research project. This formal product request will go far beyond stating the obvious, such as "There is a need for an

AIDS vaccine, a treatment, or a cure." An evaluation of what the new product must deliver is the essence of the profile. The market or marketing needs profile will project information in the following five areas:

1. State what the new product must deliver in benefits or performance. This is a product value and worth statement from the point of view of the spectrum of benefits the product must provide to be commercially viable. An AIDS treatment that helped only 10% of those treated would not be acceptable. What percentage of performance is acceptable?
2. Give details of what competition the new product may face. For most *market* needs, there is no competition. Most *marketing* needs, on the other hand, will have at least one established competitor.
3. If the new product is to be a product modification (marketing need), cost factors related to new-product introduction, education, and other marketing programs are involved. If the product is new to the market for which the need is recognized, the channel manager will provide market development and channel development costs.
4. Forecast the current and future market potential for the product. Provide estimates of sales and profitability for the first five years, if possible.
5. Give a general statement of what the product will mean to the company. Be specific as to marketing channel requirements, as well as whether current channel members will want the new product. Note how the new product will relate to existing products in the market—especially the company's own products. All sources of data used in the profile should be noted. Research and development people need specific information whenever possible. Provide these data with every bit of detail available. All data for each profile should be reviewed and updated annually or more frequently if necessary. Note the revision dates, then distribute all updated profiles as soon as possible.

The Market or Marketing Needs Format

A typical market or marketing needs profile will assume the following format. This example follows the Aero-Tec X Company marketing scenario.

1. *Title.* The title gives a name to the needed product. This profile would be named "Environmentally Safe Aerosol Propellant."
2. *Product Needed.* Include in this section of the profile all the information available that will be useful in helping to direct research and development people. Provide the requirements for product benefits. Compare to existing products, if any.
   Aero-Tec X Example. Aero-Tec X needs a new aerosol propellant that will perform as well as those currently in use. The new propellant will need to be priced at half that of current propellants. The new material must be safe to the user and for the environment. The greatest benefit for the company will

be to enable us to offer aerosols that are price competitive to trigger sprayers but are a quality product providing a better spraying pattern.

3. *Competitive Environment.* With the above-described product, the company can indirectly compete with current trigger sprayers now on the market. We expect that within the next three years trigger sprayers will be technologically improved to provide a better spraying pattern and will also cost less. A special marketing needs profile has been prepared for the development of directly competitive trigger sprayers with superior benefits to currently competitive products.

4. *Marketing Opportunity.* Aero-Tec X is losing 5% of market share annually to trigger-spray products. This trend is expected to continue and represents at least $2 million annually in lost sales. The market is growing at the rate of 20% per year. If we can stop market share losses and participate in the growth, we can turn a $2 million loss into a $4 million per year gain. Marketing has projected new product introduction costs to be 15% of net sales the first year and 10% per year for the four years following.

5. *Forecasts and Projections.* The current market is growing by 20% per year. Aero-Tec X can capture half the market growth with a new product presented in this marketing needs profile. This product can also end market share declines. Our forecast is as follows:

Forecasts and Projections: First Five Years

Year One	$50 million	20,000,000 units
Year Two	$54 million	21,500,000 units
Year Three	$61 million	27,000,000 units

Projections for years 4 and 5 are for 10% growth in units per year.

6. *Product Needs Rational.* The new propellant can provide the company with a significant cost savings. This will allow us to compete aggressively with the inferior trigger-spray products now on the market. Because of cost reduction, our profit dollars should not drop significantly even with a lower selling price. This will allow marketing programs to support the product change. In addition to the economic benefits, we will continue to use our technology, recognized as the best in the industry. We can also mount a public relations program to extol the benefits of our new "environmentally friendly" aerosol products.

7. *References.* Company market research report titled "Trigger Sprayers versus Aerosols Market Share." Industry report on market growth, "Aerosol News Report 7A."

Market and Marketing Needs Review

For those companies using a formal marketing needs profile to communicate between marketing and research, one person in the product development area and one in the marketing area are the direct representatives of each group. Frequently, a committee is formed to review progress on reaching the formalized marketing needs objectives accepted by research. This committee, which should be made up of representatives from research and development and marketing, will also verify the status of the various market or marketing needs projects. It will note changes in the profiles as well as present a progress report on all profiles.

The most important achievement of a marketing needs profile is to facilitate an organized and formal approach to the identification of specific products that are needed to improve the company's position in the market. This can be one of the most important functions of marketing channel management. When this activity is properly established, a company can achieve a higher productivity in the quest to develop new products, saving time and money in the process. One large company known to the author employs a full-time secretary for its Marketing Needs Committee. This committee consists of over twenty representatives from all areas of research, development, and marketing and meets every month of the year.

SUMMARY

Channel management activities involving product management and market management are complicated and difficult. Errors made by managers in these positions are usually highly visible and bring quick reaction. Marketing channel managers must look reality in the face and recognize this fact of life. Those who fill these management positions will wish to implement all their good ideas and plans. However, since all marketing managers compete for a share of a finite marketing budget, few managers will have all their requests for new products fulfilled, and even fewer will be provided the opportunity to try all their good channel management ideas.

Keep this in mind: Individual corporations spend tens and even hundreds of millions of dollars annually in search of unique and marketable products. Yet as intense and expensive as this process may be, there is often a lack of detailed planning for marketing these products. A large part of this important job will usually be the channel manager's responsibility. The use of the marketing needs profile can help set priorities and identify product profit potentials.

For the most part, new products marketed by research-oriented companies have a high cost for product development, a heavy financial investment, and a long-term commitment in the form of manufacturing facilities. Therefore, it is essential to correctly evaluate and project the numbers related to the competitive market environment into which new products will be placed. These projections are usually based on forecasts of sales dollars, gross profits, production capacity needs, competitive market environment expectations, product cost analysis, financial needs, the sales action plans, and personnel needs. Much of these data are collected by the marketing channel manager and are presented as the first workable business plan to top management.

Usually included in these initial projections are the added marketing costs. By this we mean costs of advertising, merchandising, product promotion, and reacting to the competitive retaliation new products must face at some point following introduction. Marketing costs are usually expressed as a percentage of the gross profit expected. This is not a heavy commitment to the marketing activity in support of the enormous investment in personnel and money required to get to this point. However, it is usually the way budgets are generated for new-product marketing.

Marketing channel managers build the foundation of the planning process with:

1. accurate, extensive, detailed forecasts
2. market research, marketing research, and even market testing of information
3. application of a logical marketing planning process
4. marketing plans that can be followed

Seldom does financial management look upon the cost of marketing the product as having more than a negative impact on profits. However, for many successful companies, the building of markets is more valuable than the building of plants and laboratories. Many industries are becoming market builders. The channel manager's job is not easy, but it is very necessary and personally satisfying. Product and market managers are always visible. They must be constantly available, and they are always expected to be the ultimate authority concerning the products and markets in their marketing channel.

QUESTIONS FOR DISCUSSION

1. List the four steps in the product and market management process.
2. What situation does the product and market life cycle identify?
3. What is the difference between market diversification and market expansion?
4. What market and product factors lead to consideration of survival objectives?
5. What management action is appropriate when a highly profitable product starts to lose market share?
6. When the market is declining, what directional objective is usually inappropriate?
7. What management actions can a channel manager implement to improve a product's competitiveness?

8. Explain how to measure growth for a market and for a product in the market.

9. What is the purpose of a marketing needs profile?

10. What are channel managers asking for when they produce a marketing needs profile for a product that is not in existence?

TEN

Marketing Programs and Pricing Strategies

Marketing programs are generally created to initiate and control the actions in the marketing channel. These actions are initiated through programs providing incentives intended to stimulate cooperation from the marketing channel members. Product promotions, advertising, pricing strategies, and programs related to competitive actions in the marketing channel are the most common. These marketing programs are directed to every level in the channel in an effort to stimulate buying, selling, and consumption or use of the products offered.

During the past two decades, the use of promotional incentives and motivational programs to stimulate group or individual response has become highly sophisticated. We have seen "price off" promotions, green stamps, blue stamps, red stamps, and even plaid stamps used as promotional incentives. There are consumer programs with on-bag coupons, in-bag coupons, magazine and newspaper coupons, in-store and mail-in redemption rebates, sweepstakes, and instant rub-off prize award cards. The fact that many states now offer a variety of lottery programs demonstrates the growing interest in incentives, motivational programs, and gaming opportunities. Also, we see a wide cross-section of the public involved. Even the U.S. Mail is saturated with credit card offers of special merchandise, insurance, free television sets, cars, and publishing house cash sweepstakes offering millions of dollars to the winner. The conclusion that incentives and motivational programs are here to stay, and are growing, is an easy one. This fact of life is well documented by daily exposure to their unending variety. Companies producing industrial products have not been immune to these programs. We find bonus packs, piggyback packaging, heavy tons, price-off's, coupons, merchandise offers, spiffs, travel, caps, T-shirts, and jackets of all kinds in neverending supply.

Probably the most uncontrolled promotional elements in marketing programs are the payment incentives. Usually these programs end up as delayed-payment incentives, that is, buy now, pay later programs. The incentive offered by producers to have their customers accept products on consignment, rather than through direct purchase, is a promotional element used increasingly for seasonal products. It is the author's observation that more money is wasted on unnecessary and unsuccessful promotional programs than on any other marketing activity. Misdirected advertising allowances fall into the same pattern as wasted promotional money.

This chapter will cover many subjects related to product promotion, merchandising, and the role played by pricing. The objective of this text is to provide direction and information to prepare the reader to become knowledgeable about the various types of marketing programs and pricing strategies. Advertising and merchandising programs are also presented as they apply to the support of promotional marketing programs. The basic elements of advertising are discussed as each contributes to the support of various types of marketing programs. Pricing strategies relate to specific types of promotional incentives as well as to product positioning in the channel.

MARKETING PROGRAMS

Marketing channel managers may be involved with many different types of marketing programs. Most of these can be collected under four headings: buying programs, selling programs, advertising programs, and competitive responses.

Buying Programs

Buying programs are promotional in their orientation. The conditions of purchase may include the product's price, terms of payment, volume discounts, promotional allowances, and other incentives to buy. The inclusion of freight allowances and warehousing allowances may also be a part of buying programs. The elements of a buying program are the product's *price*, the *terms* of the transaction, and all *incentives* offered to attract buyers.

Selling Programs

Selling programs include advertising and merchandising directed to retailers and to consumers. These programs are designed to help channel members sell products to those who are one or two steps below them in the channel structure. Wholesalers will expect programs to help them sell to retailers. Retailers expect selling programs directed to users. The wholesaler's selling programs, provided by the manufacturer, include items such as literature, displays, and sales aides offered to retailers. These items become a part of the retail selling programs. Advertising aimed at retail members and users fill out the elements of selling programs.

Advertising Programs

Although a part of the selling and buying program, advertising is a separate marketing activity. Advertising strategies are concerned with product and trade advertising, but also embrace a much broader marketing activity. Image building, channel influence, general communications and public relations may all be included under the broad heading of advertising. The focus of this text is upon advertising used in support of marketing programs, channel-building actions, and pricing strategies.

Competitive Responses

Responses to competitive programs are more reactive than those to a planned marketing program. What a company decides to do in response to a competitive promotion is to a great extent centered on the effect the competitive action will have on the company's business. Generally, three types of competitive responses are possible. These responses range from doing nothing to doing one of the following: choosing to answer a competitive promotion with a "me too" response that initiates a promotional activity to duplicate the competitive one; giving an "either-or" response in which the company offers an alternative to the competition's promotion; and, finally, retaliating, which goes beyond meeting the competitive offer by providing a program that will outdo the competitor. The details regarding these programs will be presented later in this chapter.

Promotions and Merchandising

According to the dictionary, *promotion* and *merchandising* are interchangeable words when coupled with the sale of products. Indeed, there may be little recognizable difference between the two when it comes to marketing industrial products. However, there will be significant differences between the two when dealing with consumer products. Promotional elements are found in all four types of marketing programs. A part of merchandising and promotion, advertising is the vehicle used to communicate both the promotion and the merchandising features. The types of promotions supported by advertising seem almost infinite. Generally, marketing people tend to distinguish between promotion and merchandising as follows:

Promotion. Promotion involves actions directed to a single product or a group of products to create a special stimulus to buy according to the direction of the seller.

Merchandising. Merchandising is the *visual* presentation of products to create awareness of the brand, give attention to the promotion, or accent the product's features. Generally, one should think of the promotion as the offer, and merchandising as the act of visually displaying and presenting the offer.

TYPES OF PROMOTIONAL OFFERS

The four types of promotional offers may be enumerated as follows:

1. *Price promotions.* Offering the product to the consumer or other channel members at a reduced price through discounts, coupons, or some other means of price reduction.
2. *Bonus offers.* Providing a bonus (usually merchandise) of some type other than a direct payment of money.
3. *Chance or sweepstakes programs.* Free trips, vehicles, clothing, and so on, without qualification or the need to purchase the product.
4. *Terms of sale.* Cash discounts, extended term of payment, and qualified allowances.

Price Promotion Programs

The most widely used promotional offers are those that are tied to a price reduction. Price promotions fall into two categories: *qualified offers* and *nonqualified offers*. Qualified offers may be allowances offered for services provided, or they may be an earned discount based on a specific volume of purchases. Nonqualified promotions are available to anyone and are represented by direct reductions in the product price or by promotions that offer a price reduction on purchases. There are also coupon incentives and other offers that are substitutes for the cash. Price offers and those providing incentives tied to the terms of sale may be either qualified or nonqualified offers. Promotions involving sweepstakes or bonuses are almost always nonqualified.

Price promotions are presented as a special value to be received when buying products offered at a price the buyer recognizes as a bargain. Price-related offers must be easily recognized by the buyer as a true savings. Price promotions may be directed at all channel levels. When a price offer is advertised and promoted to the user, the marketing company must be sure that the participating channel members will cooperate and will extend the advertised price reduction. However, channel members will want to receive payment for the price reductions they cover in support of the marketing program.

Promotional Discounts. All members of the channel may be included in the discount promotion. Indeed, if the discount is directed to the consumer, perhaps as a percentage off the marked purchase price, all participating channel members will be directly involved. The consumer who receives a 25% discount on a $1 item will receive the discount from the retailer's profit. The wholesaler must repay the profit lost by the retailer or cover the *margin markdown* (the loss of profit) in one way or another. In turn, the manufacturer will also cover the discount cost to the wholesaler. In general, the *promotional* discount is not an earned discount but one offered with no qualifications other than to buy the product.

Promotional Allowances. Unlike the promotional discount the promotional allowance is a qualified offer. To receive an allowance for performing a service, one must accomplish the service. Promotional allowances given for any reason must be offered to each channel member at the same level and with the same opportunity to participate. The qualifiers to participate cannot favor one channel member over another at the same level. Allowances may or may not be cash offers. Sometimes they will be a free product or an article of merchandise such as a display piece earned by showing the product on the display. A mailing allowance may be paid for including envelope stuffers that promote the company's product along with invoices.

Earned Discounts. Earned discounts, unlike allowances, are offered as cash or percentage reductions from the purchase price. Earned discounts are obtained by purchasing in volume, performing activities related to inventory accounting, providing market-building services such as prospecting for new channel members, holding training meetings, or providing technical services. Handling complaints and providing services to assure product guarantees may also earn a discount. However, services usually earn a promotional allowance rather than a discount.

Price-offs. Price-offs are different from a discount in that they are always a dollars or cents program rather than a percentage reduction. These promotions are much easier to manage than the percent reductions, since the dollar or cents amount is the same at every channel level. Rebates would be considered as a *delayed price-off* promotion.

Coupons. The last element of the price promotion is the offer of a coupon used to obtain a price reduction either on the initial purchase or a subsequent purchase. There are many types of coupons and programs to use them. In most promotional programs, coupons are directed to the user who will redeem them at the point of purchase or by mailing them to the marketer for redemption. The marketer always covers the total cost of a coupon offer, even paying channel members (usually retailers) for handling or redemption of the coupons.

Bonus Offers

Bonus offers can take on many different characteristics depending upon the products involved. In general, the bonus is given free with the purchase of the target product. Bonus offers will not appeal to as many buyers as will price offers. Bonus deals may be perceived as being of a greater value than direct price reductions. When an additional 25% of the product is packaged with the product as a bonus, the user receives full value but the manufacturer has only a 25% increase in product cost, with no added profit cost to other channel members, as is the case with cash discounts.

Some of the more popular bonuses are stamps, bonus pack packaging, merchandise, earned points for merchandise, product samples, free products, or extra services. Whatever its form, the bonus is assured to all purchasers. A garage that offers a free oil filter with a lube and oil change, for example, is employing the bonus offer as a promotional incentive.

Chance and Sweepstakes Promotions

Chance promotions are not highly motivational for most industrial product users. Chance offers are usually tied to frequently purchased items such as fast foods, breakfast cereals, or beverages. For infrequently used products, the chance element of the item is not tied to a purchase. Chance promotions can offer big prizes and attract a lot of attention. The offer of an automobile or pickup truck free will catch a user's eye even when there is a slim chance of winning. However, the legal aspects of chance and sweepstakes promotions can be quite restrictive (this subject is discussed in chapter 12).

Promotional Terms

Terms are a competitive necessity offered to all channel members with the exception of the user. The terms may *not* be identified as a promotional element when they are the standard payment discounts offered throughout the year. Nevertheless, the standard terms are price related and are tied to competitive offers. Promotional terms usually relate to an offer to extend payment provided the buyer will purchase in greater quantities. Again, these are earned discounts that are qualified by a specific action.

Terms relate to the conditions under which the sales are made. The type of payment—cash or credit—due date for payment, and early payment incentives, among other conditions, are part of the terms. When manufacturers ask a customer to buy twice the usual inventory to get a special price, they will frequently extend the payment terms to provide twice the normal time required for payment. If, for example, the normal terms require payment in thirty days, the manufacturer may offer sixty-day terms or half payment in thirty days (normal) with half payment in sixty days (extended to cover the additional purchase). Some common terms offered as purchasing incentives are extended billing, delayed billing, consignment, direct discounting of a bill if paid by a specified date, net thirty days, contracts with special terms, and graduated payment terms allowing payment as one-third in thirty days, one-third in sixty days, and one-third in ninety days. Terms offered to entice buyers to do something they normally would not do—such as buy a double order—are considered promotional terms. They may be offered in conjunction with normal terms, or they may replace them. Often other incentives (discounts) are coupled to promotional terms.

Merchandising

Usually, merchandising is an in-store activity often involving a special display referred to as a *product merchandiser*. Merchandising materials include such things as posters, banners, shelf talkers, displays, lights, video presentations, literature, signs, and specialty items—termed *dimensional materials*—such as balloons and pocket matches. In simple categories, these are as follows:

1. signs and banners
2. shelf talkers, posters, and literature
3. displays, lights, and fixtures
4. merchandise such as balloons, pens, key rings, and matchbooks

By putting together the elements of promotion and the elements of merchandising as shown in Table 10.1, channel managers can consider what they have to work with when planning a product promotion that includes merchandising.

Table 10.1
Elements of Promotion and Merchandising

Promotional Elements	Merchandising Elements
1. Price	1. Signs and banners
2. Bonus	2. Shelf talkers, posters, and literature
3. Terms	3. Displays, lights, and fixtures
4. Chance	4. Merchandise items

Channel-Level Influence on Promotion Planning

The reference to levels of promotion identifies the various audiences that are available for promotional targeting. There are three levels that can be considered when planning the motivation for promotional programs. Usually a promotion is directed to the user or consumer in the channel. The channel manager will also be involved with programs to the trade that never impact the user. Trade promotions are usually buying programs for wholesalers and retailers and selling programs to support the wholesaler's efforts to sell retailers. For the consumer, the retail selling programs are the promotional offer.

Planning a promotional program starts with the channel member to whom the promotional offer is being made. For a consumer promotion in a four member channel, the consumer is the first consideration for promotional planning, even though the manufacturer must go through wholesalers and retailers to get to the consumer. If the offer is not sufficiently motivational to entice the consumer to participate, it will fail, no matter how well the other levels in the channel are motivated to buy and sell the promotional offer.

Sometimes a strong promotion to the user (consumer) will pull through participation from the channel levels above. Sometimes a strong buying program for wholesalers or retailers will push the action all the way to the user. It is also possible to create such a highly motivational selling incentive for the producer's sales force that it will *push through* the sale's objective by a strong selling action.

Promotional Program Planning

Promotions are considered an integral part of the annual marketing plan. They are planned and executed as a part of the complete marketing effort in the channel. Promotions must be independently successful and contribute to the success of all the company's marketing programs in the channel.

Table 10.2
Promotional Planning Outline

1. Why is the promotion being planned?

2. What is to be promoted?

3. What are the objectives of the promotion?

4. If the objective is reached what are the net results?

5. Which promotional elements are to be used?

6. What are the budget requirements, and is this money available?

7. What are the major competitive assumption for this promotion?

To begin planning a product promotion, consult Table 10.2 for an outline of the considerations that must be made. For full channel promotions, the planning starts with the consumer offer.

The Consumer Offer. All channel members will become involved with the consumer offer. This is the first level of promotion. This type of promotional offer demonstrates the actions of a full channel promotion. The kind of promotion that will be attractive to the consumer depends on the consumers involved. Consumers who buy automobiles use the automobiles. Those who buy food generally eat, or consume, it. Users are more interested than consumers in the quality of a product, its performance, and its guarantee rather than the product cost. The user is, in short, *value* oriented. In contrast, consumers who actually consume the product involved in the promotion may look first to price as a motivational force. Products for consumption are purchased more frequently than those products used over a period of time, and frequent purchasing leads to familiarity with competitive brands and the satisfaction each delivers. The price paid for these products bears directly on the satisfaction of the purchase. For these reasons price is a major motivating factor for the purchase of products to be consumed, whereas quality is more important for products judged on their performance.

Start with the user or consumer, then work upward by creating a supportive trade program: This is usually the way a full channel promotional program is planned. The assumption is that if the company cannot afford or conceive of a program considered to be motivating to the user (or whoever is the promotional target), it is fruitless even to begin the promotional planning process. Key questions channel managers must consider in preparing a promotional program are listed in Table 10.2.

To simplify the application of promotional elements, consider them one at a time. One will soon discover by using them that one element is dependent upon another. Consider how each planning element applies to the fictional Chain Link Snow Tire Company in the following marketing scenario.

Why Are We Planning a Marketing Promotion?

Because the products sold by the Chain Link Snow Tire Company have a very short product use season, it is necessary to plan production well in advance of when the products are actually needed. Producing snow tires in May, June, July, and August for sales that will not take place until September, October, November, and December presents the problem of knowing which tires to produce and in what quantity. If the company knew the buying intentions of their wholesalers and retailers well in advance of the season, it could better plan production to fit the requirements of the marketing channel. The channel planning and promotional program should help provide the production group with a more accurate forecast of product needs for the short season.

What Is to Be Promoted? The three grades of snow tires produced by Chain Link will be promoted in all major snow tire markets. These snow tires are designated as Chain Link Premium, Chain Link Extra, and Chain Link Tuffy.

What Are the Promotion's Objectives? This promotion will provide information for the buying intentions of the Chain Link retailers with details listing the tire type, the tire size, and the quantity of each. This information will be developed by the Chain Link wholesalers and made available to the Chain Link Tire Company as soon as possible, but no later than April 1. Forecasts and shipping schedules for each type and size of tire will be prepared by the channel manager for each market area.

Promotional Elements

It is usually easier to plan a promotion by starting with the user or the last channel member to be included in the promotion. In this case, it is the user who buys snow tires.

Chain Link User Offer. The Chain Link user offer is not intended to create persuasion buying by wholesalers and retailers. The objective is to draw attention to Chain Link snow tires by offering a sweepstakes that will give ten free week-long vacations for two in Hawaii; the winners will also receive their purchase of snow tires free. Anyone who enters the sweepstakes will be eligible to win two free snow tires, which will be awarded to the 100 participants whose names are selected. No purchase is necessary to enter the sweepstakes (as is mandated by law for this type of promotion). Entry blanks will be available at all Chain Link retailers. The consumer offer is free tires and free vacation trips.

Buying Programs. Wholesalers as well as retailers will be offered a buying program in support of the promotional effort. The buying programs will be based on a price offer that involves a participation allowance and a bonus opportunity for retailers.

Wholesaler's Buying Program. Wholesalers who place orders of 10,000 units (tires) will receive a volume discount of 5% of the purchase price. Orders of 20,000 units will qualify for a 7% volume discount, and orders of 30,000 units or more will receive a 9% discount. All orders must be placed for shipment in full truckloads and delivered no later than May 31. An extended billing program is offered to wholesalers that provides them the opportunity to pay their invoices in three equal installments: in thirty days from shipment, in sixty days, and in ninety days. This schedule will allow wholesalers the opportunity to receive at least partial payment from retailers before they must make their payment to the manufacturer.

There is also a program for the wholesaler's sales force that is paid for by Chain Link. Because the Chain Link Snow Tire Company wholesalers represent the company exclusively in their area, Chain Link wholesalers are not in competition. The top three wholesaler salespersons—their sales measured as total tires sold—and their husbands or wives will accompany the group of ten consumers and their spouses on the Hawaii vacation trip. All expenses will be paid by Chain Link, which will also present a $500 cash bonus to these three winners. In addition, Chain Link will pay all wholesaler salespersons a *spiff* (cash bonus) of fifty cents per tire for every tire sold on a minimum *booking order*—an order placed for later shipment—of 100 units.

Retailer's Buying Program. Retailers who place a booking order for 100 units or more will receive a discount of 5% from the retailer's list price. This discount will be deducted from their invoice and is paid by the wholesaler. In addition, retailers who place a booking order for a minimum of 100 units will receive an advertising allowance of 5% (i.e., 5% of their net order) directly from the Chain Link Snow Tire Company upon proof of having placed an approved advertisement for the company's tires. Those retailers who place a booking order for 200 or more units will receive, in addition to the other retailer incentives, a lighted floor display that holds one each of the three types of snow tires offered by Chain Link. The display features the free trips to Hawaii, the free tire sweepstakes, and the selling points for the tires on display. This display, including the three tires, is a $200 value for the retailer. All retailers will receive banners, posters, and entry cards for the sweepstakes telling of the free trips to Hawaii and the free snow tire offer.

Any discounts offered retailers over the 5% allowed for 100-unit purchases will be at the discretion of the wholesalers. Again, since each wholesaler has an exclusive territory there is no price competition between wholesalers.

The Internal Sales Force Program. Chain Link is offering each of its salespersons the opportunity to participate in a sales contest. The company has three sales regions: the Eastern Region, the Central Region, and the Western Region. Each region that exceeds its quota by 10% will earn a $500 bonus for each of its sales team members and a bronze plaque declaring them the Quota Toppers—the winning team. The region that exceeds its quota by the largest percentage will send its top three producers and their spouses to Hawaii as the company representatives for the one-week consumer vacation trip. Further, these top three regional representatives, as well as all members of the top region, will receive a $1,000 bonus rather than the $500 the other Quota Toppers will receive.

Promotion Discussion. The Chain Link Snow Tire Company promotion has price, bonus, chance, and terms offered to at least one of the four levels of the marketing channel. Every level of channel member will participate in the promotion. Motivational incentives will be provided to each to ensure the best possible result. Budgets will need to be set for each element of the promotion and compared to expectations for sales production. Channel managers will need to make a competitive assumption statement related to what counteraction, if any, is anticipated from the competition.

Promotions involving several levels of channel members require planning to be sure all participants are involved and are satisfied with the reward they receive for the work they are being asked to perform. Not all promotions need to include all channel levels, of course, and many companies promote only to their direct customers and offer them nothing but buying programs.

Long-Term Promotional Programs

Some companies do not include their long-term programs in the promotion category. For this reason, "programs" rather than "promotion" is the designation used here for long-term promotions. These programs may be termed *buying* programs or conditions of sale. Generally, they are a part of the policy aspect of selling products. Long-term programs will fit under the definition of a promotion if their objective is to create sales according to special directions or stimuli provided by the terms of sale or other buying conditions that are a matter of policy. Such long-term programs are important to channel managers in maintaining their competitive position.

In some promotional situations, a program will become unwelcome if the manufacturer's terms are not consistent with the terms the wholesaler or retailer must extend to support the primary promotional program.

Table 10.3
Types of Long-Term Programs

1. Season- or year-long terms	5. Guarantees
2. Volume discounts	6. Return policy
3. Special earned allowances	7. Shipping policy
4. Purchasing qualifiers	8. Competitive position

Channel managers must be alert to the role played by standard long-term promotional policies, credit extension, terms of payment, guarantees, and the other elements of the long-term programs that must support short-term promotional actions. Most of the elements of long-term programs are included in Table 10.3.

It is critical that the company's long-term programs do not become *demotivating* to channel members, turning them away from the programs and the company's products. The long-term programs should not be a factor in the acceptance of shorter-term, high-profile, promotional programs.

As an example, if a product is highly freight-intensive, one must sell full truckloads, railcar loads, or barge loads, or one must sell by contract on a "make and take" basis. To buy in these quantities requires an incentive. Usually, this would be a volume purchase. One might also offer the qualifier that after reaching 50 tons, a shipment will earn a special price. All purchases thereafter, regardless of amount shipped, will be billed at the 50-ton price. This can also be done with case quantities, or it can be based on unit purchases as in the Chain Link snow tire promotion.

The long-term promotional activity must be examined carefully by the channel managers, since it can be very costly. Remember that money for promotional activity comes from the marketing budget. The implication is that budgets are limited, and once money is committed, *it is gone.* Long-term promotional programs require long-term budget commitments.

Discussion of Long-Term Programs. Budgets for long-term programs are usually accrued as a percentage of net sales. As an example, consider a company that offers a 2% discount for invoices paid within ten days. An analysis is made based on historical use of the 2% discount, and the budgeted cost will reflect this percentage. This company may find that the cost of the 2% discount for ten-day payment is actually only ½% of net sales. If so, the budget will be calculated as ½% of the forecasted sales for the year and *reserved,* or allocated, as a cost of sales charged for every transaction. This budget figure is never available to marketing to

Table 10.4
Short-Term Promotional Programs

1.	Bookings	6.	Introductory offers
2.	Loaders	7.	Discontinuation sale
3.	Special price	8.	Bonus packs, two-for's, tie-in's
4.	Coupons	9.	Free goods
5.	Sweepstakes and drawings	10.	Merchandise, travel, and point programs

use for any other purpose, since it becomes a fixed charge against profits and the marketing budget.

Short-Term Programs

Ten types of short-term promotional programs useful to channel managers are listed in Table 10.4. Short-term promotions have a definite time period, budgeted cost, and specific action objectives. Short-term promotions try to make something happen that would otherwise not happen—usually an increase in sales. However, sometimes inventory reduction, preemptive selling, or some other objective is the primary promotional focus. For the Chain Link Tire Company, the promotion provides essential information for production purposes.

The promotional programs listed in Table 10.4 are not all-inclusive. They represent about 90% of what is effectively used by industrial products companies. Several programs may be combined to make them more attractive. As an example, a farm store retailer offering a special price during a two-day truckload sale of livestock feed may enhance the motivation by giving away balloons, caps, coffee, and donuts. Also, a coupon worth 5% extra discount to the first fifty buyers could be mailed to his customer list to help increase early buying. Because there are so many promotional possibilities, it is essential to know precisely what one wants to accomplish *before* deciding how it is to be done.

Selecting the Most Effective Promotion. Selecting the most effective program is a fine objective, yet many times it is governed by what can be accomplished within the available budget. As shown in Table 10.5, there are some basic rules a manager can follow to select an effective promotion.

Discussion. Do not promote a product unless there is a clear objective and need. An unnecessary promotion may discourage the sales force, since it creates more work with less reward. Unneeded promotions may also create unnecessary expectations from the trade as well as confuse

Table 10.5
Basic Rules of Promotion

1. Keep it simple.	6. Clearly communicate to channel.
2. Define promotion objectives.	7. Train & equip presenters.
3. Be logical.	8. Involve everyone necessary.
4. Make it profitable to participate.	9. Kick off on time.
5. Provide advertising and merchandising.	10. Evaluate the results.

the user. Using a promotion sends the signal that something special is being offered for a distinct reason. Of course, manufacturers may choose to use promotions for a number of reasons. Companies initiate promotions to:

1. meet a competitive situation
2. introduce a new product or service
3. reduce inventory
4. shift buying from one period to another
5. preempt competitive buying
6. increase volume of sales
7. sell short-dated product
8. create new users
9. capture market share
10. meet an objective otherwise unattainable

But there are also reasons a manufacturer or marketer should *not* promote. Promotions cannot solve basic marketing problems. Common sense should be followed in making the decision to promote. Using the old rule, "When in doubt, don't," is usually good advice. Since promotions require special budgets, the flexibility to promote is not always a choice. Indeed, there are some common reasons why manufacturers should not promote. Companies should not promote:

1. when the cost would be more than the benefit
2. when the objective can be met without the promotional cost or exposure
3. for volume increases, when business is shifted from one period to another with no other benefits
4. with a lower price when the reduced price will not increase product consumption

5. when promoting a short-dated product will reduce sales of normal inventory (there are exceptions)

6. when introducing a new product at a reduced price sends the wrong message about the product's worth

7. to solve one problem but create a new one related to competitive responses

8. with a low-profit item if it will hurt sales of a higher-profit item

9. when the need is underpromoted; it is better to do nothing if the action planned cannot be successfully completed

The Competitive Promotion

There are occasions when it is necessary to launch a promotion in order to meet a competitive situation. Many times members of the sales force ask channel managers to do something to help when a competitor is taking business from the company's customers. Channel managers should be cautious in assuming that the reports received from the sales force are complete and factual. Frequently, the effect of the competitive promotion is not accurately reported. Channel managers need to contact reliable sources in the channel to ask them the pertinent questions. Marketing channel managers especially need to ask if channel members have acted on the competitive promotion and to what extent. *Usually, the best way to treat competitive promotions is to do nothing.* Many times an offer made to counter a competitive action causes a new round of problems to face rather than solves the current ones. The most effective way to deal with a successful competitive promotion is to do the following:

1. Get accurate information on how the company's sales are affected.

2. Get copies of all materials concerning the competitive offer.

3. Create a response that will quickly stop the negative effect of the competitor's offer.

4. Establish a goal—to regain the business or market share you have lost. Do not try to gain all that your competitor has accomplished, since some of that business comes from other marketers in the channel.

In short, the channel manager should react to the competitive promotion only if it is truly hurting the company's position. When that happens, follow the outline given for competitive pricing promotions. The channel manager's action may not be directly price related, but the action response is the same. The four points of action are these:

1. Get all the facts.

2. Stop the sales loss.

3. Reestablish the company's position.

4. Regain the market share.

It is also necessary for channel managers to be sure that the activity they prepare in answer to a competitive promotion will not prompt retaliation from the competitor. Keep your response low profile, but effective. The answer to a successful competitive promotion is to nullify its effects on your business, not to create a new level of competition. The use of one of the three promotional actions related to price promotions— me too, either-or, and retaliation—is also an appropriate response to any other type of competitive promotion. Indeed, these are all any channel manager can plan to do.

Budgeting for Promotions

Every company has its own rules on budgeting for promotion. Usually, these rules are not flexible. In many cases, the budget comes first and the promotion is built around the available money. Promotions created to fit the available budget may not always be effective, since the reason for promoting, as well as the objectives set to accomplish the promotional need, becomes secondary to the availability of money. The best way to determine the proper budget level is first to decide what the appropriate promotional action will be and then to project its results along with the related cost. Deciding whether to promote depends upon the benefit to the company and the marketing channel members.

Once again, channel managers have to look at reality rather than the ideal. Reality says promotional money is limited, so it must be well spent. However, there is unlimited promotional money that through proper planning may be generated by the promotion itself. This unbudgeted money is self-generating, with every transaction from the new profit actually created by the promotion. This is *pay-as-you-go* budgeting.

To understand the pay-as-you-go promotional budgeting, consider this short philosophy on promotion. *Money spent on promotion that does not create the predicted response is wasted.* There can be no quarrel with this statement. The pay-as-you-go promotional budgeting plan provides that if the promotion does not get the response expected, the promotional money is not spent. Only by acceptance of the promotional offer will the promotional money be spent. Those who do not respond to the promotional offer buy on regular terms at normal prices. We have now described an open-ended budget that generates its own money based upon the success of the promotion. The following example may be helpful in understanding how this works.

Open-Ended Budget Example. The entire budget needed to run this promotion is generated from new business. There is no cost if no one buys into the program. If the promotion exceeds expectations, the additional costs come only from additional profits.

The fictional Waxes and Resins Manufacturing Company (W & R, Inc.) produces a special ingredient that may be incorporated into floor waxes to provide an anti-skid feature. It is used primarily in schools, offices, hospitals, and other public buildings with vinyl plastic flooring. W & R sells the anti-skid product along with basic waxes and resins to most major floor wax manufacturers. A specialty chemical company that is a competitor to W & R introduced a promotion on their own anti-skid ingredient, giving a 10% discount for a sixty-day period on orders of 500 gallons or more. The competitive product has the same basic characteristics as the W & R product, but with its promotion some of W & R's largest users have placed orders with the competitor. Five hundred gallons will last about three months for these users. W & R wants to address the competitive price promotion offer with an either-or response rather than a general price reduction to all customers for all of the "Anti-Skid" they sell. To meet a short-term competitive promotion would cost more than the benefit will produce. The new product has taken about $50,000 in business away from W & R, which sells $500,000 of the product annually. Until the promotional offer, large users bought Anti-Skid from W & R along with their regular requirements for waxes and resins. The anti-skid product is the only product sold by the competitive specialty chemical company to the floor wax manufacturers.

The W & R response was to offer a 10% discount (me too) on Anti-Skid to any of its customers ordering a combined 500 gallons of all W & R products (not just Anti-Skid) during the promotional period. W & R also extended the promotional period to ninety days. This is the length of time a 500-gallon order of Anti-Skid would last. W & R's counter-promotion was highly successful in stopping the competitor. Customers ordered a normal supply of products without investing in an overstock of Anti-Skid to get the discount. The 10% discount was paid only on the promoted item and only for the promotional period. If they did not buy the promoted item, there was no cost to W & R. In addition, there was nothing the competitor could do to create another level of competition that W & R could not match or better.

Margin Markdown Sharing. There is another way to generate promotional money without increasing the budget. This method is used extensively in food marketing (grocery) and for many mass consumer markets. It lends itself well to short-term promotions for seasonal products of any type. This promotional budget is generated by what is termed *margin markdown sharing.* This is a fairly complicated method, but once understood it can be very useful. Consider the following example of how it works.

In this marketing scenario, the Hand Tool Company is offering a pre-season buying program to the trade (the channel intermediaries) for garden rakes. This promotion is scheduled to end about the time gardening activities begin. The timing is different in the three marketing zones identified as the Southern Zone, the Central Zone, and the Northern Zone. This is a *pass-through* promotion to the user, who receives a 25% discount off the listed price if the product is purchased before the cutoff date. These rakes retail for a normal price of $20 each. The discount represents a margin markdown to the retailer of $5 per unit. The retailer's normal profit is 40%, or $8 per unit. The margin of profit on the sale price of $15 is $3, or a margin of only 20% on the selling price ($3 ÷ $15 = 20%). To restore the retailer's margin of profit to 40% on the promotional selling price of $15, the retailer would need an additional $3, rather than $5, representing the *dollar* markdown. Since this is a pass-through promotion, the wholesaler would give the retailer $3 credit for each rake purchased during the promotional period. This allows the retailer to make the normal 40% profit ($6) on the sale of rakes at $15 each.

Wholesalers in this example make a margin of 25% on their sales to retailers. The regular wholesale price for the rakes—that is, what retailers pay—is $12 per unit. Wholesalers make 25% of $12, or $3, for rakes that cost them $9 each. During the promotion, the wholesaler must sell rakes to retailers for $9 to restore the $3 margin loss. The $9 price to retailers leaves the wholesaler with no profit. The normal $3 profit was used to reduce the retail price to $9 from $12. The manufacturer must reduce the price paid by the wholesaler to ensure the normal 25% profit on the selling price to retailers, or 25% of $9 = $2.25 profit for the wholesaler. Each of the channel intermediaries has thus made a full margin of profit on sales of promotional merchandise. Each has also contributed to part of the cost of the promotion through the margin markdown. The Hand Tool Company has offered a $5 discount to the user for a total cost to the company of only $2.25. The retailer gave up $2 of profit, the wholesaler gave up $.75, and the manufacturer $2.25. This is margin markdown sharing.

In this example, the Hand Tool Company is assured it will not spend promotional money for the margin markdown in excess of $2.25 per unit. Of even greater importance, the company is spending its money only for units purchased by the retailer, not for units purchased by the wholesaler for inventory. A word of caution is necessary on margin markdown sharing: These programs are not easily understood, and they are difficult to administer. This type of program is used only when the budget is limited.

Table 10.6
Motivation for Channel Members

Motivational Interests

1. Management	Profits, terms, volume allowances, training programs, selling help.
2. Purchasing	Terms, volume discounts, good prices (cost).
3. Service people	Product quality, timely delivery, regulatory support, guarantees.
4. Salespeople	Price, commission, spiffs, bonuses, merchandising aids, competitive marketing programs.

MOTIVATION FOR THE CHANNEL MEMBERS

An important element of any promotional program is planning how to motivate each channel member to fully support the promotional program presented. Selling the program to the channel is sometimes more difficult than selling to the target audience. Even the best-planned promotions must have full channel support to be successful.

Marketing channel managers need to be well informed about the motivational differences of the three major groups in the channel: the internal sales group (the manufacturer's people), the wholesaler's sales force, and the retailer's salespeople. None of these sales groups can be overlooked in the promotional planning.

Motivation for the Trade. The intermediary members of the marketing channel, referred to as *the trade*, include the wholesaler and the retailer. Wholesalers and retailers each have management groups, purchasing people, service people, and their own sales force. The motivational programs required to be effective with each must be considered. The most critical motivational interests of those in the trade are outlined in Table 10.6.

For most companies involved in the promotion of industrial products, we seldom find a channel with more than one wholesale level and the retail level. If there are other levels in the channel, as is the case in some industries, they too need to be considered for motivational support of the program.

Channel managers must know the identity of the decision makers who influence the buying decision at each level in the channel. It is logical to think that the person who controls the action is the most important.

Internal Level. For the internal level, it is the manufacturer's salespeople who can most greatly influence the buying decision of the company's

Table 10.7
Performance Measurements

1. Percentage by which the previous year's sales are exceeded (dollars or units).

2. Dollars increase x % increase=index. The highest index indicates the greatest performance.

3. Last year + growth %=quota in either dollars or units. Measure performance against quota as a percentage.

4. Percent increase in sales over previous year times total dollars sold. This method equalizes large- and small territory opportunities.

customers in the channel. Sometimes management is reluctant to provide cash incentives for the sales force. When this is the case, other motivational incentives may be implemented. Those who may be involved in internal motivational programs are the sales force, sales management, and people who may be performing customer services.

Performance Awards and Measurements. How the company determines who wins the sales awards for a motivational program critically affects whether or not the sales force will in fact consider the program motivational. Goals should be fair and possible for everyone to reach. More importantly, the rules governing how the promotion is run should be perceived to provide all participants an equal opportunity to reach the goal or quota.

Using a specific dollar level for all to reach is easy for the big sales territories but is tough on the small ones. It is a good idea to stay away from specific dollar increases as a means of measuring performance. The use of percent increases, rather than dollar goals, makes the playing field level for big and small alike.

One word of caution is needed in considering what motivation to offer a sales force: Do not ask the salespeople what they want. The answer will be different for everyone. Usually a salesman offered a choice between $1,000 cash award and a weekend in Las Vegas with his wife will say, "Give me the money." His wife will say, "Give me the trip." It is up to the marketing channel manager to determine what will work and then offer no choices. Consult Table 10.7 for alternatives.

PRICING METHODS AND ANALYSIS

Pricing and pricing strategies have been discussed thus far only in the context of marketing promotions; however, there is another side to pricing that channel managers must control. We refer to the basic pricing concepts and strategies associated with product positioning.

There are three basic pricing methods used by most companies marketing industrial products: *cost-plus, value pricing,* and *product position pricing.* These same pricing methods are also used extensively by consumer products manufacturers. Channel managers need to be familiar with their own company's pricing practices as well as the practices of members at each level of the marketing channel. The success of marketing programs in the channel are dependent upon the basic pricing strategies of a company and the promotional pricing programs of the marketer.

Cost-Plus Pricing Method

The most basic concept for pricing a product is to determine its cost and add to that a figure for profit, resulting in the selling price. This is the cost-plus method of pricing. There is considerably more to it however than that simple calculation. Arriving at a products cost requires knowledge of many factors. The same can be said for setting a profit figure or percentage of profit.

The cost-plus method is preferred by manufacturers who have excellent control over the product's cost. It is also the method of choice for channel intermediaries and marketers who buy from contract manufacturers and have a fixed product cost. Cost-plus will not always provide the seller with the highest level of profit obtainable from the sale of a product. Making the expected profit when using a cost-plus pricing method requires that the marketers maintain close control over product costs and marketing expenses or, when costs increase, be willing to accept a lower profit if the selling price is to remain stable. In most cases, the selling price is more flexible for cost-plus pricing than for the other two methods.

Retailers who buy products and put them into inventory at a price that will not change frequently use the cost-plus method by the addition of a standard markup to the product cost. Food markets use the markup method because products are bought and sold very rapidly with frequent price changes. However, the operating costs are stable for food market operations. When the cost of doing business is stable and the cost and prices of the products sold change rapidly, the markup method of cost-plus pricing is a good choice.

Standard Markup Pricing. In standard markup pricing, the selling price is the result of adding a fixed profit percentage, called markup, to the fixed cost of the product. The profit percentage is always calculated as a percentage of the product cost.

EXAMPLE A. A product with a $1.00 fixed cost and a 50% profit markup has a selling price of $1.50. The calculations for markup pricing are simple: $1.00 (cost) $\times$ .50 (markup %) = $0.50 profit. The selling price is calculated as follows: $1.00 product cost + $0.50 markup profit = $1.50 selling price.

EXAMPLE B. The second cost-plus pricing method calculates the margin of profit based on the selling price rather than as a markup from cost, as in Example *A*. The same product with the same cost will provide only a 33.3% profit margin at the same selling price. The profit margin is expressed as a percentage of the selling price. Calculations for the margin of profit are as follows: $1.50 selling price − $1.00 the product cost = $0.50 profit ÷ $1.50 the selling price = 33.3% profit margin. Here, the margin of profit is *always* based on the selling price, not the product cost.

VALUE PRICING

Value pricing starts with the market rather than with the product. Just as there are two methods of cost-plus pricing there are two methods of value pricing: the *cost-to-benefit method* and the *return-on-investment method*. Value pricing is a strategy based on the known value of the product related to a measurable benefit to the user. The cost-to-benefit pricing method is based on the profit benefit received from using the product, whereas the return-on-investment pricing method is centered on cost improvements or savings attributed to using the product.

Cost-to-Benefit Ratio Pricing

Corn farmers who control their weeds with a chemical herbicide destroy weeds and thereby conserve for the corn the moisture and fertilizer that is available in the soil. The value of performing this function is directly related to the use of the herbicide and requires the farmer to judge the value of the product they use. If farmers calculate they can spend $10 per acre on herbicide and receive a $30 benefit, then the cost-to-benefit represents a ratio of 1 to 3. This value is the *cost-to-benefit ratio*. For each $1 of cost, a benefit of $3 will be expected. The greater the benefit received to the cost paid, the more value there is from using the product. The perceived product value can be converted into a strategy for pricing to reflect what the user will pay and still receive a benefit for the price charged. The cost-to-benefit ratio is applied to each use of the product. Current factors of evaluation will apply to each transaction: they will be different for each situation. The cost-to-benefit ratio must be easily understood by channel members who can determine a clear value from using the product. As a further illustration, consider the cost-to-benefit value for automobile collision insurance. If the policy costs $1,000 per year and the car is worth $25,000, the cost-to-benefit ratio is 1 to 25 and a good value can be perceived. If the car is worth only $2,500 and the policy costs $500, the cost-to-benefit ratio drops to 1 to 5 and the value of the insurance is questionable. The five key decision factors concerning the cost-to-benefit pricing method follow.

Cost-to-Benefit Ratio Factors

- The decision to buy is a value judgment based on the profit benefit or increased production from using the product.

- The buying decision is based on current use conditions and is evaluated on the benefits received from each use of the product.

- A firm control over the product cost is essential to maintain a stable selling price.

- A value judgment must be established that is quickly acceptable to the user.

- A price that would provide a low cost-to-benefit ratio may limit the number of buyers. If the benefit is high enough to stimulate a decision to use the product, then the product choice is tied to other product characteristics.

Return-on-Investment Pricing Method

The return-on-investment method is significantly different from cost-to-benefit pricing. Both are variations on the value pricing method. The considerations for return-on-investment pricing must be made with a much longer payout period. These strategies are usually based on cost savings rather than upon increased benefits. They may also be directly measured in increased productivity. Cost savings may be spread over an entire production period or over the lifetime for a piece of machinery. The value of a product is based on its ability to increase the production rate or provide a lower per-unit cost.

As an example, consider a manufacturer who can produce 1,000 units of production each day with the existing equipment in the factory. The manufacturer has learned of a machine that can produce 2,000 units per day using the same amount of energy and human resources as the existing machine. The decision to be made is whether or not to invest in the new equipment to increase production. What are the key points related to this decision for investment in the new machinery?

The most critical factor in this example is the cost per unit of production, considered in terms of the time it takes to pay for the new machine, compared to continuing with the old machine. Also involved in the decision is the debt service factor. The old machine may be completely depreciated, whereas the cost of debt service for the new one will have to be deducted from the investment benefit. Another key decision factor is to calculate the benefit of twice the production rate to determine if it is needed. Other factors relate to the per-unit cost of energy and human resources and whether or not the savings will result in new business. Also to be determined is whether the quality of the product would benefit the manufacturer entailed with the new machine. A final consideration may be what to do with the old machine.

In general, companies that price their products using the return-on-investment method to justify their pricing strategy will have considerable information to present to potential buyers. The pricing strategies are set for long-term investment and continuous benefit of the investment through the lifetime of the product. These savings may be expressed in terms of energy use, running time, quality enhancement, work efficiency, labor savings, and even pleasure from the operation of a more efficient unit.

Product Position Pricing

The product position pricing method tries to·establish prices relative to specific competitive products as well as against specific companies that are competitors. The competitive pricing relationship, or product position in the market, is a choice. The strategy may be to price products *equal to* the competition. It may also be to price products *lower than* most competitors to attract the price buyers. Lower pricing is considered *economy price positioning*. Alternatively, the pricing strategy may be to price higher than competitors of similar products. Higher pricing is sometimes referred to as *quality pricing*. The strategy in this case is intended to imply the higher price is there for a good reason.

With product position pricing, a company will determine its major competitors' pricing strategies and price its products in relationship to these companies. The new prices will be either higher, lower, or equal. The company will then try to maintain the planned strategic pricing relationship as a basic pricing position for most products in the company's line. If the company believes it offers superior quality and product uniqueness that provides a favorable cost-to-benefit ratio when compared to the products of competitive companies, then it may, as a standard, set prices that are higher than those of their competitors. This will probably be a price that is always higher than the competition by a set percentage. When companies choose to position their products equal to the predominant prices in the market, they do not wish pricing to be a consideration in the buying decision. Companies with well-recognized brands will frequently take pricing out of the picture and price equal to competition as a basic strategy. Other companies using the product positioning pricing strategy may choose to be recognized as the economy choice. They will offer their products at a lower price and try to give value for the quality they offer even though quality may be lower than some competitors. Not everyone shops for Cadillac products. The key to using the competitive positioning pricing strategy is to be sure the target audience agrees with the position the manufacturer has chosen. A company that wishes to be recognized as the high price, quality line, must be easily recognized to deserve this position. The use of competitive positioning, relative to the company and its competition, will have an impact on the company's image. Utilization of competitive positioning as a pricing strategy should be understood and supported by both the internal organization and all of the channel members.

Inventory and Pricing Considerations

A product price increase will affect inventories in the channel positively, since all inventories will be worth more. On the other hand, a price decrease will adversely affect the value of the channel member's inventories if nothing is done to protect their value. For this reason, programs involving price decreases must address the inventory problem that may be created. Two programs may be used to alleviate inventory problems brought on by a price decrease: *inventory protection* and *inventory cost averaging*.

Inventory Protection. A manufacturer may decide to protect the value of inventory from price decline as a matter of channel management policy. Such a policy would be necessary to encourage channel members to accept loading programs offered by the company. The following example illustrates how a 100% inventory protection policy works.

A wholesaler who has fifty cases of a product in inventory at the time of a $5-per-case drop in the wholesale price would receive a $250 credit to "equalize" the inventory value with the new price ($5 × 50 = $250). This provides the wholesaler with 100% price protection of the inventory value. When the price decline is directed to retailers, however, a completely different set of circumstances comes into play. In the following example, the objective of the marketing company—the group that must provide inventory protection to the channel members—is to protect the wholesaler's profit percentage on sales to retailers.

Example. A general price reduction of $10 per case is offered to retailers by a major competitor on an item costing $100 per case. The company decides to "me too" this competitive offer and reduces its suggested price to retailers by $10 per case. Wholesalers, who make 25% profit on the price at which they sell to retailers, will receive an inventory protection credit of $7.50 per case (75% of the price decline) for each case *in stock* in the form of a credit of $7.50 ($10 less the profit of $2.50 on the price reduction). With this policy, the wholesaler can sell to retailers for $10 less and will still make a 25% profit even though the percentage represents fewer dollars. These statistics appear as follows:

	Old Price		New Price
• Retail price	$100.00	New retail price	$90.00
• Wholesalers' inventory cost	$ 75.00	New inventory cost	$67.50
• Inventory credit allowance	$ 7.50	Adjusted old inventory cost	$67.50

Inventory protection attempts to eliminate the price change effect on the wholesaler's profit percentages. If the price reduction is at the user level, then retail prices may also need to be protected. Frequently retailer price protection is in the form of inventory price averaging, not direct credit to offset the price differential.

Inventory Price Averaging. Inventory price averaging is usually employed to equalize a price decrease at the retail level. This method of inventory cost adjustment can be used with wholesalers but it is much less common for wholesalers than direct inventory protection.

Inventory price averaging is calculated to allow the buyer an opportunity to buy new inventory at a price sufficiently *below* the new lower inventory cost to result in an average total inventory cost equal to the new lower price. This action allows the retailer to make a normal profit percentage on all sales of the product, whether from inventory on hand at the time of the price change or from newly purchased inventory.

Example. A retailer has 100 units of a product in inventory that normally sell for $10 per unit. The retailer makes 40% profit, resulting in a cost of $6 per unit. The marketer of the product introduces a $2 per unit price-off promotion to users in order to meet a competitive offer. The new consumer price is $8 per unit, or a 20% price reduction from the normal $10 retail price. If nothing is done to adjust the on-hand inventory cost, the retailer will lose half its profit ($2) when selling the inventory.

The method of determining an inventory adjustment for the margin markdown calculation is as follows: The selling price reduction is $2 per unit. The retailer's margin of profit on the $2 price reduction is $0.80 (40% of $2). The retailer's profit is the amount the manufacturer will mark down the $2 price reduction, which results in an adjustment of $1.20 per unit. The adjustment is *not* available as a cash payment. Rather, the retailer is offered an opportunity to buy new inventory equal to the number of units on hand. The adjusted price of $3.60 per unit is calculated thus: The new price of $4.80 is reduced by $1.20 (the adjustment), resulting in a price of $3.60 per unit. This provides for an average inventory cost of $4.80 per unit for the entire 200-unit inventory and a profit of 40% on all sales.

One problem with inventory cost averaging is that it can create an excess of inventory at the retail level. Of course, the assumption made by most companies involved in price reduction programs is that the lower price will stimulate increased usage or consumption of the product and allow the retailer to sell inventory faster.

Commentary. Pricing policies and strategies involve everyone in the marketing channel. Seldom will managers find an issue over which more controversy is generated than with price changes. What a company does in managing its pricing policies is visible to everyone and will make some channel members happy and leave others aggravated. Channel members should accept the fact that not everyone will be satisfied with how pricing and pricing problems are handled. Rely on the points made regarding why a company should initiate a promotion or pricing action as well as the basic rules of promotion shown in Table 10.5. With thorough planning and documentation, a channel manager can usually provide acceptable justification for an action even if it is not popular with everyone.

ADVERTISING

Throughout this chapter, advertising is referred to as an activity of communication for marketing channel managers. This is true in that all forms of advertising attempt to attract attention and project a message. Much more than the simple act of communicating is involved, however. Advertising also solicits a specific response to the message it conveys through various media.

The marketing channel cannot operate without accurate and frequent intercommunication. There are direct communications with users through many media sources. There are also indirect communications disseminated to channel intermediaries who carry the message to users. Indirect communication may be as subtle as the label design for a product or as graphic as a video presentation on product use.

Advertising Tasks

The advertising department is involved in numerous tasks, including

- *creating materials* for all types of channel communications
- *producing graphic materials* such as ads, displays, literature, selling sheets, sales aids, and product presentations
- *planning advertising actions*, including media selection, copy message, communications frequency, market reach, testing and evaluating promotional materials, and budgeting
- *developing training materials* such as audiotapes, videotapes, training manuals, movies, and meetings
- *planning trade shows*, along with developing booth construction, handout materials, displays, programs, and meetings
- *performing internal tasks* related to acting as a marketing advisor as well as overseeing the production of the company paper or magazine, and company meetings and conventions
- *planning channel member meetings*, management meetings, sales meetings, and other group functions

Table 10.8
Advertising Tasks

1. Identify the *target audience* of the advertising objective.

2. Create the *message* that will be the theme of the communications.

3. Select the *media* to be used to *reach* the target audience.

4. Determine the *frequen*cy at which the message must be presented to make the needed *impressions* and establish *notation*.

5. *Pre-test* the ad with members of the target audience for understanding and notation.

6. Perform follow-up *research* with the target audience and in the market for responses.

To select the most important tasks of the advertising group that apply directly to channel management, see Table 10.8.

Planning and Managing Advertising Actions. The need to use advertising with promotions and other marketing programs is obvious. Advertising managers form a part of the marketer's or manufacturer's management group. The advertising manager's advice and skills are important in establishing effective channel programs.

In general, media programs are directed either to the trade—that is, to channel intermediaries—or to users of the company's products. The advertising task to the trade is to present a message that will create support for the company and its products. The message should also promote participation in all the company's marketing programs. All channel managers should be familiar with the advertising tools as well as the process used in producing effective communication. Based upon the advice of the advertising department that will create the media materials, the marketing channel manager will establish parameters for the advertising tasks necessary to the advertising campaign. These tasks are listed in Table 10.8.

Target Audience. Who is to be reached? The target audience is identified and described (profiled) by the channel manager. Although this group is generally recognized as one category of users or consumers, one message may be directed to rural populations, and a significantly different message may be directed to metropolitan audiences.

Message. The message strategy is a theme selection centered on price, value, product satisfaction, utility, or some other product benefit or program advantage. The message content will be tailored for the audience to which it is directed.

Media Selection and Reach. Once the target audience has been identified and the message theme has been decided, how to reach the target is the next concern. Which media should be employed? Use print publications, radio, television, direct mail, meetings, telephone, or whatever communications tool available that will reach the target audience and effectively carry the message.

More than one medium, may be selected for the communications. Radio and print media may be supplemented with a direct mail campaign, for example. If print publications are selected, which magazines or newspapers should be used? The readership data available from the publications should show a high percentage of the target audience in the figures. This would indicate a high probability of reaching those who would most favorably respond to the message. Often it is necessary to use several publications to accomplish the "reach" objectives, usually measured as a percentage of the total target audience *reached* over the duration of the campaign with the media mix that is employed.

Frequency. How often and over what period of time must the message be presented to get the action response desired? Simply put, the advertising message must be placed, broadcast, mailed, phoned, or viewed often enough for the company to obtain the percentage of notation desired.

Impressions or Notation. Notation means that an impression has been made on the target audience. Notation is measured two ways: The most desired impression is the unaided recall of the advertisement's message. An aided response also qualifies as a notation, but this type of recall has a much lower *buy ratio* than the unaided response. The buy ratio is the percentage of those who noted the advertisement and then bought the product as the message directed. One should know how many impressions are made on the target audience with the media used, the reach, the frequency, and the message. Research during the ad campaign can provide this important measurement.

Pretesting the Ad. Research groups will perform the job of pretesting the ad for understanding and response to the message, should it be necessary. The more one knows about the effectiveness of the advertisement, the more one can predict with confidence the success of the program. Because pretesting is expensive, it is not used when the advertising effort is small or short term.

Research. When the advertising and promotional campaign is over, the channel manager must research the market to determine what parts of the program were the most successful. It is well to canvas all marketing channel participants for their opinions regarding any major promotion. It is just as important to determine what did not work. Learning where not to spend promotional money will save the budget for those programs that bring results.

Using the Professionals. To use advertising properly requires professional judgment. Depending on the size of the company, its advertising budget, and the products involved, the advertising manager will be able to establish resources to help in making advertising decisions. Numerous facilitating agencies are available to perform tasks involving everything from designing corporate logos to the production of a movie or video. The company's advertising manager will provide the liaison with these agencies as needed.

Channel managers should be involved in the planning of advertising action and evaluating the results it produces.

Comments on Communication. The tasks of communicating are an integral part of promotional planning. These tasks must also be a part of channel management actions and channel planning activities. Channel managers must be sure promotions are communicated to the trade as intended and on time. Probably the greatest error that can be committed by channel managers concerning advertising relates to timing. Never allow the promotion to start before the planned advertising support is in place. It is a waste of money to have advertising break in the media before the channel members have been advised of the promotion. These errors occur frequently because of poor communications.

QUESTIONS FOR DISCUSSION

1. Why are price or discount promotions usually short term?
2. Before one reacts to a competitive promotion, what should be done?
3. List five reasons why a manufacturer should plan a product promotion.
4. What incentives are used to motivate wholesalers? retailers?
5. Explain the difference between markup profit and margin of profit.
6. Explain the basic concept of product positioning.
7. What is meant by open-ended budgeting for a promotion?
8. Discuss how to plan a self-generated promotional budget.
9. What are five basic elements in planning an advertising program?
10. Define how the terms *reach* and *frequency* relate to the target audience.

ELEVEN

The Marketing Channel Planning Process

Every company has its own format for writing marketing plans. Any process used that produces effective plans is acceptable. What one company requires for documentation and planning layout may be quite different from what another company requires. Yet there are certain basic elements that should be a part of any planning method. The purpose of this presentation is to provide a process for gathering information, evaluating it, structuring it in the correct sequence, and logically presenting it in the form of a marketing plan. When followed, the process presented will provide reasonable marketing channel planning process objectives with strategies and action plans to accomplish them. The marketing channel planning process must be sufficiently detailed to chart the action path. It must also be simple enough to follow.

Much has changed in the way business is conducted since Henry Ford said, "Nothing happens until something is sold." Had this thought been strictly adhered to, the Ford Motor Company would have failed. This idea was inspired by a manufacturing approach to the market. In the past, a car was first ordered and then produced. Even today, assembly lines will manufacture cars according to customer specifications of available options. Henry Ford was also credited with saying, "I'll give them any color they want . . . so long as its black." Shortly after Chrysler-Dodge came out with gray and dark blue, Henry Ford decided he could do that too. The competitive influence is a part of marketing planning and of considerable importance in the selection of marketing channel strategies.

In the 1880s the first flush of consumerism prompted Marshall Fields, the great Chicago department store entrepreneur, to say, "The customer is always right" and "You never win an argument with a customer." This concept was a giant step in the direction of developing a marketing function. This thinking reflected the realization that the customer (channel member) has needs and wants that go far beyond the product and its price. The consumer's needs and wants are also considered in the channel planning process and are documented in the opportunities and obstacles section of the plan.

Marketing plans provide for the functions and programs necessary to ensure the satisfaction not only of the customer's needs but also those of all marketing channel members. These plans also employ every avenue of channel communications in creating a product message that offers the perception of value and satisfaction to the user. These promises are included in the programs that create the motivation to buy.

Since the success of marketing planning is dependent upon information gathering and analysis, the computer and its many applications is an essential tool for this activity. Historical data, forecasting, and the projecting of probabilities dependent on specific assumptions lend themselves well to computer applications.

Many millions of dollars are spent each year in support of marketing programs and strategies. Experienced managers know that it takes more than just money and accurate data to produce success. It takes detailed planning and preparation to turn information into an action that wins. This kind of planning also produces the expected profits for all those involved in the marketing channel. Establishing a profit plan is a critical part of the channel planning process. The marketing channel planning process offered in this text will show how to integrate all the necessary data compiled to improve the chances of reaching the predicted outcome in profit and performance. There are seven steps in the marketing channel planning process.

THE MARKETING PLANNING PROCESS

Each step in the marketing planning process is an independent activity built upon the steps established before. For this reason, it is highly important that each step be developed in sequence. As the plan develops, it must have continuity and integrity. It must present facts and planned actions in the sequence of logical occurrence. The plan's integrity is assured by incorporating into each step the foundation necessary to support the conclusions or actions presented in the next step. Similarly, for example, one would not try to collect money from a sale before the trans-

Table 11.1
Seven Steps in the Planning Process

1.   *The Mission Statement.* This step names the plan and establishes the direction of the planning activity.

2.   *The Situation Analysis.* In this step all the historical data related to the planning mission are collected and presented as facts to validate and facilitate the planning mission.

3.   *Opportunities and Obstacles.* Based on the facts developed in Step Two, identification of viable opportunities and potential obstacles to reaching them are presented.

4.   *Goals and Objectives.* Goals are established by selecting from the opportunities in Step Three. Objectives are the interim check points on the way to a goal.

5.   *Strategies for Action.* To reach the goals and objectives in Step Four, specific strategies for action are planned for every major activity.

6.   *Action Plans.* To accomplish the strategic actions of Step Five, provide assignments for action responsibilities. Establish budgets, seek authorizations, set schedules, provide controls and supporting actions to initiate the plan.

7.   *The Profit Plan.* Documents the financial expectations inherent in the plan; project expenses and produce a budget requirement.

action was concluded, nor would one attempt to make a withdrawal from an account in which deposits have not been made. The marketing planning process provides for the identification of the most logical objectives, the preparation of potentially effective programs, and the development of the most successful strategies for accomplishing the goals adopted. Each step in the planning process, along with a brief explanation of its purpose, is listed in Table 11.1.

The marketing planning process is like the combination to the vault. When worked in the correct sequence, the combination can unlock resources stored away in market statistics, competitive analysis, product and market evaluations, trend data, pricing strategies, and the action potential of people in the marketing channel.

This process applies to any type of marketing planning—promotional, organizational, or motivational. The process may even be applied to long-term strategic planning. Some modifications may be needed for specialized planning tasks, but the elements presented here are basic to most marketing channel planning requirements.

Planning Responsibilities

Before trying to work with the details and elements of the process, consider the contributions that may be made by various marketing channel managers.

Upper-Level Marketing Managers. Although the top marketing managers may be involved with several parts of the marketing planning process, they will usually reserve the adoption of marketing strategies as their domain. This group may act as a review and approval group for all the planning activities.

Product and Market Managers. Managers at the product and market level are the most directly involved management group in marketing plan development. Both market and product needs are addressed by these managers. This group is the best resource for opportunities and obstacles information because they maintain close contact with the marketplace and with product development resources. Market and product managers are also involved with goal setting, action plans, and the development of the profit plan.

Advertising and Promotion Managers. Advertising and promotion managers plan how to communicate with both the channel intermediaries and the consumers of the company's products. They are involved with four of the planning activities: setting goals and objectives, determining strategies, developing action plans, and contributing to profit planning.

Market Research Managers. Market and marketing research are both market oriented and program oriented. The key role of research is in the development of the situation analysis. By providing trend data, research may also facilitate decisions relating to the selection of opportunities, strategies, action plans, and the profit plan.

WORKING WITH THE PLANNING PROCESS

Step One: The Mission Statement

The mission statement sets the direction of the marketing plan development. This first step is sometimes referred to as the *planning premise.* In general, the mission statement answers the question, "Why is this plan to be written?" The statement should be made in one paragraph with as few sentences as possible. This is a directional statement. It is almost a subject title.

Mission Statement Example. A manufacturing company is about to prepare the marketing plan for the coming year. The following mission statement was provided by the marketing director to all involved in the preparation of the plan:

Growth by our company during the period of this plan will represent a 15% increase in sales dollars with a 2% increase in net profit before taxes. Ten percent of the dollar growth will come from new-product introductions and 5% from our current products. Since several new products will soon be available for marketing, it will be up to the channel managers to compete for the money available for a new-product introduction budget. Budgets for new-product introduction will not exceed 15% of the profits expected from these products in their introductory year.

This brief statement gives direction and indicates what type of marketing activities and information needs will be presented in the plan. The mission statement may point to what the plan will present, but it cannot say how it expects the plan to evolve except in very general terms. This planning premise statement, for the manufacturing company, could have been as general as simply stating that the company intends to show substantial growth during the plan year. It is better to have something more definitive, but it is not always necessary. If the planning team finds the premise statement to be so vague as not to provide a clear direction, it will need to seek more specific language before trying to move to the next step.

Annual marketing channel plans that strongly rely on the documentation of the previous year tend to be more specific in the premise statement. Plans for short-term project planning require less directional detail. The manufacturing company in this example would need to include a new-product introduction plan as a part of the overall planning document. The new-product introduction segment would probably be started months or years prior to the annual marking channel plan in which it will become active. The new-product introduction plan may have a very general mission statement, such as "Our company has the capability to develop new products that will have a significant impact in improving our sales." This statement simply says, "We can do it!" The plan that follows will answer what, why, when, and how and will explain its impact on the company as well as its position in the market. The mission statement simply points the direction in which the marketing planning process will move.

Step Two: The Situation Analysis

The situation analysis provides all the historical documentation required to follow the direction of the mission statement. Step Two covers products, markets, distribution, competition, capabilities, costs, prices, trends, and any activities that *have already occurred* that relate to the mission statement. As a minimum, all the five *P*'s of the marketing mix must be covered in the development of this step. Step Two: *The Situation Anal-*

ysis, must state all conditions known that would influence future opportunities related to the plan direction. This step deals *only* with facts that have been historically documented. The channel manager's database will provide much of this information.

In the beginning, the situation analysis collects and documents pertinent data to facilitate the planning tasks that come in the steps to follow. The situation analysis does *not* make projections or enumerate assumptions. It deals only with what has already happened. It may analyze the significance of the facts or present comparative data, but it does not speculate or project trend data. At times data based on known situations may be included. Trend data are not projected into the future but represent current trend directions. The situation analysis is the one place in the planning process where no one should be able to question what is stated. It is the historical foundation upon which the plan is built, and it must be made of solid unquestionable facts.

Many channel planners will spend fully one third of the planning time and half or more of the planning costs in developing the facts of the situation analysis. Since most historical data are gathered in an ongoing systematic process, it is not necessary to start writing the new situation analysis from scratch every year. The process is usually an "add on and analyze" one as new data are made available to the channel manager and added to the database.

The first obligation of the situation analysis is to provide all the data necessary to accurately support the opportunities and obstacles developed in the third step. In Step Three: *Opportunities and Obstacles*, the planners must start to make assumptions critical to the success of the entire plan—assumptions projected from the facts developed in the situation analysis. If the facts presented in this step are inaccurate or incomplete, the entire plan will risk failure.

Some companies are willing to use *projected* trend data in the situation analysis to support opportunities identified in Step Three. This practice is risky, as trend forecasts are not based on fact but, rather, are speculative concerning existing facts that indicate what could happen in the future. If trend data are to be used in the identification of opportunities, managers should verify at the last possible moment, before the plan is adopted, whether the trend data are accurate and sustainable. Companies that have had good experience with trend forecasting are the most inclined to use projections to support opportunities.

The final statement presented in the situation analysis must directly support or reject the mission statement of Step One. In the case of our example concerning the manufacturing company, this direct statement is usually based on market research data and may include the following comments:

Market Research Report Example. The current five-year market figures show a growth trend of 5% per year in market size, expressed in dollars. This trend would support a growth expectation of 5% for our current product line during the plan year. The growth in unit sales volume has not been evaluated. Research reports show the market has a significant need (actual numbers should be presented) for products like those that our company is developing and will introduce during the plan period. If new products can be introduced early during the plan year, they should capture a 10% market share as indicated in Step Two. Based on these facts, the mission statement is supported by the situation analysis.

The scope of the situation analysis will vary with the need for channel planning. Annual planning for the whole product line will be extensive. At the very least, each step of the situation analysis should cover the elements of the marketing mix, namely, products, prices, programs, physical distribution, and people.

Step Three: Opportunities and Obstacles

Determine which specific opportunities are viable. List known obstacles to the achievement of these opportunities. Step One identifies the direction the plan will follow. Step Two provides the pertinent facts of the current situation for the environment in which the plan will operate. Based on these historical facts and knowledge of the current situation, one can project which opportunities are possible and identify the obstacles that may stand in the way of adopting these opportunities as goals to be achieved.

Specific opportunities must be identified as factually and as completely as possible. If a new-product introduction is projected at a specific time in the plan period, then this opportunity must be specifically stated. It must also be supported with research reports and market data related to the new product's capability to fulfill the opportunity identified. This is the step that identifies what may be done. Whether or not it should be done comes in Step Four: *Goals and Objectives.* How to do it will be found in Step Five: *Strategic Planning.* Who takes the responsibility for specific actions is in Step Six: *Action Plans,* and results are expressed in financial terms in the final step, *The Profit Plan.*

Step Three is simply a compilation of the capabilities available to move the plan in the indicated direction. Manufacturing companies may list strengths and weaknesses in evaluating their capabilities, and they may identify many opportunities that will not be pursued even if their capability to do so is unquestioned. When identifying opportunities, immediately follow each one with a statement related to any known significant obstacle in pursuit of that opportunity. It will be necessary to make assumptions at this time and it is *appropriate* to do so. In the next step, where goals are set, assumptions may *not* be used to support a goal that the plan recommends. Any assumption made in the identification of an opportunity must be listed as an assumption and not presented as fact in the text of the opportunity statement. Assumptions must also be supported with factual data from the situation analysis. If supporting data do not substantially justify the assumption, delete the assumption and reevaluate the opportunity.

This method of plan development for opportunity identification also adds a factor for a risk and reward assessment. The selection of one opportunity over another may be made based on the least risk rather than on optimum opportunity factors. This analysis is made not in the opportunities and obstacles section but in the goals and objectives section. Providing the necessary information for risk assessment and for the potential rewards of the opportunities is essential, since this information makes the selection process possible.

Step Three should result in the tabulation and risk assessment of several viable opportunities in order of a *value factor* to the company, such as cost to develop or profit potential, but no priority selection should be claimed at this time. Since Step Four will result in the selection of opportunities for which goals and objectives may be established, it is best *not* to set priorities of opportunities.

The final task for identification of opportunities and obstacles is to verify that each opportunity presented is supported with a direct reference to the situation analysis. All opportunities must be fully supported by the facts in Step Two.

Since channel management deals with the elements of the marketing mix, each opportunity should assess product and market opportunities, price options, program potential, physical distribution impact, and the people-related needs. In the example of the manufacturing company, the list of opportunities and obstacles would contain the following:

Opportunity. Introduce Product *A* on May 1 of the plan year. This product will be ready for market by March 1, with manufacturing to begin February 1. Manufacturing has confirmed this production schedule (Joe Josephs, production coordinator, memo of 12/1/–).

The marketing mix impact is as follows:

1. *Product comparisons* for quality and utility show our product to be equal or superior to those in the market (channel managers will present the actual product comparisons).

2. *Prices,* as projected in the introduction plan, show that our product is priced competitively yet still exceeds our profit objective by 10% (actual price comparisons are presented).

3. *Programs* normally used by our competition, including advertising and promotional programs, are not expected to have a negative effect on our sales projections. These competitive programs have not spent more than 10% of the

market share dollars in the past (market research report, Norm Beals, 5/1/–). Our expected promotional budget of 15% of the new product's profits should be adequate.

4. *Physical distribution* capabilities, which are currently established, will be sufficient to handle the new product and its introduction program (memo of 3/23/–, Sally Swift, Transportation and Distribution Department).

5. *People* requirements for the new product present no special training programs, since the product is a type already in use by our channel members and our sales force.

Obstacle to the Introduction of Product A. Cost projections used in the product introduction profile have not been verified and will not be available before production begins. Materials management has assumed that the numbers for cost and profit will be within a plus or minus 5% factor from those used in the introduction profile. The risk factor for this opportunity is considered no more than the identified 5%. Marketing assumes that this small variable can be accommodated by some flexibility in the introductory pricing strategy if necessary.

Analysis of Product A Opportunity. This opportunity is clearly supportive of the mission for the plan (Step One) and is consistent with the data presented in the situation analysis (Step Two). Each of the five elements of the marketing mix has been addressed and presented along with the supporting documentation. The one obstacle mentioned is evaluated as having only a minor impact in product cost and presents a minor risk factor.

Opportunity. Product B should be ready for marketing sometime in the third quarter of the plan year. This is potentially a more profitable product than Product A, and all figures on cost and profitability have been verified by the accounting area. Product B will not have a direct competitor according to market research report A-77:1, dated 9/1/–.

The marketing mix impact is as follows:

1. *Product* features and benefits for this new product offer a breakthrough in the marketing channel and will require channel education in its use and handling, as well as a new cost-to-benefit ratio. The cost-to-benefit ratio of 1 to 10 has been tested by market research, as indicated in reported A-77:1, and has been found to be fully acceptable to channel members.

2. *Price* evaluations show that our new product will be higher than competitive products, but the benefits are far in excess of the cost difference. Profits are much higher than Product A and may be compromised to be competitive.

3. *Programs* for the introduction of this product fit into our long-term marketing programs as a part of the product line. Short-term promotional programs will not be used during the introductory period; rather, the new product will be introduced through normal advertising activities.

4. *Physical distribution* plans for the new product include a testing program for special packaging that will be required to ensure delivery without damage.

5. *People* qualified to train new operators of this equipment will need to be added to the technical service staff. All channel members as well as our own sales people must be trained in the handling and use of this new product. This is an important step in the marketing channel plan which has not yet been evaluated as to cost.

Obstacles to the Introduction of Product B. Product B is not cleared for marketing but is now in the final review process. Normally this process would take six months to complete. We assume Product *B* will not run into any problems and will be ready for a third-quarter introduction. Training the sales force at all channel levels will be an important task. A risk assessment will need to be completed in Step Four for this new product.

Analysis of Product B Opportunity. This product offers channel members and our company an exciting breakthrough-product introduction. Although the profit per unit is high, no calculation of the market size or volume has been made in the opportunity statement. And although training needs are substantial and a risk assessment is needed, the opportunity is supported by all the preceding steps in the plan.

Review of Examples. These two opportunity and obstacle statements provide the involved marketing channel managers with sufficient information upon which to set priorities for the selection of goals and objectives in Step Four. The goals and objectives must be supported by the statements in Step Three.

Step Four: Goals and Objectives

Identify, list, and set priorities for the specific goals and objectives expected to be reached by the plan. Each goal and objective must be the result of an opportunity identified in Step Three.

Reaching specific goals is the final accomplishment of any action plan. It is hitting the target. It is the fulfillment of the plan. Objectives are the critical path checkpoints or intermediate accomplishments that must be reached on the way to the goal. If the objective is to introduce a new product into the market by May 1 and to support a sales goal of $1 million in new sales by September 30, one would identify the May 1 introduction date as a critical checkpoint objective. Should the introduction be delayed for a month or two, the goal of a million would more than likely need to be modified. The effects of failure to reach a specific objective at a specific time may be a part of the objective statement. In the example given for the May 1 introduction, failure to reach the objective may be identified in one of two ways: First, the delay may be expressed as resulting in lower sales dollars produced by the September 30 checkpoint. Second, the failure to launch the introduction on time may be expressed as a delay in reaching the $1 million goal by a specific time. Missing a critical checkpoint objective always requires the channel manager to make alterations in the plan.

The goal-setting activity tells how far we expect to go in the agreed direction and may indicate a time frame as well. The objectives are the checkpoints en route and may even become a formal system of review along the way. Establishing intermediate objectives provides the means to perform two critical plan activities: *review* and *control* of the plan's progress. Some companies tie the availability of certain budgets, such as advertising or promotion spending, to the review and control part of the plan. Every part of a plan that is committed should include a review and control process stated as critical milestones. The critical path review method of evaluating progress for the plan should be written into each action that is required to reach an objective or goal. In the example of the manufacturing company, the following goals and objectives may be indicated as a starting point:

Goal. Introduce Product *A* during the plan year. This product is to contribute a 10% increase in sales dollars.

Objectives. Introduce Product *A* into the market by May 1. Reach sales of $1 million by September 30. Price Product *A* as planned in the product introduction profile. The risk factor for this product introduction lies in the initial cost of the product, which is not considered to be more than a 5% plus or minus variable according the manufacturing group. If necessary, marketing assumes that this variable can be accommodated by flexibility in the initial pricing strategy.

In Step Four, we must provide specific goals and well-defined objectives. A good marketing plan will include goal setting in all areas of the marketing mix. Table 11.2 shows the areas for goal or objective setting as well as the related involvement of the marketing mix.

In general, the goals and objectives selected should cover the markets, products, prices, programs, physical distribution, and people needed in facilitating the plan. The need for services such as manufacturing, financial, and technical support provided by the company may or may not be a necessary part of the plan at this point. Usually references to the support groups in the company will appear in Step Six: *Action Plans.* In situations where there are obstacles that require the cooperation of other areas outside the marketing planning group, the reference to the area involved is a part of Step Four. (In the case of the manufacturing company, the cost estimates needed to complete the profit evaluation are a part of the obstacles mentioned and therefore must be a part of Step Four.)

Since Step Four is not the area of the plan that deals with how to

Table 11.2
Areas for Goal or Objective Setting

1. Sales volume (price)	6. Budget requirements (programs)
2. Profit making (price)	7. Training and technical services (programs)
3. Market and marketing (programs)	8. Product introduction (programs)
4. Manufacturing schedules (product)	9. Distribution needs (physical distribution)
5. Manpower needs (people)	10. Competitive impacts (programs)

accomplish the goals and objectives, the planners can and must be scrupulously objective in setting dates and using numbers that when reached will provide the results of that stated plan. How these results can be obtained is provided in Step Five: *Marketing Strategies.*

Unlike Step Three, where all the viable opportunities are identified, whether intended as goals or not, Step Four lists only the goals and objectives that are to become part of the plan.

The final statement for setting each goal and objective is related to the opportunity that supports it in Step Three: *Opportunities and Obstacles,* where *all* the needed assumptions to support an opportunity are listed. If applied to an adopted goal, these assumptions may need references in Step Four. They may also need modification to fit time schedules or enable commitment of resources for the company to perform each goal.

New assumptions, not introduced in Step Three, should not be made in setting goals and objectives in Step Four, since the initial assumptions are based on facts identified in Step Two. If modified in Step Four, the original reference must be rechecked to verify the support it provides. If several goals are included in the plan, list the priority for their adoption. Budgets may not allow channel managers to follow all their dreams at the same time.

Step Five: Strategy Planning

Strategies are planned actions and activities calculated to result in reaching specific goals and objectives. Strategies must be established for each goal identified in the plan. Strategies must clearly define the course of action, how it is to be implemented, and the expected result of the action.

Writing the strategic plan is the point where most marketing channel managers like to start. The efforts that precede the writing of strategies—

Step One through Step Four—are much less exciting than planning the action. Nevertheless, it is the quality of the work that goes into the preparatory steps that limits or facilitates the creation of strategies that will produce planned actions and activities that will be successful in reaching specific goals.

It is human nature to jump from recognition of a problem or acceptance of a challenge to making a response. As an example, consider the situation that follows.

Strategy-Planning Example. A car is driving down a city street. Following the sound of a small explosion, it swerves to the right and comes to a stop with the right front wheel a good six inches lower than the rest of the car. One of the passengers says, "Darn, a blowout, now we'll be late getting to the office." The other passenger says, "O.K., let's get the spare on, no sense sitting around crying about it." They have jumped from identification of the problem (with no investigation of the facts) to a strategic action they assume will solve it (putting on the spare). The driver says, "Wait a minute. Just as that truck passed by on our left, it backfired. I reacted by pulling to the right and applying the brakes. We stopped because the wheel dropped into a hole in the pavement." He then asks his passengers, "Do you still want to go to the office?" (basic mission: direction). The passengers agree that they do. The driver continues, "I know the noise was a backfire from the truck. I pulled to the right on purpose and stopped with the wheel in a hole" (historical data). He then gets out of the car, examines the wheel, and looks at the street ahead. Upon entering the car again, he states, "The tire is O.K. and not damaged. Also, the street ahead is smooth and has no more holes in it" (current situation analysis). He goes on, "If we intend to get to the office on time, going ahead on this street is our best opportunity and there seems to be no reason we should not" (opportunities and obstacles). He continues, "Our goal is to get to the office and our first objective is to make it to the end of this street" (goals and objectives.) The driver asks, "Should we back out of the hole and avoid getting a rear wheel into it or pull forward in low gear?" (strategy). They all agree to back out.

Do you remember that the first strategy (action) suggested was to put on the spare? It is obvious that this strategy, formed without the detailed information in the first four steps of the planning process, would be a waste of energy.

Strategies must always deal with specific procedures that will bring the results needed to reach planned goals and objectives. To ensure that actions are specific to the need, Step One through Step Four must be followed in detail. Even after recognizing the folly of trying to solve a problem without first determining if there is one, many will immediately jump from recognizing that something needs to be done to attempting to provide the answer. Marketing channel managers must steel themselves against this temptation. One quick check to identify whether the "how to" is appropriate is to ask a very critical "Why?" to whatever action is suggested.

Developing effective strategies is highly important. Yet to define the strategies before specific goals are established and objectives set is difficult, and the wrong strategies can result in disastrous consequences. We can, however, consider the areas where strategic planning is likely.

Product Issues for Strategic Planning. Pricing strategies considered for *positioning* products in the line are product issues. In addition, competitive share and market share strategies are typical strategic planning objectives that are related to products. Strategic packaging considerations are usually related to product size. New packaging design is part of the product strategy. Packaging strategies may be cost and program related when bonus packs are used for a product promotion.

Product claims, benefits, features, guarantees, and mix variations may each be included with strategic plans. The strategic selection of the product feature or benefit to be emphasized can have a great bearing on the perception of the product's effectiveness, competitiveness, value, or capability to satisfy the user's expectations.

Pricing Issues and Strategic Planning. Product positioning is primarily a pricing strategy. In planning new product introductions, the channel manager should have the option to position the new product unlike the rest of the product line. This is not easily accomplished. Normally a strategic price position is related to competitive products in the channel. Whether or not a new product can independently sustain a special position in the market is questionable. New products should be consistent in market position with others in the line. If a company has positioned its products to be in the *economy* price range, it would be difficult to introduce a new product at a *quality* price.

The use of short-term pricing strategies is usually tied to promotional programs. Long-term strategic pricing is a part of the usual terms and volume discounts offered as standard policy. Long-term price strategies are coupled to competitive programs to remain equal, better than, or different in some advantageous way. Discounts, costs, profits, and the competition all contribute to pricing issues. Pricing strategies may be related to product introduction, promotion, value perception, cost association, profit objectives, and competitive influences. Pricing strategies can change from one selling period to another and are also responsive to the competitive influences of other companies. The development of cost-to-benefit ratios is related to pricing strategy.

Marketing Programs

Communications. Strategies related to marketing programs speak to the very reason why the programs are designed and used. Each program has its own strategy to achieve specific objectives or goals. Marketing program communications is one area where strategic planning can find some consistency in channel plans. These are the strategies employed to find the most effective avenue of communications. The advertising message, media selection, reach, notation, frequency, and target audience profile are the communication choices in advertising. Always a part of strategic planning, communications is such a comprehensive topic that it needs to be referenced to specific situations for critical analysis of the strategies involved.

Promotional Programs. A major part of marketing program strategies is directed to product users and the channel members. Here again, the strategies behind the use of specific promotional programs are directly related to the product and the market situation in which the promotional strategies are designed to function. Promotions are usually tied to increasing sales for a specific period, inventory reduction, dealer loading (inventory building), seasonal use needs, or competitive situations. In general, these are the buying and selling programs.

Program Timing. The strategic timing of advertising and promotional programs is critical to their success. If the program is not in place by the time the new product is introduced, to some extent it will be wasted. Promotions are designed to produce specific results within a set period of time.

Training Strategies. The recognition of a need for strategic training is tied to products, programs, and services. Training needed for a new product introduction must be a part of the strategic plan. Usually strategic training is part of an ongoing marketing program.

Budgeting Strategies. The strategic use of money in the support of marketing programs is one of the most necessary and disciplined parts of the planning process. Strategies for the best use of money are essential for plan approval. Money in marketing planning is usually allocated between people, programs, products, distribution costs, and market investments or motivation. Using the self-generating promotional budget for a promotion is a strategy decision.

Physical Distribution

Strategies for product distribution, warehousing, shipping, and marketing channel development are a part of channel planning. When the physical distribution task or marketing channel involvement changes, strategies must be written to support the new activities.

People Issues and Strategic Planning. The motivation and use of internal personnel and external channel members is a part of strategic planning. As in the military, where the deployment of personnel is one of the most studied topics, in business the strategic use of personnel is critical. It is essential to the success of a company's marketing plans and programs. The cost of personnel is one of the greatest expenses for most companies.

When writing strategies, remember that the result must be to reach the plan's goals and objectives. Strategies do *not* replace policies or obviate them. Strategies show how specific actions should take place.

Strategic Plan Flexibility. Unlike any of the four steps in the planning process that precede it, strategic planning should be flexible. If strategies are not working, or if they can be made more effective, they should be changed or modified. All changes must be communicated to the involved parties before they are implemented. Strategies need to be flexible to reflect the changing dynamics of the market, whereas the objectives they are to support, such as budget commitments, may not necessarily be flexible. Strategies are intended as the way to reach the goals and objectives. Goals and objectives are not intended to support strategies.

A separate strategy must be written for each approved objective and goal. These strategies will be linked together in the marketing plan documentation, which will contain rationales or assumptions for each strategy adopted.

Step Six: Action Plans

Plans for action, support requirements, authorities, schedules, controls, measurements, and responsibility assignments are considered in the action plan. Action plans are required to implement the strategic actions detailed in Step Five. Each strategy should have a detailed action plan, along with the accompanying schedules and support requirements, to assure its success. Some marketing planners like to write the strategic action assignment, sometimes called *tactical plans*, following each strategy. This method has the advantage of making a cost analysis possible for the development and execution for each strategy. Writing action plans in support of strategies is not difficult. These *assignments*, or action responsibilities, are a part of the job requirements of those involved and in many cases are performed routinely.

Step Six: *Actions Plans* ensures that all needed actions are planned, assigned, scheduled, budgeted, and *accepted* by the responsible parties. When the actions and responsibilities are included in the strategy planning, rather than the action planning, they tend to get lost. It is also necessary that channel managers have a checklist of who does what, when, and how. Control of the budget is made easier when all those who share in the expenditures are identified on one list. Some channel planners list actions along with the strategy they support, as well as write a separate action plan for each action.

In many cases the action plan will involve several people. Assigning the planning task to the functional marketing area means it can be shared as needed under the direction of the manager for the specific marketing function involved. Staff marketing managers, product and market managers, advertising and promotion managers, and those involved in market research may all be involved with action planning. The following lists show the actions appropriate for each marketing function.

Action Plan Responsibilities

Staff Marketing Managers or Directors

1. Make the assignments for action plans and responsibilities.
2. Control budgets and allocate resources.
3. Approve the manpower requirements.
4. Receive reports and coordinate actions.
5. Evaluate and control all action plan activities.
6. Obtain all authorizations necessary for plan implementation.
7. Establish the review and control activities and responsibilities.
8. Report on plan progress to all functional areas involved.
9. Act as the *plan manager* or coordinator.

Product and Market Managers

1. Take responsibility for all product-related actions and programs.
2. Assume the responsibility for all market-related actions and programs.
3. Accept responsibility to be sure regulatory and legal guidelines are communicated.
4. Prepare periodic reports for staff managers.

Advertising and Promotion Managers

1. Take responsibility for all communication actions.
2. Facilitate the implementation of promotional programs and trade motivation.
3. Direct the production of all merchandising materials for action plans.
4. Prepare periodic reports for the marketing channel managers.

Research Managers (Market and Marketing)

1. Produce all historical and current demographic data in support of action plans.
2. Monitor, test, measure, and analyze data collected on action plan progress.
3. Produce current market or marketing activity data, as required by channel managers.
4. Prepare periodic reports for the channel managers.

Action plans provide for the allocation of all the resources needed to accomplish the strategies adopted. This makes the action plan almost a supplement of the strategic plan. Step Five and Step Six always work in concert with each other.

Step Seven: The Profit Plan

The profit plan—or *business plan*, as it is called in some companies—documents financial expectations based on reaching the plan objectives and goals as presented. This activity provides for the detailed preparation of a marketing budget required to accomplish the plan.

The final and most critical planning step in the entire process, the profit plan documents in detail the costs of every function and action. It also projects the profits that can be expected if the plan reaches the goals. Finally, it produces the detailed budget required to reach the plan goals and objectives.

This final step may also provide an economic report concerning the cost of money, situation analysis of the business environment, review of corporate capabilities, and commitments to support the plan's financial needs along with an analysis of the expected sales and marketing performance. This economic projection is done independently of any plan assumptions or conditions of the situation analysis. It is meant to be a critical review of capabilities and expectations from the point of view of corporate interests and is usually prepared by the head of the marketing department with help from all corporate departments involved.

In many companies, a preview of the profit plan will become Step One and will precede the presentation of the annual marketing plan. Upper management does not care to deal with an evaluation of goals, objectives, strategies, and action planning if the result expressed in financial terms would be unsatisfactory. A review of the results produced by reaching the plan goals and objectives can be provided in a profit plan preview before any of the marketing planning is started. If the figures are acceptable to upper management, the marketing channel planning process can begin. The detail of the profit plan becomes Step Seven.

At the very least, the profit plan must provide a detailed sales forecast, cost estimates for all areas involved, and the gross and net profits expected before taxes. A quarterly cost and profit projection will provide cash flow expectations and budget needs for the period. An approved profit plan will provide a preliminary budget figure for planning purposes. Once top management has agreed to both revenues and budgets, it is ready to look at the complete marketing plan. Upper-level managers will determine the probability of reaching these financial goals by the strategies, actions, and assumptions in the complete marketing channel plan. The appropriate documentation should always accompany finan-

Table 11.3
Profit Plan Preparation

Management Activities	Contributing Areas
Sales Forecasts	Channel Managers, Market Research
Product Cost	Channel Managers, Manufacturing
Marketing Costs	Channel Managers, Product Mgt. A&P & Research
Profit Projections	Channel Managers, Product Mgt., Finance
Economic Assumptions	Channel Managers, Research
Competitive Assumptions	Channel Managers, Product Mgt., Market Research
Regulatory Assumptions	Channel Managers, Product Mgt., Legal
Production Scheduling	Channel Managers, Manufacturing
Inventory Control	Channel Managers, Product Mgt.
Product Action Plans	Channel Managers, Product Mgt., Market Research
Manpower Plan	Channel Managers, Human Resources
Budget Request	Channel Managers, Financial

cial planning of any kind. The profit plan, prepared as a pre–marketing plan document, must clearly identify the source of statistical information it has used in support of the plan.

The profit plan is produced by the collective collaboration of all marketing channel managers. In addition, managers from several other corporate departments will be asked for critical information to help produce the profit plan. Profit planning will usually require 25% of the time required to produce the marketing plan. The major elements of a typical profit plan are listed in Table 11.3, along with the contributing marketing functions involved and other outside source participants. There may be other functions represented depending on the scope of the plan. Each company will have different departments dealing with specific areas of activity. Those listed in Table 11.3 are typical but not all-inclusive.

The marketing channel management and planning process is simply a way of helping management make good decisions in an organized and timely fashion. The important commitment is the *act* of decision making. Without decisions, nothing is planned and no action is taken.

SUMMARY

To present a reasonable summary of the marketing planning process applied to channel management actions would require repeating the process itself. Managers must realize that the act of planning is a commitment to discipline and hard work that will provide a road map for marketing actions. Good work will provide a map that can take one to the destination desired. Poor work will result in a map that is never referred to or followed.

The marketing plan should become the most dog-eared document in the channel manager's possession. It should be a reference for all and any significant actions to be taken. The fortunate fact is that a well-written annual marketing plan can be revised and updated as the basis for the next year's plan. It is not necessary to start over every year to produce a well-written marketing plan.

The planning process presented may be used for short-term promotional planning as well as for long-term strategic plans. The process is the same with changes only in the details for longer-range plans. The longer the range of the plan, the less detail is needed.

Accuracy in Step Two: *The Situation Analysis* is essential for a well-written and documented plan that can deliver the objectives. This is the heart of the planning process. It is the one place where everyone must agree with what is written. With a good start in Step Two, the rest of the planning will be well worth the effort. Without a good start, nothing else in the planning process is worth doing.

Decisions

Will you win or will you lose?
You'll never know if you don't choose.

Will you smile or stand there grim?
Will you fail or will you win?

Will the others call your name?
Will you fill with pride or pain?

Will you be the one about
Whom others raise their cheer and shout?

Will you run to win the race?
Will you stand in the victor's place?

Or, will you watch as a stander-by
And hear them shout for the other guy?

You'll never know if you don't choose,
To laugh or weep, to win or lose.

Above all else, there's this one fact,
You'll never know . . . if you don't act.

The paradox of decision making is simply this: If you don't make a decision, the answer is always no. If you don't take action, then you have surrendered to the actions of others. The currents in the marketing channel are swift. Change is frequent and sometimes dramatic. It is much better to manage the direction of the marketing channel by good planning than to forever react to the changes planned by others.

QUESTIONS FOR DISCUSSION

1. Actual channel planning starts with the development of data for the situation analysis. Where is the basic information found for this activity? Who compiled these data?
2. How much of the marketing planning effort and expense is involved in the situation analysis (% estimate)?
3. Should planners include opportunities or list obstacles for situations they do not intend to recommend? Explain.
4. What are the differences identified between goals and objectives?
5. Marketing planning must be sufficiently flexible to react to competitive situations. In which steps of the plan can the need for flexibility be expected?
6. Can the action plan be considered a separate plan from the marketing plan? What about the profit plan?
7. How frequently should the marketing plan be consulted or revised and by whom?
8. When a segment of the plan is revised, what action must immediately follow?
9. Why is the situation analysis *not* considered a channel planning function?
10. The most important aspect of any plan is that it must be understood and followed. How is this accomplished?

TWELVE

Legal Issues in Channel Management

The legal issues included in this text are founded on federal legislation affecting marketing channel structure and management. Also included is a discussion of frequently raised questions concerning legal issues related to marketing programs and actions. The comments presented are intended as a general guideline based on the author's understanding and experience concerning these issues. *No statement in this text should be construed as legal advice.*

The legal environment and interpretation of existing law is under constant change. Thousands of new bills are drafted by senators and representatives every year. Fortunately, only a few hundred are ever considered, and fewer yet become law. State and city regulations may also be a part of the marketing channel manager's concern. Even with a concerted effort by many companies and trade organizations to standardize such critical regulations as those governing packaging and labeling, there are still differences from state to state. For these reasons, marketing channel managers must constantly seek advice from those individuals in their company who are charged with the direct responsibility for legal and regulatory matters.

FEDERAL LEGISLATION

There are five federal acts that establish the basic legal relationships in the marketing channel. Some sections of these five acts have been interpreted in various ways over the years, but in general they provide a clearcut philosophy of how channel managers may establish federally acceptable programs for working relationships between channel members.

Sherman Antitrust Act

In 1890 Congress passed the Sherman Antitrust Act, a major piece of legislation making it illegal to establish or operate a monopoly. The thrust of this legislation, sometimes referred to as the "restraint of trade" act, was to encourage competition in the marketplace for the welfare of the general public. The first section of the Sherman Antitrust Act forbid contracts or business combinations that restrain interstate or foreign commerce. The act also provided federal courts the power to break up or dissolve those companies proven to be monopolies. Criminal penalties are established for individuals who are involved in the creation or operation of illegal monopolies. The term *illegal* is used because legal monopolies were preserved for utilities, telephone companies, and a few other industries. The deregulation of several industries, such as airline and telephone companies, broke up many monopolies that were previously permitted.

Clayton Act

The Clayton Act was the first of two important pieces of federal legislation to be passed in 1914. This legislation attempted to strengthen the Sherman Act by clarifying specific actions considered to be in restraint of trade. Practices such as interlocking directorates of competing companies were singled out for regulation. Furthermore, price discrimination, tying clauses (forced buying), exclusive dealing, and intercorporate stockholding between competing companies was restricted. The basic philosophy of the Clayton Act was to be sure that those practices of business that restricted competition, whether directly or indirectly, came under the federal jurisdiction.

Federal Trade Commission Act

The second important legislative act passed in 1914, the Federal Trade Commission (FTC) Act provided the investigative and enforcement arm for the federal government in order to prosecute those who violated the Sherman and Clayton Acts. The FTC Act went even farther than either the Sherman Act or the Clayton Act in that it included not only those illegal actions stipulated in Sherman and Clayton but added any other actions that provided "unfair methods of competition." The FTC Act put the federal government firmly in control of interstate commerce.

The Robinson-Patman Act

The Clayton Act was amended in 1936 with the passage of the Robinson-Patman Act, also known as the "unfair price discrimination" act. For companies involved in interstate commerce, Robinson-Patman prohibits price and terms-of-sale discrimination for goods of like grade and quality if the price and terms substantially lessen competition or encourage the formation of monopolies. This broad coverage of Robinson-Patman substantially and forever changed the way products were priced throughout the marketing channel.

This act did, however, recognize specific conditions under which price differentials for special customers could be established. These conditions were established under Sections 2-a and 2-b of the act.

1. Price differentials may be established to different customers when the increased or lowered price does not exceed actual costs to the manufacturer. In short, manufacturers may pass on to their customers the cost increases and cost savings that the manufacturer experiences as a direct result of doing business with specific customers.

2. Of significant importance to marketing channel managers is the provision in Robinson-Patman that allows for a manufacturer to meet changing market conditions with pricing action. Actions are allowable if changes in the market necessitate the need to
   a. avoid obsolescence of seasonal merchandise
   b. dispose of perishables
   c. conduct *legitimate* closeout sales
   d. conduct court imposed distress sales

   The provisions of sections 2-a and 2-b of Robinson-Patman are highly important for companies producing agricultural or industrial products.

   Section 2-c of the act is involved with the payment of unearned commissions or brokerage fees. Providing any payment in connection with a sale that creates unfair competition is prohibited.

   Sections 2-d and 2-e address potential price discrimination when providing such things as promotional allowances, advertising allowances, warehousing allowances, payments for display, catalog listings, training programs, and other services that are paid for in a discriminating way. All these services may receive payment, but payments must be available to all competing channel members on a proportionally equal basis.

3. So long as meeting the competitive price is not intended to injure competition, it is a legitimate marketing action.

Example: Proportional and Equal Treatment. A large national company that sells its products directly to retailers recognized three separate categories of retailers. One category was the traditional retailer, such as a hardware store. A second type of retailer was as the promotional department store, such as K-Mart. The third category was the traditional department store, such as Sears or J. C. Penny's. Each type of retailer had its own methods of buying and promoting products. The company designed separate programs for each to accommodate its needs. The principal criterion was that each program provide proportionally equal prices, allowances, and services to ensure that no competitive advantage be given to any segment of the marketing channel regardless of the type or size of the business.

The Robinson-Patman Act has been the most tested and challenged of all interstate commerce legislation. Unfortunately, its language is not clear in all areas it regulates. It is, however, clear in its intent to prohibit unfair price discrimination in the restraint of trade.

Celler-Kefauver Act

Following the thrust of Sherman, Clayton, and Robinson-Patman, the Celler-Kefauver Act of 1950 continued to clarify the meaning of restraint of trade by unfair competition. Celler-Kefauver broadened the scope of the Clayton Act to include mergers and acquisitions that tend to create monopolies. This act was particularly directed to the vertical integration practiced by companies that intended to suppress competition substantially by merger or acquisition.

Celler-Kefauver did not affect internal vertical integration from growth and the development of new capabilities, only merger and acquisition activities.

Example: Vertical Integration. In 1970 International Telephone and Telegraph Company (ITT) bought the O. M. Scott Company. At the time, Scott enjoyed a market share of 40% to 50% of the specialty homelawn fertilizer products sold through retailers to homeowners. As a condition for approval of this acquisition, the FTC advised ITT that it could acquire no other companies in the homelawn and garden business that had a market share exceeding 10%. Acquiring further companies with a greater market share would have been a form of vertical integration through merger or acquisition, having the potential to restrain trade and reduce competition.

LEGAL ISSUES IN CHANNEL MANAGEMENT

In agribusiness, there are many legal issues worthy of illustration. Some of the most interesting have been the result of the changing marketing channels for agricultural chemicals, farm equipment, animal health products, and animal feeds. Most manufacturers may not dictate or impose vertical integration restrictions on their channel intermediaries in an attempt to restrict competition in the channel. Manufacturers cannot require exclusive dealing or impose territorial boundaries or price controls on any channel member. Consider the situation where a manufacturer of animal health products sells the same products to over-the-counter distributors, as are sold to the professional veterinary distributors selling only to veterinarians. Such dual distribution is not illegal as such under federal antitrust laws. However, if the pricing to one channel restricts the other channel, a problem of legality may be created.

Much has been written and spoken about the cost of prescription drugs manufactured and marketed under the major pharmaceutical brand names compared to that of generic drugs of the same compound. A company selling its drugs in both professional and over-the-counter channels will probably offer different prices to each channel. This is considered legal because the two channels do not compete directly, since they are not in the same market.

A bigger question of legality comes from the practice by some wholesalers of owning a chain of retail outlets that are in direct competition with independent retailers whom they also supply. Even when the retail stores owned by the wholesalers are separate corporations, the question of interlocking corporate directorates may still apply. When the retail stores are not involved in interstate commerce, however, they can avoid federal involvement. This practice has caused channel managers to deal with a significant amount of conflict.

Payment of Unearned Commission

There is another situation where retailers, representing the products of a nationwide manufacturer, have asked for and received a cash allowance for the business conducted by the manufacturer that sells directly to the user in their trade area. This payment is made to keep the good will of retailers even though the retailers know the manufacturer's trade policy is to sell directly to consumers as it wishes. When the manufacturer sells directly to consumers in the local dealer's trade area, the manufacturer pays a "participation allowance" of about 1% to the nearest local retailer. The retailer performs no service for the payment. Since this is a local, rather than interstate commerce transaction, it is permissible. Even so, if the manufacturer were to pay the allowance to only one retail outlet in the trade area to the exclusion of other competing retailers, the company would most likely find the FTC in its shadow looking for unfair trade practices. When allowances are unearned and paid with selective discrimination between competing channel members, the giving of the allowance or commission is not allowed under section 2c of the Robinson-Patman Act.

Fair Trade Pricing and Meeting Competitive Prices

In 1970 the "fair trade" laws were abolished by the repeal of the Miller-Tydings Act of 1937 and the McGuire Act of 1952. These acts allowed states to exempt retail price fixing by the manufacturer. By allowing manufacturers to dictate the price at which their products would sell to the consumer or user, retailers who did not follow the consumer price schedule could be restricted from buying the manufacturer's products. When fair trade was abolished, many manufacturers tried to *suggest* selling prices to channel members. This could be considered an act of coercion.

Coercive tactics are frowned upon by federal law. Even so, the laws do not leave manufacturers without recourse when it comes to price cutting or meeting a competitive price. The ability of channel managers to meet competitively lower prices legally also carries with that privilege the obligation to verify *in writing* that price cutting is taking place. Price cutting is rampant in some businesses where the only established price in the channel is the one at which the manufacturer sells. This leads to little or no profitability for some channel members and presents significant problems for the marketing channel managers. Abolition of fair trade pricing by the states made price cutting a legitimate marketing action so long as it did not create unfair competition. If a wholesaler decides to sell a product priced below other wholesalers, he may do so. The low price, however, must be offered to all on a proportionally equal basis. To carry this situation one step further, consider the following example of meeting a competitive price.

Example: Meeting a Competitive Price. Two wholesalers sell Brand X rubber boots to the same market. They are keen competitors. Both wholesalers sell to farm store retailers. One wholesaler specializes in horse care products and carries the Brand X rubber boots only as a "line filler" of little importance to his business. The other wholesaler does not sell horse care products but depends on the dairy farmers for most of his business. Dairy farmers buy rubber boots and many other items from farm stores. For convenience, some dairy farmers will buy rubber boots from the tack shop that has horse care products. The dairy wholesaler sells his Brand X rubber boots to the tack shop as well as to the farm stores that are its major retailers.

The horse care products wholesaler decides to cut the price by 15% on Brand X rubber boots to his retailers. The dairy wholesaler meets this lower price only for its sales to the tack shops. Is this creating unfair competition in violation of the Robinson-Patman regulations? Probably not, as long as the dairy wholesaler is doing no more than meeting the lower price in retail outlets where the price is established. There may be considerable conflict created in the channel with this tactic, yet it may not be illegal.

When equipment retailers sell a discontinued model or last year's model below listed prices, even though the model is new equipment, is this price cutting? Yes, but this action is allowed as disposal of obsolete merchandise. Again, it should be noted that these are local situations. They do not involve interstate commerce or scrutiny under the FTC enforcement. Even when the factory authorizes and underwrites the discounted price nationally, it may be secure under the Robinson-Patman provision for such actions involving obsolete merchandise.

Volume Discounts

Most companies who sell products have a schedule of volume discounts. A large-volume buyer can buy at a better price than a low-volume buyer. Volume discounts are permitted under federal law if the discount does not exceed the direct volume-related cost savings enjoyed by the manufacturer, and if the volume categories do not establish a discriminatory price situation. The application of cost savings related to volume purchases is strictly identified by FTC regulations. Savings on selling and marketing costs may not apply, whereas manufacturing and freight cost savings may apply.

Example: Volume Discounting. A large lumber mill ships its lumber into a major market for home building. The mill sells its products through five established lumber and building supply wholesalers. One very large- and four medium-sized wholesalers make up the lumber mill's account list in the market. For years the lumber mill has sold its products priced on the basis of truckload purchases. Truckloads of mixed lumber products were priced a little higher than the amount charged for the truckloads containing only one type of lumber. This practice was justified by the extra cost of product selection and loading time for the mixed-car shipments.

Recently the mill established a new volume discount for shipments of five truckloads on one order. This purchase volume fit only the one large wholesaler, who had plenty of room to store the lumber. Since the volume discount was restrictive and created an unfair price advantage, the FTC would not allow it to remain in force. The FTC pointed out that in addition to establishing a restrictive volume level, the new volume discount passed on no legal cost savings to the wholesaler that bought the five truckloads. Loading and shipping costs remained the same whether one carload or several carloads were sent. Since the lumber mill had no savings to pass on, the discount for a purchase of five truckloads of lumber was simply not cost justified.

There are many examples of volume discounts in the industrial products area that would be difficult to cost justify according to FTC standards. However, manufacturers are permitted to let many of these unjustified discounts remain in force as established competitive practices, since they generally fall under regulations that allow marketers to meet established competitive prices.

Conducting Legitimate Closeout Sales

Robinson-Patman allows a company to close out a product at any price it wishes, even when unfair competitive advantages are created in the marketing channel. It is unnecessary to offer the closeout products to all competing retailers in equal and proportionate amounts. It appears that for these products, manufacturers may handle disposal in any way they deem best for their business.

Exclusive Representation and Full-line Forcing

The law under the Clayton Act states that manufacturers are not allowed to force a channel member to handle only their line of products. Neither can manufacturers dictate which brands a customer may or may not handle. Exclusive dealing arrangements are prohibited by the Clayton Act if, as defined by the FTC, such arrangements substantially lessen competition or foster monopolies.

Mutually exclusive contracts may be entered into for good business reasons, however. Manufacturers of large pieces of equipment, such as those used for highway construction, may wish to have exclusive representation in protected territories. These mutually exclusive contracts may be established when they do not violate the Sherman Act, the Clayton Act, or the FTC regulations concerning the limiting of competition between companies.

Full-line forcing is similar to exclusive dealing in that the manufacturer is attempting to control the channel member's buying practices. Full-line forcing requires channel members to take the manufacturer's entire line whether they want it or not. The idea is to stop "cherry picking" the fast-selling items in a line while ignoring lesser products. When the stocking requirements of a company force a channel member into a position where he cannot sell competitive lines of products, the antitrust issue emerges. Some manufacturers require a specific number of shelf-keeping units (SKUs) to be stocked by their customers. In these cases, the manufacturers will not designate which products must be stocked, but they will require the purchase of a sufficient number of the company's products to provide reasonable line representation. So long as the SKU level is not competitively restrictive, it may be employed.

Restrictive Selection of Channel Intermediaries

In 1919 a landmark Supreme Court case, *United States vs. Colgate & Company*, resulted in the *Colgate doctrine*. It decided the legality of private companies to do business with whomever they choose. The case concluded with the following argument:

The Sherman Act does not restrict the long recognized right of a trader or manufacturer to exercise his own independent discretion as to the parties with whom he will deal. And of course, he may announce in advance the circumstances under which he will refuse to deal.

Channel managers must be cautious in exercising this right of restrictive customer selection for establishing a marketing channel. For example, one must use discretion in the use of coercive force to keep channel members in line. The threat to discontinue doing business with a channel member that does not follow suggested prices, buy certain products, or perform some specific service is considered coercive. The manufacturer may indeed discontinue selling to any channel member, but the act of discontinuing the business relationship must be unconditional and final.

Companies that use a threat to discontinue, or "cut off," a customer to extend their control over the customer are clearly in a dangerous position with section 1 of the Sherman Act. In 1967 the Supreme Court case of *United States vs. Arnold Schwinn Company* established once and for all that manufacturers part with dominion over their product's destiny in the market when they give up title and risk.

Included in this area of antitrust law are *tying agreements*. A manufacturer who requires the purchase of one product to qualify for the purchase of another has created a tying arrangement or condition of purchase that is likely to be considered in violation of the Sherman Act.

Franchise operators come under close scrutiny in regard to the tying agreement regulations. Franchisers may contractually establish the quality standards for products sold under the franchise name. However, the franchise may still buy products of the same type, grade, or quality from other suppliers. When no other supplier can provide products with the required quality or product specifications, then the tying agreement is likely to be considered legal.

Vertical Integration

For many industrial product manufacturers and food producers, vertical integration is well established. This is particularly true with operations that involve mining or natural resources. Companies involved with steel production may produce their own coke made from coal. They may make pig iron, use it in the production of various grades of steel, and even produce finished steel products for sale. This type of vertical integration is internal integration. It does not deal with acquisitions and mergers, which are part of external integration. Internal vertical integration will usually not violate the Celler-Kefauver Act or the Sherman Act. Companies that develop their own vertical integration capabilities—for most often, economy of scale or to control product availability and quality—may have no antitrust concern. However, when a company seeks to buy established facilities to create vertical integration, it may come under the Celler-Kefauver Act. If the planned merger or acquisition substantially lessens competition or creates the formation of a monopoly, it can be in trouble.

The Involvement of the Channel Manager in Legal Issues

Channel managers are not expected to be expert in matters of the law. However, they should be aware of situations where legal concern may alter their marketing actions. The key for the channel manager is to know when to ask for expert advice. Channel managers should know when to question a program or marketing action. They must be ever aware that in marketing channel management there are legal restrictions concerning pricing, products, programs, distribution, and people—these are the manageable elements of the marketing mix. The basic federal acts that have been discussed in this chapter are a guide to where specific information may be found. The basic federal acts with which channel managers should be familiar follow in Table 12.1.

In many companies, the legal department must review all promotions and marketing programs. The legal department will also wish to write and approve the initiation of customer contracts, distribution agreements, and purchasing contracts. The interpretation and application of law should always be left to the professionals. Use the legal advice of the company's attorneys. The comments in this chapter are intended to make the reader aware of areas where professional advice may be needed.

Marketing channel managers have the responsibility to produce programs that bring profits to the company. For this reason, they will often take some risks. The legal area is not one that condones risk taking, however. As a general guide to risk-free management action in the marketing channel, follow these simple rules:

1. When creating programs that include the elements of pricing or motivational incentives to the product user and buying or selling opportunities for channel members, provide the same opportunities to all, whether large or small.

Table 12.1
Federal Acts Affecting Channel Management

<u>Federal Acts in Force</u>

1. The Sherman Antitrust Act of 1890.

2. The Clayton Act of 1914.

3. The Federal Trade Commission Act of 1914.

4. The Robinson-Patman Act of 1936.

5. The Celler-Kefauver Act of 1950.

<u>Federal Acts Repealed</u>

6. The Miller Tydings Act of 1937.

7. The McGuire Act of 1952.

2. Regardless of their size, never place one retailer in the channel at a competitive disadvantage to another.
3. Wholesalers should adhere to the principal of proportionally equal treatment to all.
4. Be sure all allowances are earned and volume discounts are cost justified at each channel level.

Build a "level playing field" for all members of the marketing channel, and the legal considerations can fade to invisibility. Those marketing channel managers who try to find a way to offer special deals and privileges to certain accounts or influential channel members will find their programs on the edge of legality. These managers will also create dissension in the marketing channel. To settle discord takes management time and money. Even when resolved, conflict may leave hard feelings and make those who feel wronged open to competitive enticements.

QUESTIONS FOR DISCUSSION

1. What did the Sherman Act try to establish?
2. How did the Clayton Act expand the influence of the Sherman Act?
3. What is the role of the FTC?

4. In what respect does the Celler-Kefauver Act deal with mergers and acquisitions?

5. Give an example of how a manufacturer may legally impose discriminatory pricing action. Which federal act is involved?

6. How can a marketer legally meet competitive pricing?

7. Can a company offer bigger (greater %) advertising allowances to its bigger customers? Explain.

8. When are volume discounts legal? When are they illegal?

9. Can franchising companies require their franchisees to buy all their materials from them? Explain.

10. What general rule may be applied to managing prices, products, distribution, and programs that will significantly reduce legal risks for the channel manager?

REFERENCES

Sherman Antitrust Act
U.S. Code 1976
Title 15, paragraph 1 et seq.
July 2, 1890, c.647 Stat. 209

Clayton Act
U.S. Code 1976
Title 15, paragraph 12 et seq.
Title 18, paragraphs 402, 660, 3285, 3691
Title 29, paragraphs 52, 53
October 15, 1914, c.323, 38 Stat. 730

Federal Trade Commission
U.S. Code 1976
Title 15, paragraph 41 et seq.
September 26, 1914, c.311, 38 Stat. 717
March 21, 1938, c.49, 52 Stat. 111

Robinson-Patman Act (price discrimination)
U.S. Code 1976
Title 15, paragraphs 13, 13a, 13b, 21a
June 19, 1936, c.592, 49 Stat. 1526

Celler-Kefauver Act (acquisition of corporate stock)
U.S. Code 1976
Title 15, paragraphs 18, 21
December 29, 1950, c.1184, 64 Stat. 1125

Annotated Bibliography

Boone, Louis E., & James C. Johnson. *Marketing Channels*. Tulsa: Petroleum Publishing Co., 1977.

This book deals with case studies for retail marketing and channel development. It points out the importance of channel selection to the success of marketing programs. The classic corporate and marketing channel topics of channel conflict and cooperation with the effect on marketing efficiency are detailed in simplistic terms.

Significant examples of channel control, its problems, and its successes are covered in relationship to organization, distribution, marketing programs, and social systems.

Marketing channels for industrial goods, franchise operations, and international marketing are discussed from the legal view point and the organization structure for distribution and retailing.

Bowersox, LaLonde, and Smykay. *Readings in Physical Distribution Management: The Logistics of Marketing*. New York: MacMillian, 1969.

This is a collection of significant articles written on the subject of physical distribution. Special attention is directed to the marketing implications of the various articles as they relate to freight, transportation, warehousing, materials management, protective packaging, inventory control, plant and warehouse site selection order processing, market forecasting, and customer services.

These subjects are organized into three areas: Part 1 deals with physical distribution and the market; Part 2 is involved with physical distribution design; and Part 3 encompasses organization, administration, and control. The articles presented offer a balance between what academicians and practitioners have to say on the subject of physical distribution.

Boyd, Harper, and William Massey. *Marketing Management*. San Diego: Harcourt Brace Jovanovich, 1972.

This is a significant and comprehensive volume covering the entire field of marketing management. The significance of a marketing approach to market development and management is detailed with reference to marketplace behavior, market resources, development and control of market strategies, and development of a marketing organization. Both the theoretical and practical points of view are accommodated in this volume. The market and its participants in channel structure are discussed from the functional impact of participant contribution to the marketing system and market environment.

Distribution is covered primarily from the design aspects in consideration of specific marketing objectives rather than physical distribution services.

A full chapter is devoted to the functions of a marketing channels approach and strategies related to the development of a system involving manufacturers, middlemen, and consumers.

Debelak, Dan. *Total Marketing*. Homewood, IL: Dow Jones–Irwin, 1989.

The main thrust of this book is in providing information for writing a marketing plan. In essence, what is provided is the organization and writing of detailed profit plans rather than complete marketing plans. The market development aspects of marketing planning are practically ignored. The typical product life cycle is presented with no reference to the market. Product-planning strategies are offered in respect to their competitive reference. Marketing channel managers will find the Getting Your Customers to Notice chapter of value. This chapter provides useful information on advertising and communications functions applied to a marketing channel system.

The most significant reference to marketing channels is related to the channel of distribution structure. Using "exclusive dealing" as a channel strategy and employing direct sales force involvement in training channel members are noted as significant activities. Many examples and references to what companies have done or are now doing in marketing program development are offered as examples of strategies that have or have not worked for the reasons noted.

Haley, Russell I. *Developing Effective Communications*. New York: John Wiley & Sons, 1985.

The results of over 120 studies conducted in "Benefit Segmentation" are presented in this book. The central issue discussed throughout the text is in how a company, or any organization, can discover an effective communications strategy and, once discovered, execute it for the desired effect on the market.

In general, the reader is presented a broadside of how advertising works, how attitudes are measured, how effective communications strategies are developed, and how one organizes to perform studies and tests for "Benefit Segmentation." Case histories are presented as examples of successful "Benefit Segmentation" programs.

Hass, Robert W. *Industrial Marketing Management*. Wadsworth, IL: PWS-Kent Publishing Co., 1989.

This textbook concerns itself with the subject of industrial product marketing management rather then the usual consumer product orientation. Recent emphasis on market segmentation is highlighted. The basic differences between industrial and consumer product marketing are a common thread throughout the discussion of such topics as market behavior, marketing management and organization, the marketing mix, and case studies.

Over twenty-five case studies provide examples of management practices and offer an analysis of the results expected and accomplished.

Formulating industrial channel strategy starts with the determination of channel objectives and works its way through direct and indirect channel development, establishment, and control management activities.

Kollat, Blackwell, and Robeson. *Strategic Marketing*. New York: Holt, Rinehart & Winston, 1972.

Strategic Marketing is a text for the study of developing planning objectives and techniques. A valuable discussion of channel programs deals with marketing channel development in a changing business environment. A systematic approach is offered as a method for channel development. The authors indicate that knowing a company's corporate objectives and strategy is necessary before a channel structure can be suggested. No "best channel structure" can be suggested independently of this information.

A second topic of interest to marketing channel managers deals with developing alternative physical distribution systems. The authors maintain that physical distribution systems should recognize physical distribution as "inventories in motion." This is a total systems approach from the manufacturer to the consumer. The discussion of physical distribution concludes with a very useful method of evaluating the effectiveness of various distribution systems.

Kotler, Phillip. *Marketing Management*. Englewood Cliffs, NJ: Prentice-Hall, 1980.

Phillip Kotler is one of the most recognized and respected writers on the subject of marketing management. His text covers the subject from an academic point of view, with the interjection of over 300 references to real-life situations in business. Kotler draws the reader's attention to the application of theory through analysis. He demonstrates the process of marketing planning and functional control in marketing management.

This text is primarily centered on developing a usable understanding of marketing management and the tools it uses in the performance of its management tasks. Special emphasis is placed on analyzing marketing opportunities, planning marketing strategies, assembling the marketing mix, and administering marketing programs. Special topics cover some of the aspects of international marketing.

Chapters are devoted to a discussion of marketing channels decisions and physical distribution decisions, respectively.

Mallen, Bruce. *Principles of Marketing Channel Management*. Lexington MA: Lexington Books, 1977.

Oriented to consumer products, this book offers the reader a rather basic understanding of management concepts related to the marketing channel and the channel of distribution. The usual references to the marketing mix are integrated into marketing systems, functions, decision areas, channel structure, and economic development.

Distribution structure involves wholesaling and retailing concerns and offers many tables on market types, their sales volume, and their position in the various markets listed.

A traditional coverage of the market environment, governmental and legal impacts, pricing, channel design, channel relations, and conflict and power issues are all discussed and annotated with many references for further reading.

Onkvisit, Sak, and John J. Shaw. *Product Life Cycles and Product Management*. New York: Quorum Books, 1989.

A very useful reference in providing a foundation for product management, this volume details the product life cycle, noting the inevitability of "what goes up must come down" with an application of reality to theory.

Product planning with regard to consumer acceptance and behavior deals with the new product and existing product strategies as well as with demographic applications.

Pellegrini, L., and S. Reddy. *Marketing Channels*. Lexington, MA/Toronto: Lexington Books/D. C. Heath and Co., 1986.

Although not a comprehensive study of marketing channels in general, this book does contain some interesting and valuable observations on vertical marketing agreements. It also details the relationships that develop between the various channel levels in exclusive purchasing arrangements and those with less emphasis on channel management control.

A significant amount of this book deals with location strategies and forecasting demand levels for various retail situations. The forecasting of seasonal demand for individual products offers some interesting, though rather complicated, forecasting equations.

Rosenbloom, Bert. *Marketing Channels: A Management View*. Chicago: Dryden Press, 1991.

This current revision of the original 1978 text is a broad anthology on the subject of marketing channels. With an orientation to consumer rather than industrial products and markets, the text offers a full range of subjects with examples and references to what has been done in the development of marketing channel structure and management of channel problems, opportunities, and special situations. The many examples and case studies of different types of companies offer a link to the real world of business. This link, however, is limited to the examples used and is not applied in general to business dissimilar in origin and with different marketing structures.

Much of the language of this text is very academic and does not read well. It thus has limited application to the business world, where the vocabulary is more pragmatic and descriptive.

Serri, Italo S. *New Product Development and Marketing*. New York: Praeger, 1990.

This volume offers a practical guide to new-product planning, product definition, implementation of new-product introduction, and evaluation of the success of the planned introduction. Since managing products is a large part of the marketing channel process, this book offers the reader some very useful "how to" steps in the determination of the answers to the *why, what, how, who,* and *when* concerning new product introduction.

Shapiro, Benson, Robert Dolan, and John Quelch. *Marketing Management—Strategy, Planning and Implementation*. Homewood, IL: Richard D. Irwin, 1985.

The extensive use of Harvard Business School case studies makes this volume live the lessons it provides for the reader. The marketing process is profiled using Pepsi Cola and Kenics Corporation cases.

Implementation of the marketing process uses five separate case studies to provide examples of "how it is done" in various corporate situations. Programing, budgeting, and allocating is covered with case studies from four major companies, including the AT&T Long Lines program for marketing telemarketing to its customers.

This book offers market research techniques, a product line planning process, and market strategy planning from both domestic and international case study settings. The reader has the opportunity to note what diverse companies have done in strategy development, planning, and implementation of marketing programs. Conclusions are offered after each case is presented.

Tarrant, John J. *Drucker: The Man Who Invented the Corporate Society.* New York: Warner Books, 1976.

Tarrant has collected many references to the activities and actions of Peter Drucker, "the man who invented the corporate society." Peter Drucker's writings are referenced and noted as examples of pronouncements on the effectiveness of management practices. The management performance comments are particularly useful in noting what may be expected from managers at all levels of the marketing channel.

Walters, C. Glenn. *Marketing Channels.* The Ronald Press Company, 1974.

This text explores the concepts and theories of marketing channel development and existing management practices. It relates to what is (or was in 1974) in place regarding channel development and management activities. The text identifies its five primary areas of interest as:

1. Channel management: Concepts, opportunities, and responsibilities.

2. Channel structure: Institutions, design, and selection.

3. Management of channel operation: Product assortment, purchasing, pricing, and logistics.

4. Management of channel communications: Information systems and promotions.

5. Channel leadership roles: Conflict, motivation, control, and special situations for international marketing channels.

This is a very basic and simplistic study for the development and understanding of the subject called marketing channels.

Index

About the Author

RUSSELL W. MCCALLEY is an adjunct professor in the School of Agribusiness and Environmental Resources at Arizona State University. He has held a number of positions in business and is the founder of R. W. McCalley and Associates, a management consulting firm based in Arizona.